ANIOMA

ANIOMA

≋

*A Social History
of the Western Igbo People*

by DON C. OHADIKE

Ohio University Press
Athens

Library of Congress Cataloging-in-Publication Data

Ohadike, Don C.
    Anioma : a social history of the Western Igbo people / by Don C.
Ohadike.
        p.   cm.
    Includes bibliographical references (p.   ) and index.
    ISBN 0 8214 1073-5 (cloth ; acid-free paper). — ISBN
0-8214-1073-3 (paper : acid-free paper)
    1. Igbo (African people)—Origin.   2. Igbo (African people)—
History.   3. Igbo (African people)—Social life and customs.
I. Title.
DT474.6.I34O33   1994
960'.0496332—dc20
                                                    93-31029
                                                    CIP

DEDICATION

≋

To the people of Anioma
    who brought me into this world
    and gave me love

And to my children
    Azuka, Nenna, Nonye, and Nnamdi
    who share this wonderful gift with me

CONTENTS

~~~

1   CHAPTER 1. ANIOMA ORIGINS

Where did the Igbo people come from? Archaeology and the origins of the Igbo people. The diffusion of the Igbo people. Anioma origins. Ogwashi-Ukwu and Ogboli origins. Ibbuzo. Asaba. Ubulu-Ukwu. Obiarukwu and the Umu Akashiada confederacy. Abbi. How do the Anioma people perceive themselves?

33   CHAPTER 2. BENIN-IGBO WARS AND THE SETTLEMENT OF EDO- AND YORUBA- SPEAKING PEOPLE IN ANIOMA

War and diplomacy among the Igbo. Wars on the borderlands. The rise of militaristic Benin. The first Anioma-Benin encounters. The first Edo immigrants in the Igbo culture area. Olukunmi: A Yoruba community in the Igbo culture area. The war between Benin and Ubulu-Ukwu (1750). The Exechima flight: Obamkpa. The Benin-Agbor wars. The historical importance of the Benin-Anioma wars.

69   CHAPTER 3. SOCIAL AND POLITICAL STRUCTURES, A.D. 900–1900

Social and political institutions. The council of elders and the age-grades. The impact of Benin on the precolonial social and political organizations of Anioma: The Ika example. The impact of Iglala on Anioma. The precolonial social classes of Anioma. Paramount chiefs: Obi. The titled chiefs: *Ndi eze* or *Ndi ozo*. Women's titles. Slaves.

MAPS

≋

ACKNOWLEDGMENTS

≈

THE RESEARCH AND WRITING of this book took many years to complete and benefited from the experiences of many people, too numerous to be mentioned here. I must, however, specifically thank Elizabeth Isichie, my mentor at the University of Nigeria, Nsukka, who urged me to undertake a serious study of the Western Igbo people. Others that I must not forget to mention are Donald D. Hartle, who taught me archaeology and ancient civilizations at the University of Nigeria, and Anthony G. Hopkins, my supervisor and instructor in the economic history of West Africa at the University of Birmingham, England.

I also wish to thank the present and past directors of the Africana Studies and Research Center of Cornell University—Locksley Edmondson, Robert Harris Jr., and James Turner—whose kind and amiable dispositions enabled me, despite the anxieties of life in a foreign land, to cope with a particularly heavy academic commitment at Cornell. My special gratitude goes to my other colleagues in the department, especially Sandra Greene, Abdul Nanji, Salah Hassan, N'Dri Therese Assie-Lumumba, and June Richards, who made available to me very useful materials on African social history and anthropology.

I would like to thank Patricia Ukoli, Kunirum Osia, Chima Anyadike, Marvin Williams, and Henri Boyi for consenting to read the earlier drafts of the Anioma manuscript and for offering valuable suggestions. My gratitude also goes to Tom Weissinger and Eric Acree of the Africana Library of Cornell University for their assistance, and to Dan Britz, Patricia Ukoli, and Angelia Johnson, of Northwestern's Melville J. Herskovits Library of African Studies, for responding promptly to my "long-distance" requests for references.

Finally, I wish to thank Sheila Towner for the endless hours she spent typing the first and final drafts of the Anioma manuscript.

Without these and many others whose names I have not mentioned, this book would never have been published.

FOREWORD

≈

PROFESSOR DON C. OHADIKE'S book has, indeed, filled a void in the
historiography of the Anioma people. With grace, subtlety and imagi-
nation, he has reconstructed a sense of historical presence for a people
who have been burdened by the lack of documented and interpreted
history. His study has given, not only the Anioma people, but also
other people, a mirror to look at themselves now and into their past,
to retrieve a wealth of history and culture that served them for a mil-
lenium or more.

This study is not only placed in the Igbo, Nigerian and African
contexts, but also in the world context. Professor Ohadike dismisses
with scholarly incisiveness the ethnocentric hubris and cultural arrogance of the Western world which has too long distorted the significance of African systems.

The virtue of this study lies in the skill with which Professor Ohadike has provided a "sense of self" to and a context of meaning in
which the Anioma people can locate themselves. He has answered the
questions surrounding the origin of the Anioma people. He has shown
the importance of 'culture contact' and how it has enriched the people's worldview. Whether it is the Benin-Igbo wars, the settlement of
Edo and Yoruba-speaking people in Anioma, the precolonial social
and political structures, the religious encounters—Christianity and
traditional religion, the British conquest and Anioma resistance, slave
trade, influenza epidemic, subsistence economy, Anioma women,
Anioma men, polygamy and so forth, these factors have merged in a
sort of sociological gestalt to generate a history of a people who see
themselves not only as one people but as distinct from their immediate
neighbors.

While not denying their Igbo origin, the Anioma people wish to
emphasize their distinctness believing that 'culture contact' has broadened their worldview. Even in our daily life, we effortlessly incor-
porate cultural motifs and norms, and make them our own. Likewise,
Anioma people's contact with the Edo, Igala Yoruba, et cetera, has re-

sulted in the classificatory system of their socio-political structure which differs from those of other Igbo-speaking people of Nigeria.

By dividing the Anioma history into digestible time periods, by writing it in such lucid, vivid, forceful and precise language, Professor Ohadike invites and entices his readers to pick up the book and read it from the introduction to the conclusion.

The notion of relevance as far as the study is concerned, is created by the real situation it documents, which is, the totality of the people's experiences. Hence, the designation of the area and the people as 'Anioma' accords relevance and meaning to their aspirations and experiences. There comes a time in the evolutionary history of a people that they cast away imposed order. History is replete with such actions. There was a time when Ghana was Gold Coast, Zimbabwe was Rhodesia, Zaire was Belgian Congo, Burkina Faso was Upper Volta, and so forth. Anioma is a people and they have chosen to be called as such.

Professor Ohadike has not only legitimized 'Anioma' but also provided logic and authenticity to the aspirations and experiences of the people. *Anioma: A Social History of the Western Igbo People* provides an interpretive map to guide readers, students and scholars through a very fascinating history of a people who cherish their uniqueness.

October 1993   Kunirum Osia
                                 Maryland State Department of Education
                                 Camp Spring, Maryland

Abbreviations

≋

ADC	Assistant District Commissioner
ADO	Assistant District Officer
CMS	Church Missionary Society
CO	Colonial Office (London)
DC	District Commissioner
DMO	District Medical Officer
DO	District Officer
FO	Foreign Office (London)
NAE	National Archives Enugu (Nigeria)
NAI	National Archives Ibadan (Nigeria)
PRO	Public Record Officer (London)
RCM	Roman Catholic Mission
RNC	Royal Niger Company
SMA	Societé de Missions Africaines (Society of African Missions (Rome)

Introduction

≈

ON THE WESTERN SIDE of the Lower Niger River live some Igbo-speaking groups. Their social history can be traced to the tenth century A.D., when some of their ancestors, whose original homelands in the Anambra valley and the Orlu and Isuama areas, began to respond to the ecological crisis that was afflicting their hometowns by crossing the Niger River to seek better farming and hunting grounds in what was soon to become the western part of the Igbo culture area. They came in small numbers, bringing with them certain notions of social and political organization which guided them as they established their new settlements. In later centuries they were joined by immigrants from a wide range of places and went by several names: *ndi Aniocha, ndi Ukwuani, ndi Ika, umu Ezechima, umu Isu, ndi Odiani, ndi Oshimili, and umu Nshi* (or *Nhi* or *Nri*). However, when these people came under British rule at the end of the nineteenth century, the British colonial administrators grouped them together under the name *Western Igbo,* presumably because they spoke the Igbo language and occupied the western part of the Igbo culture area, or perhaps to distinguish them from the Igbo-speaking people who lived on the eastern side of the river. Throughout the colonial period, they remained known by the British and the other Nigerians as Western Igbo people.

After the achievement of independence by Nigerians in 1960, a new form of consciousness began to spread in the country and many groups began to redefine themselves. Some felt that the names they had been given by the British were either meaningless or even derogatory, while others felt that the regions or provinces into which they had been put did not guarantee them peace and happiness. For instance, the Tiv rejected the name *Munchi* by which the British sometimes referred to them in official documents. Also, in view of certain historical, religious, and sociological considerations, the Tiv asked that they be removed from the former Northern Region of Nigeria. These requests were granted, and today, the Tiv live happily with the name and in the region of their choice.

Like many groups in Nigeria, the Western Igbo people began to seek a new identity. The name they chose for themselves was *ndi Ani-oma,* which literally means "those who live on the good and prosperous land," a term that they coined in the 1970s when they began to agitate for their own separate state within the entity known as Nigeria. Although the name *Anioma* is not well known within intellectual circles outside Nigeria, it is a familiar one there.

Believing that every people should be known by the name it chooses, I have decided to address them in this volume as the people of Anioma, a term they prefer, rather than as the Western Igbo people, which was imposed on them by the British. Moreover, the Igbos historically have not described themselves as western, eastern, northern, or southern Igbos, but as the children of such and such a person, or as those who occupy such and such a land; hence, for example, a group might be called *umu Ezechima* (the children of King Chima), or *ndi onu iyi* (those who live on the bank of the river). Further, the Igbos generally would describe non-Igbos by the languages they speak; hence, for example, *ndi Hausa* (those who speak the Hausa language), or *ndi Yoruba* (those who speak the Yoruba language). In keeping with this custom, the terms *east* and *west* will be used in this volume only with reference to geographical locations and not to peoples. We may, for example, speak of Igboland, east of the Niger, and not of eastern Igbo people.

The early history of Anioma is distinguished in one particular respect; it shares a common heritage with the wider Igbo history of which it forms a segment, and yet has significantly been influenced and modified by the Edo, Igala, Yoruba, Urhobo, Ishan, and Ijo cultures. One cannot therefore appreciate the origins and development of Anioma history without making reference to these other cultures. Both oral and written records confirm that by the fourteenth century A.D. the Anioma region had been effectively occupied by the early Igbo immigrants and that beginning from the sixteenth century, some Bini residents, who had left their homelands because of certain political changes occurring within the Edo country, began to arrive and were soon followed by other immigrants from Igalaland, Yorubaland, Ishanland, Ijoland and Urhoboland. Wherever they might have come from, these immigrants were admitted as full citizens of the Anioma communities in which they settled.

The social history of Anioma spanned four historical periods, each coinciding with one of four major experiences. The first was the period from about A.D. 900 to 1500, when the history of Anioma was largely an extension of the wider Igbo history. During this time some men and women in the Igbo core area, in and around the Anambra valley, began to cross the Niger River to escape from the deteriorating soil conditions in their ancestral homelands. Most of them were farmers, hunters and craftpersons. On arrival in the new western territory, they built compact settlements that were well ordered and adequately supplied with food and other necessities of life. At the same time, they evolved complex relations of production that aimed at ensuring a fair distribution of roles and appropriation of surpluses. The emergent social relations were consistent with their agricultural system, religious practices, and political ideologies, all of which had their origins in Igboland, east of the Niger. In short, this period was marked by the reproduction of the basic Igbo institutions in Anioma.

The second era was a period of cultural clashes that lasted for two and one-half centuries, from about 1500 to 1750. This was the period when the people of Anioma became involved in the histories of the Edo, Igala, Yoruba, Urhobo, and Ijo people. The period was also marked by territorial expansion from the direction of Benin and Anioma resistance to it, by population movements and settlement, by the Atlantic slave trade and the provisioning trade, by the spread of the Igbo kingship system based on the *ozo* title, and the Edo political system based on obiship. Indeed, it was a period of rapid social transformations and class differentiation.

The third period of Anioma history coincides with the years 1750 to 1900. This was the time when Anioma became involved with the continued expansion of the overseas slave trade and the provisioning trade that was based on yam, maize and palm oil, together with the politics of the abolition of the slave trade, gunboat diplomacy, European "civilizing missions," and the wider world crisis instigated by European imperialism. For the people of Anioma, it was a period of initial conflicts with Christian missionaries and adjustment to the new international commerce based on palm oil and kernels.

The fourth period was the colonial period that lasted from 1900 until 1960. It was marked by the crisis generated by colonial conquest and economic exploitation, together with the continued resistance and adjustment to western cultural, political, and economic imperialism in Africa.

As we shall see in the chapters that follow, the precolonial history of Anioma presents the historian with a number of paradoxes. First, it deals with a people who occupied a region that was both fairly densely populated and situated on one of the busiest trade routes in Africa (the Niger River); further, the Anioma shared common frontiers with large kingdoms, such as Benin and Igala. Yet they never cared to build large kingdoms themselves. Instead, they organized themselves in small-scale republics, ruled by their elders in association with titled chiefs, age-grades, secret societies, and women's associations. It is equally strange that even though the people of Anioma participated in the Atlantic slave trade and in the provisioning trade, their political institutions remained almost unchanged by the facts of those trades. How, then, did they escape those influences that stimulated state formation in many parts of West Africa?

The answer to these questions could be found both in the traditional religions of Anioma and in the absence of small kingdoms which were ambitious enough to serve as the foundations upon which large states could be built. The traditional religions of Anioma were mediative and pacific in the sense that they recognized and respected the autonomy of each descent group and clan. They abhorred the spilling of human blood which, in turn, discouraged the kind of large-scale wars necessary for territorial expansion and consolidation. Thus, neither military threats from Benin and Idah nor the attraction of the Atlantic slave trade induced the communities of Anioma to embark on state formation. The people of Aboh, for example, participated in the highly profitable Atlantic slave trade and built a formidable military force but did not use it to gain political domination over the less powerful groups. Instead, they used it to protect the weak against such restless intruders as the Ijo river pirates. The chiefs of Aboh also used their military force to protect their spheres of trade and influence on the Lower Niger, and to collect tributes from traders who ventured into their territories.

As we shall see, most known military forces of Anioma were developed primarily for defense, and while they trained to contain the aggression of their non-Igbo neighbors, they tried as much as possible to maintain friendly relations with the other Anioma communities. Thus, even though some polities, such as Agbor, Ubulu-Ukwu, Issele-Ukwu and Ogwashi-Ukwu, emerged as small chiefdoms which would have served as the foundations upon which more ambitious political units might have been built, their inhabitants chose not to extend their authority beyond the confines of their hometowns. Their military forces remained small in size insofar as the communities themselves remained almost entirely segmentary and autonomous.

By contrast, the rise of Benin from a small political establishment to a large empire in the fifteenth and sixteenth centuries affected Anioma in three principal ways. First, it created a series of wars that triggered population movements from the direction of Benin toward the Igbo heartland. Second, it resulted in the introduction and emulation of Benin political institutions in the forms of title systems. Third, mainly because of the need for defense, the people of Anioma congregated in compact villages and towns which they based on war-readiness.

The Anioma people's meeting with the Europeans in the nineteenth and twentieth centuries was very violent and destabilizing. The suppression of the Atlantic slave trade and its substitution with the palm oil trade could not have been achieved without great pains both to the people of Anioma and the Europeans. The gunboat diplomacy and the trade competition which the British imperial agents, traders and missionaries introduced into the Niger territories eventually ruined the African merchants and weakened the political authority of the traditional chiefs. The colonial period in particular was one of political strife and social insecurity. The overt military conquest of Anioma, together with the imposition of alien cultures, disrupted traditional institutions and customs. The European intrusion radically dislocated the agricultural cycles and modified the ideologies and rituals that had previously regulated social relations. The first few decades of the colonial encounters produced a noticeable trend toward food shortages, and by the third decade of the colonial period, food had become scarce and expensive. Direct taxation and new forms of labor obligations provoked a strong tendency toward labor migration, which compounded the food crisis. To ward off hunger, the people of Anioma experimented with cassava, an inferior food, and were soon to become the foremost growers of the crop in Nigeria. It was, indeed, an interesting historical turnaround when the very people who had grown the largest quantities of yams for provisioning during the era of the Atlantic slave trade became the leading producers of cassava in the twentieth century.

The main purpose of this book is to illustrate how certain decentralized (or small-scale) African societies like the Igbos functioned in the precolonial periods, how their settlements grew from a few individuals to tens of thousands of people, how they admitted and integrated outsiders into the host communities, how they responded to the opportunities and crises generated by both internal African developments and external world political and economic forces, and how they made the transition from the traditional to the "modern" market economy. It is also a study which aims at demonstrating that the various African societies responded differently to similar stimuli. We shall see, for instance, that while the Atlantic slave trade transformed the economic and political structures of many West African communities, it made little or no impact on Anioma social structures despite the latter people's active participation in it. I shall demonstrate that it was not the Atlantic slave trade, but its ending, that caused so much problems for the people of Anioma. I will also show how the people of Anioma responded to the British colonial conquest of Nigeria, and how they adjusted to the indirect rule system. In fact, the whole social history of Anioma can be described as one of resistance and adjustments to change. This volume is written with a view toward not only in the Igbo and Nigerian contexts, but also toward the wider African and world contexts. I hope that it will serve the needs of educators, students, and the general public.

1

~~~

ANIOMA ORIGINS

WHERE DID THE IGBO PEOPLE COME FROM?

ANECDOTAL EVIDENCE FROM virtually every historian, ethnographer, anthropologist, or Christian missionary who worked in southern Nigeria indicates that the earliest known inhabitants of Anioma came from Igboland, east of the Niger. Before these early Igbo people came over, there might have been small groups of non-Igbo residing in the area but these were driven off or assimilated. We do not have sufficient evidence to support this assumption even though one might argue that the region could not have been entirely unoccupied before the Igbo immigrants arrived. We know, for example, that the Aboh and Illah traditions of origin mention the Akri and the Ukala, whom the founding ancestors met on arrival, but it is not certain whether these people were Igbo-speaking or bore the kind of specific names that other Igbo groups bear like Nri, Ngwa, Ezza, Otanzu, and Ikwerre. Whatever the case might have been, it is only logical that we begin our search for Anioma origins in Igboland, east of the Niger. In this chapter we shall follow Anioma people to their original birthplaces. To do so satisfactorily, however, we must be prepared to examine two of the exciting, yet unresolved, questions about the Igbo-speaking people themselves, namely, who are the Igbo people, and where did they come from?

Simon Ottenberg, one of the leading scholars and pioneers of modern Igbo studies, has noted that the Igbos "are one of the most unusual peoples in Africa," a people known for their "high achievement skills."[1] The precolonial Igbo were one of the most numerous ethnic groups of Africa and yet one of the least understood. Their

1

homelands had one of the highest rural population densities in the continent, reaching a thousand persons per square mile in some districts. This high density could not have been sustained without a complex and yet stable political system and the availability of abundant food staples. Basil Davidson, a leading African historian, has rightly observed that in historical times, the Igbo "have shown a quite outstanding capacity for political and economic adaptation, social coherence, and ideological self-assurance."[2] Furthermore, Thurstan Shaw, the renowned archaeologist to whom we owe much of our knowledge of the early culture and civilization of the Igbo people, has noted that the high density of Igbo population could be explained in terms of "the antiquity and effectiveness of yam cultivation and the exploitation of the oil palm."[3] He wondered if it was a coincidence "that the densest populations in sub-Saharan Africa are in southern Nigeria where the combination of yam cultivation and the exploitation of the oil palm, providing complementary food values, have been most highly developed?"[4]

These observations are clearly borne out in the social, economic, and political organizations of the Igbo. Until well into the twentieth century, each town or village, whether large or small, remained reasonably democratic and independent. Also, even though the Igbo political structures and gender relations suggest some amount of stratification, most people enjoyed personal freedom. A stable political system ensured adequate food supply which in turn encouraged the development of an elaborate interregional trade and a sophisticated craft industry that produced bronze and brass objects such as those that were unearthed at Igbo-Ukwu. A highly developed culture flourished in the Igbo core area and its major towns of Nri, Enugwu-Ukwu, Igbo-Ukwu, Awka, Isu, and Orlu. An elaborate commercial relationship was established between the Igbo people of this region and the outside world.[5]

The Igbo are one of the most ancient groups in Nigeria and have occupied their present locus for such a long time that no one knows where they came from. In a sense, one could say that even the Igbos themselves, despite the great importance they attach to their past, are not certain about their origin. For, as Elizabeth Isichei has pointed out, "No historical question arouses more interest among present-day Igbos than the inquiry, 'Where did the Igbos come from?'"[6] Despite the curiosity, the origin of the Igbo people has remained elusive, resulting in a wide range of speculation. The first European visitors to southeastern Nigeria, for example, were baffled by the sociopolitical structures they encountered among the Igbo people, and wondered how freedom could have reigned in a situation that looked anarchic, how a population that was so dense could have functioned without some monarchies or standing armies or police force. Some of them lavishly praised the Igbo culture, arguing that it could not have been the product of internal development but must have derived from some existing advanced civilizations. Some insisted that the Igbo people came from the Middle East, and others pointed to what they considered to be striking similarities between the Hebrews and the Igbos.

George T. Basden, an agent of the Church Missionary Society (CMS) who spent forty years in southern Nigeria, compared the customs of the Igbo people with those of the Israelites and found many similarities, especially in regard to language, the law of sanctuary, circumcision, propitiation rituals, and the belief in supreme beings.[7] Relying partly on evidence provided by Richard F. Burton in his *Wanderings in West Africa*, Basden argued that the Jews themselves adopted the custom of circumcision from the Egyptians and suggested that the Igbo must have acquired the custom from the same original source.[8] Like Burton and other European visitors, Basden believed that at some remote time, the Igbo either actually lived near, or had very close associations with the Semitic peoples, but the successive waves of invasion which started in northeast Asia and were carried down through Egypt triggered a population movement which pushed the Igbo into Sub-Saharan Africa. Having finally settled down on the Lower Niger, the Igbo retained ideas and customs handed down from generation to generation.

Percy Amuray Talbot, another British visitor, compared Igbo cultures with those of the people of North Africa and concluded that Igbo cultures either derived from North African cultures or were influenced by them. Commenting on the Earth Spirit, variously termed *Ale, Ala, Ana, or Ani,* Talbot stated that she occupied the second most important position in the Igbo pantheon. "She is the great Mother Goddess, the spirit of fertility, the nearest and dearest of all the deities. Some of her statues in the Ibo Mbari temples . . . with a child in her arms or on her knees and a halo round her head and with the crescent moon often depicted on or near her, are reminiscent of some Italian Madonnas and still more of Ast [Auset] or Isis with her son Horus. The attitudes of the two goddesses are very similar. Often also, as with the Cretan goddess, snakes are modelled in attendance on her."[9]

The works of these and other European observers were cited in scholarly texts, which created in the minds of the Igbos themselves the impression that their ancestors and their cultures were of foreign origin. For example, the well-known Igbo historian, Modilim Achufusi, argued that the Igbo people probably migrated to their present location from the Lake Chad region during the first millennium A.D.[10] Other Igbos, especially those who had received a strong Christian upbringing, paraded themselves as the descendants of one of the lost tribes of Israel, apparently echoing Olaudah Equiano and James A. Horton who claimed that the Igbo culture, including their religion, contained strong elements of "Hebrewisms."[11] Horton thought that *Ibo,* which was spelled as *Heebo* or *Eboe,* by some eighteenth-century writers, was a corruption of *Hebrew.* Horton went on to describe the Eboe as a "lost race of Israel who had occupied parts of Egypt during the days of Moses."[12] These attempts to invent some strange origins for the Igbo people compounded the confusion rather than clarified matters. Nor did Igbo scholars themselves help to resolve the problem. This "slothful" attitude of Igbo scholars caused Simon Ottenberg in 1961 and Adiele Afigbo in 1972 to lament the deplorable state of Igbo studies.[13] Nine years later, Afigbo was still disturbed that "Scholarly research into Igbo culture history has lagged far behind research into Yoruba or Edo culture history."[14]

Some recent publications have helped to widen our perceptions of the origins of the Igbo people even though there are still a number of unanswered questions. Austin Shelton has suggested that the problem of reconstructing the Igbo origins emanated from the fact that the Igbo had no professional historians like the *griots* of the Western Sudan, nor did they have professional storytellers. The result was that each descent group transmitted its own traditions in its own way.[15] The absence of professional historians and storytellers may well explain the confusion that characterized the early history of the Igbo people. New traditions could have been invented as circumstances warranted. A researcher might return to a settlement some years after his or her first visit to chance upon different sets of traditions. This phenomenon must have contributed to the contradictions that we find even in "scholarly" Igbo history.

ARCHAEOLOGY AND THE ORIGINS OF THE IGBO PEOPLE

It was at Ibadan that some scholars began in the 1950s and 1960s to make conscious attempts to scientifically rehabilitate the Igbo past. This initiative was first taken up, not only by historians, but also by archaeologists, anthropologists, and linguists who collected valuable archaeological, ethnographic, and linguistic data; interpretation of these historical records was painfully interrupted by the Nigerian civil war of 1967–70, however, and many valuable materials that had been collected were destroyed before they could be analyzed. After the civil war, a new breed of archaeologists emerged at the University of Nigeria, Nsukka, admirably following the footsteps of Thurstan Shaw and Donald D. Hartle, who had pioneered some major archaeological works in the Igbo-Ukwu, Nsukka, and Afikpo areas. There was also Michael Onwuejeogwu, whose anthropological works at Agukwu Nri and other settlements in the Anambra valley revealed a civilization of considerable antiquity.

Since neither oral traditions nor written records provided definite answers to Igbo origins, the archaeologists intensified their efforts to "dig them up." They began by bypassing the theories of an "Eastern origin" and the hamitic hypothesis which had influenced such speculations, and went on to focus their attention on Igboland as the original home of the Igbo people.

Although our concern in this chapter is with the Igbo people, we must make reference to the wider African historiography in order to understand the considerable problems involved in reconstructing the Igbo past. The first point to mention is that contemporary African historiography is predominantly Eurocentric. It is a negative image, a product of European cultural arrogance and racism. It is also the product of the hamitic hypothesis which, among other things, is based on the assumption that Africans had no historical past to exhibit, and that everything of value ever found in Africa was brought there by the hamites, allegedly a branch of the caucasian or white race, or some wandering, "pastoral Europeans."[16] One imperial historian, Hugh Trevor-Roper, a professor of history at Oxford University, was bold enough to write in 1965 that there was little or no African history to teach, but only the history of Europeans in Africa. He said that the African past was nothing but the unrewarding gyrations of barbarous tribes in picturesque but irrelevant corners of the globe.[17]

For most of the colonial period, most African historical writings were those that concerned themselves with the activities of Europeans in Africa, never with the Africans themselves, except for those moments when these ethnically biased authors considered it necessary to show how "barbarous" Africans were or how deserving they might be of European charity. To most Europeans, the most attractive books about Africa bore such titles as *Sir George Goldie and the Making of Nigeria, or Cecil Rhodes and the Making of Rhodesia.* The educational curriculum was geared toward making Africans half Europeans or assimilated "natives"; as God made man in his own image in the Garden of Eden, so would the Europeans make the Africans in the European image in the jungles of Africa.

The tendency to deny Africans their heritage and their contributions to world development became an European obsession despite the fact that the European, Asian, and other chroniclers and travellers who came in contact with Africans in ancient, medieval, and early modern times spoke highly of the Africans they met. They also gave highly impressive descriptions of Africa as they saw it. Herodotus, Homer, Ibn Battuta, Ibn Hawqal, Ibn Khaldun, Leo Africanus and the Portuguese and Dutch explorers ranked Africans as highly as, and sometimes higher than, Europeans in terms of civility and overall humanity. But by the mid-nineteenth century, these positive images had turned negative. Africa had become the "Dark Continent" and its people, uncivilized.

This sudden change of attitude has been traced back to 1798 when Napoleon of France and his scientists raided Egypt and looted the treasures deposited in the pyramids. In the process, however, they found there the evidence of a civilization that was more ancient than the civilizations of Rome and Greece. They found evidence that the beginnings of science, art, mathematics, astronomy, navigational science and writing were in Egypt, and that the originators of these activities were Africans. Over time a consensus developed among scholars and scientists that: the Egyptians were Africans,[18] not Europeans or Asians; the civilization they built in pre-Christian and pre-Islamic eras was African; and this ancient civilization had its origins, not even in Egypt itself, but in the regions south of the fifth cataract, that is, in Nubia, Kush, Abyssinia, Somalia and the regions around Lake Victoria, in present-day Uganda. In fact, the ancient Greeks had no doubt whatsoever that the Africans they knew were "the favorites of the gods," that Osiris, Isis, and Horus were African deities, that the concepts of the trinity and virgin birth were African, that the Egyptians were merely a branch of the Somali, Ethiopian, and Nubian people, and that Pythagoras, the greatest of the Greek mathematicians, learned from the Egyptians what the Egyptians had learned from the Ethiopians.

These revelations were too bitter a pill for the new breed of European intellectuals and clergy of the mid-nineteenth century to swallow, since they contradicted certain ideologies extant in Europe at this time. This was the period when pseudo-scientific racism and Social Darwinism were gaining wide acceptance in Western Europe and North America. The European racists constructed an imaginary ladder of human evolution, placed themselves on top of it, and consigned the

Africans to its lowest rungs. Having done this, they went on to argue that if the Africans were so base, how could they have originated the most advanced civilization the world ever knew?

Since the Eurocentrists could not suppress all the evidence that kept surfacing, they had to explain it in other ways. For example, without any justification, they argued that a nomadic way of life was superior to an agricultural one and that the nomadic groups in Africa originally were not Africans but wandering Europeans. They went on to assert that the nomadic groups were the carriers of high cultures, and that it was they who taught the Africans the art of orderly government.[19] They also claimed that the Fulani people of West Africa, together with the nomadic Gala, Massai, and the other pastoral groups of Eastern Africa, looked like Europeans and therefore were either their cousins or some of "the lost tribes of Israel."

But these Europeans had a real problem dealing with agricultural African communities that exhibited what they termed "high cultures." They tried to circumvent the problem by attributing these cultures to non-African origins. For example, they claimed that the Yorubas of southern Nigeria, because of their complex political systems and highly developed customs and religious practices, originally were not Africans, but immigrants from Yemen, or Mecca. As already mentioned, some compared the customs of the Igbo people with those of the Jews and found many "Hebrewisms" in both. Likewise, the Great Zimbabwe, Europeans claimed, was not the product of internal African development but that of some existing advanced civilizations; Eurocentrists therefore had no difficulty attributing the Great Zimbabwe to the Phoenicians, the Syrians, and the Indians.

From these declarations, one can see a deliberate attempt to remove sections of Africa and their people from the African continent. European "scholars" invented the meaningless term *negroid*, to confuse, divide, and rule the Africans. For, once the term had been accepted within the dominant western intellectual and political circles, it was easy to speak of "black" and "white" Africa, and of Supra- and Sub-Saharan Africa. Even today, some Eurocentric Africanist scholars have no problem speaking of "Bantu Africa," another meaningless term.

What the European writers focused on proving was that the Africans were incapable of starting or inventing anything of value, that only those groups in Africa who were related to the Europeans, or looked like Europeans, or had had prior contacts with the Europeans or their cousins, the Semites, could. The Twa or Mbuti or M'Baka, whom the Europeans called Pygmies, together with the Khoi and San, whom they called Hottentots and Bushmen, respectively, were described as the "cousins" of the Negroes, and therefore true Africans. This is understandable, for if the "Pygmies" and the "Bushmen" and the "Hottentots" had built pyramids or Zimbabwan-type stone structures, perhaps they would have been described as some of the lost tribes of the Anglo-Saxons.

Unfortunately, the myth that the Africans had no history waxed strong, giving rise to two dominant attitudes toward native Africans. Some thinkers and writers believed that the Africans had to be brought under European political domination in order to benefit from European civilization. Other Eurocentrists thought that the Africans were one of the fallen races of mankind who could be uplifted through works of charity. These two attitudes gave rise to such concepts as the "white man's burden," "trusteeship," and "civilizing missions," by which the Europeans arrogated for themselves the role of the custodians of the Africans. These prevailing beliefs also sanctioned the appropriation of African land by violence.

Edith R. Sanders, together with other Africanist scholars, have demonstrated that the hamitic hypothesis and the myth of African barbarity were founded on misconceptions and were calculated to mislead.[20] In fact, since the birth of the new African studies in the 1940s, African scholars have endeavored to demonstrate that Africa had a glorious past that was worthy of scholarly investigation. But their efforts have sometimes been counterproductive, for rather than emphasize the historical facts, most would begin with the time-consuming attempt to prove that Africans had a meaningful past. In short, since the Europeans had spent so much effort proving that the Africans were uncivilized, African scholars had to prove, one way or another, that the opposite was true. These exercises only helped to retard the pace with which African history was being rehabilitated. It certainly retarded the reconstruction of Igbo history by diverting the attention of the first generation of modern Igbo historians away from Igboland as a possible original home of the Igbo people.

While some Igbo people represented themselves as members of some of the lost tribes of Israel, archaeologists at Nsukka avoided this unrewarding theory by carrying out numerous excavations in Igboland, a number of them revealing spectacular finds. When tested, some finds confirmed that Igboland had been inhabited for at least 60,000 years. Further studies revealed that many of the material cultures of the present-day Igbo people resembled those of the early inhabitants who had occupied these sites over the past millennia. Archaeologists were able to show how these ancient cultures developed, stage by stage, to produce what we know today as the Igbo culture.

The oldest archaeological site so far discovered in Igboland is the Ugwuele pre-historical site of Uturu near Okigwe. Archaeologists described it as a "stone-age site" because of the spectacular stone tool specimens they found there. Among these were several heaps of early stone-age artifacts, mainly hand axes, cleavers, stone knives, and other small tools. Archaeologists believe that the Uturu stone-age culture was contemporaneous with the Acheulean culture. They also believe that the types and technology of the tools found at Uturu belonged to the great "hand axe" culture which was worldwide and which archaeologists believe flourished from 1.6 million to 50,000 years ago.[21] Similar Acheulean sites have been found on the Jos Plateau of central Nigeria.

Archaeologists also believe that it was toward the end of the Acheulean period that men and women in Africa discovered the use of fire. This was a major contribution to world culture. With fire, they burned bush and trapped animals. With fire, they drove animals out of caves to make room for their habitation, and could convert previously indigestible plants into food. With fire, men and women produced better tools. In fact, it was with the discovery of the use of fire that humans, in due course, began to produce metal implements. Because of the large number of stone tools that archaeologists recovered at Uturu, they have described the site as the largest stone-age axe factory in the world. Francis Anozie, an archaeologist at the University of Nigeria, Nsukka, is of the view that no other site has yet been discovered in the world with such a large quantity of stone artifacts.[22]

This does not in any way imply that the occupants of the ancient site of Uturu were Igbo or that the present-day Igbo cultures derived from the Uturu stone-age culture. What it intends to show is that Igboland (a geographical location) was one of the earliest centers of mankind's physical, technological, and cultural evolution.

Archaeologists carried out more excavations in southeastern Nigeria in the 1970s and 1980s. The interpretations of their finds confirm that many parts of Igboland had been occupied for a long time. The data also revealed that the occupants of these sites, in addition to stone tool manufacture, developed such skills as iron working and pottery and bead making. For example, some pieces of *tuyere,* or clay nozzles, a number of pit or bowl furnaces, and pounding implements were discovered at Lejja, a small town situated about ten miles south of Nsukka. An archaeological study of these finds confirms that Lejja was an iron-working settlement and that the technique of smelting used there was the pit or bowl furnace which archaeologists believe was the earliest and most primitive technique of smelting.[23]

The Lejja finds are unique in the sense that they suggest that iron was being worked in Igboland before iron technology was said to have been introduced into Sub-Saharan Africa from the Middle East. If the dates of the Lejja finds are confirmed, they would strengthen the evidence that iron smelting was indigenous to Africa, south of the Sahara. Archaeologists at Nsukka believe that iron-smelting, like all inventions, could have been discovered accidentally or independently in Africa. They are therefore sceptical of any thesis which might claim that iron working was difficult and complicated, and that no group of people could have discovered the process without first passing through a bronze age.[24]

Other important archaeological discoveries in Igboland include Donald D. Hartle's finds at Afikpo, and Vincent E. Chikwendu's discoveries, also at Afikpo and later at Amichi and Ichida.[25] Interpretation of these finds confirms that a definite Igbo culture and a peculiar Igbo personality began to evolve about five thousand years ago from a mosaic of cultures and people that occupied the forest and semi-grassland belts running from southeastern Nigeria to the Niger-Benue confluence.[26] During this period, many of the groups gave up hunting and gathering and adjusted to an agricultural mode of living. At one of the Afikpo sites, for instance, stone implements decreased as the number and variety of pottery increased. Also, archaeologists have evidence that when this ancient community at Afikpo reached a fully agricultural stage, it experienced a "population explosion." One finds in this region a continuity of cultural development illustrated by the fact that the Afikpo pottery of about 3,000 B.C. resembles the pottery of present-day Afikpo, while the *ichi* face marks found on terra cotta heads of ninth century A.D. Igbo-Ukwu resemble the *ichi* face marks of present-day Umunri.

These archaeological interpretations strongly corroborate Ottenberg's own works in the Afikpo area. Ottenberg stated that "the Afikpo society has undergone constant changes through its discoverable past," changes which produced cultural variations that became more identifiable in the more recent centuries. He reported that the earliest inhabitants of Afikpo might not have been Igbos or might have been related to ethnic groups in the Cross River estuary. Whatever their origin, these people hunted and fished but did not travel or trade extensively.[27] However, Ottenberg suggested, until the slave trade was introduced into the Bight of Biafra, many patrilineal Igbos moved into the area from the Okposi and Okigwe areas, and were followed by farmers and traders from the Arochukwu area, causing a population buildup. When the slave trade became the dominant economic activity of that region, the Aro, together with the economic and political systems they operated, transformed Afikpo into a center for the slave trade, which in turn was linked in economic and political interdependence with the other major slave markets at Uburu, Uzuakoli, and Arochukwu.[28]

From the works of Ottenberg, Hartle, Chikwendu, and Anozie, one can see how the earliest inhabitants of Afikpo and Uturu might not have been Igbos but over the centuries or even millennia, the population acquired strong Igbo characteristics due to the influx of Igbo-speaking people.

Meanwhile, by the first century A.D., the evolution of the Igbo culture had begun to accelerate rapidly. The widespread use of iron tools enabled the Igbo people to further tame the forest. Archaeologists and anthropologists are of the view that the first people to make the transition to "higher civilizations" were those groups who rapidly changed from the use of digging sticks to iron tools. With iron tools, Igbo farmers spread the cultivation of yams and cocoyams and, in due course, introduced the new crops of southeast Asian origin, such as bananas and plantains.

The use of iron tools and the rapid spread of agricultural production resulted in the evolution of a sophisticated culture in the Igbo core area. They also encouraged the expansion of both internal and external trade. The elements usually associated with this culture are iron working, bronze casting, divination, status attainment, yam cultivation, and the yam cult. As these early people travelled from home, they carried with them the major traits of the Igbo culture, including agricultural practices and rituals. Scholars concerned with Igbo studies believe that the core area is the cradle of the Igbo people where *Chukwu*, the Great Creator, gave them the gift of yams.

THE DIFFUSION OF THE IGBO PEOPLE

The rapid agricultural change of this period manifested itself in a population explosion in the Igbo heartland. As the centuries rolled by, men and women began to respond to the problems associated with soil depletion and a progressively unrewarding agricultural activity by

moving into more favorable locations. The result was that from about
the ninth century A.D. some lineages and clans in the Igbo core area began to fan out in all directions, almost imperceptibly at first, but more
rapidly later. Michael Onwuejeogwu has been particularly fascinated
by this diffusion process which he labelled *migrations* and classified
them into six categories based on the approximate dates when they
began and ended.[29] The more recent movements out of this core area
occurred during the last thousand years or so, when some Igbo men
and women moved south into the Niger delta, some east into the
Cross river estuary, and others across the Niger River. My personal research in the western part of the Igbo culture area has convinced me,
however, that these movements should not be conceived as large-scale
migrations but as an occasional breaking up of family groups due to
civil disturbances, land exhaustion, wanderlust, or the desire to fulfill
certain ritual obligations, and the departure of some of the members
to some uninhabited districts nearby.

My assumptions about Igbo diffusion are confirmed by oral traditions. Elders in the Igbo core area have no definite recollections of any
distant immigration of their people. Some recall nearby towns, not
more than forty or fifty miles away, as their original hometowns. On
the other hand, elders in the periphery of Igboland point to settlements in the core area as their ancestral homelands. This is particularly the case with the traditions of origin of many Anioma groups
who point to Nri, Isu, Nteje, Achala, and Ogidi (all in the Igbo core
area) as their ancestral homelands.

I therefore have chosen to regard these movements as diffusion, to
distinguish them from migrations proper. Those oral historians and
ethnographers who still conceive of these movements as migrations
might have been influenced by the biblical story of the tribes of Israel
who roamed about in the wilderness for forty years only to cover a distance of forty miles—from Egypt to Israel. We shall presently see how
this scenario of endless wandering was played out in the somewhat dramatic "migrations" of the Umuezechima clan, a migration that began
from Benin City, or its vicinity, to Issele-Ukwu and Onitsha, a distance
of sixty or eighty miles, but took several generations to complete.

Whatever happened in the remote past, the search for better agricultural lands must have been the most compelling reason for the diffusion of the Igbo people into Anioma. Parts of Igboland still carry
some of the highest population densities in Africa. For such a spectacular population explosion to have occurred, the aborigines must have
developed certain skills that enabled them to conquer a particularly
difficult environment and subsequently to fan out in all directions, to

secure fertile lands, raw materials, and to establish local and long-distance commerce.

Movements out of the core area having begun, they continued, filling up all available space, until the Igbo people came in contact with other ethnic groups. In the north the Igbo came in contact with the Idoma, Igala, and Tiv. In the east they met with the Ibibio, Efik, Yako, Mbembe and the other ethnic groups in and around the Cross River valley. In the south, the Igbo continued to expand into Etche and Ikwerre areas but were stopped just north of the delta and coastal swamps where yams could be cultivated, but only with the greatest difficulty. In the west the Igbo crossed the Niger River to occupy sites on the opposite bank, where they were variously known as *ndi Oshimili, ndi Aniocha, ndi Ika,* and *ndi Ndokwa.* Their movement in this direction brought them within close proximity of Benin City, the Edo capital (See map 1).

Oral traditions confirm that the arrival of each Igbo-speaking group was contested by neighboring inhabitants. The result of each contest, however, was determined by the strength of the opposition. In the northern borderlands, the Ezza and Nzam struggled with the Idoma, Igala, and Tiv for land but after some centuries, the groups came to recognize a "no-man's land." In the eastern borderlands the Igbo pushed the Ibibio and the other groups further east and south, between the Imo River and the Cross River estuary. Some territories in the northern and eastern borderlands are still disputed.

In the south, the Igbo did not meet with any strong opposition largely because they did not move into the coastal swamps and islands where the Ijo had established themselves as fishing and salt-making communities. Because these regions were unsuitable for yam cultivation, the Igbos stayed out of them. In the seventeenth and eighteenth centuries, however, many Igbo people moved into some eastern delta settlements, not to grow yams, but to participate in the Atlantic slave trade which was so vigorous that it resulted in a population explosion in the Niger Delta city-states. Alarmed by the endless streams of immigrants into this region, the rulers of Bonny, Okirika, Kalabari, and Nembe adopted certain strategies to contain what has been described as "the Igbo peril," that is, the influx of Igbos into these communities. The Ijos also insisted on the rapid acculturation of strangers, but neither of these measures succeeded in checking the rapid population growth. By the mid-nineteenth century, the Ijos had begun to reconsider their ancient attachment to their fishing and salt-making environments and soon began to head for the mainland. By the early twentieth century, after the establishment of British colonial rule, the

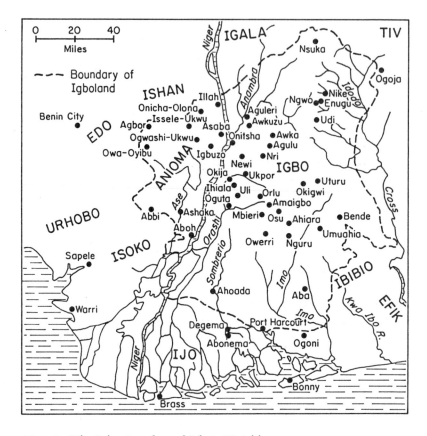

Map 1: The Igbo People and Their Neighbors

Ijos began to dispute with the Igbos over lands on the mainland, especially at Port Harcourt, around the railway terminal and harbor which formally bore the Igbo name, *Ugwu ocha.*

In the west, the arrival of the Igbo was not immediately contested until the rise of Benin as a powerful kingdom in the sixteenth century. Traditions state that during the reign of Oba Esigie (1504–50), many Igbo groups in the Edo-Igbo borderland were driven back toward the Igbo heartland. The people of Onitsha and Aboh were among those who were so displaced. These conflicts, which manifested themselves in the Anioma-Benin wars, will be examined in detail in the next chapter. There were other important Igbo movements during the era of the Atlantic slave trade, but most of them were directly or indirectly connected with the activities of the Aro, Abam, Ohafia, Edda, and Nike, which we shall also examine in the next chapter.

ANIOMA ORIGINS

Anioma people may therefore be rightly regarded as a branch of the wider Igbo community who live on the western side of the broad valley of the Lower Niger. They may also be regarded as the descendants of those Igbo men and women who, because of a combination of land shortages and population growth, began to cross the Niger in the ninth century A.D. to occupy some inviting sites on the west bank of the river. In their new homelands, they had the Edo-speaking groups as their western and northern neighbors, and the Isoko, Urhobo, and Ijo as their southern neighbors. As time went on, people from these communities began to join the established Anioma communities.

Our knowledge of the precolonial history of Anioma is limited, however. This is largely because these people did not write down all the elements of their history. Much of what is known about them today is derived from three sources, namely, oral traditions, the written accounts of the first European visitors to the Niger valley (explorers, traders, and missionaries), and the ethnographic reports of colonial administrators. A detailed study of these sources shows that most of the Anioma people, as we know them today, began to occupy the subregion during the last thousand years. One interesting thing about these sources is the revelation that most communities trace their origin to nearby settlements. Thus whereas some Nigerian groups may claim origin from such distant places as Egypt, Mecca, or Yemen, Anioma people still recall that their founding fathers and mothers migrated from places which were not more than two or three days' march away. This assertion is well illustrated by the early histories of such large Anioma communities as Ogwashi-Ukwu, Ogboli, Igbuzo and Asaba.

OGWASHI-UKWU AND OGBOLI ORIGINS

The Ogwashi-Ukwu and Ogboli traditions of origin state that the founders of Ogboli-Igbuzo and Ogwashi-Ukwu were born of the same parents. They were the sons of Eze Nshi (Eze Nri Agu), whose period of reign has yet to be determined. Their mother was one of the many wives of the king. Both brothers lived happily with their parents at Nshi until the senior one, Odaigbo, committed murder.

Spilling the blood of a kinsman was a serious offense and, according to the law of the land, the offender must either go into exile or be hanged. Eze Nri Agu and Odaigbo's mother chose exile for their son. They prepared a pot of medicine for Odaigbo and instructed him to settle down anywhere the pot fell from his head. Edini, Odaigbo's younger brother (some accounts say that Edini was, instead, Odaigbo's sister), volunteered to accompany the exile; Edini was also presented with a pot of medicine and given similar instructions. It is believed that Odaigbo and Edini were accompanied into exile by a sizeable party of volunteers in order to lighten their pain and loneliness.

The group left Nri and travelled westward until they got to the Niger River and were ferried across by some riverine traders. They journeyed further west but when they got to Ani Udo, barely three miles from the Niger, Edini's pot fell to the ground and broke. He and his companions cleared the bush and founded there a settlement that later took the name of Ogboli.

After a few days, possibly months, of rest at Ani Udo, Odaigbo and some of his companions resumed their journey westward. Balanced on Odaigbo's head was his pot of medicine. When the party got to Eke, somewhere near the present site of Ogwashi-Ukwu, Odaigbo's pot fell from his head and broke. The party stopped, cleared the bush, and founded a new settlement there.

The years rolled by and Odaigbo became the father of four sons: Dei, Eshe, Ase, and Etumukwu. Odaigbo became a prosperous man and built an *ogwa* (a shrine or meeting shed) in memory of his father and the home he left behind. This *ogwa* was very large and because it was fashioned after his father's meeting shed at Nshi, passers-by spoke of it as *ogwa ukwu nwa eze Nshi*. This term was equally applied to the settlement which grew around it. In later days, however, this term was shortened to Ogwa-Nshi-Ukwu, which the British mispronounced as Ogwashi-Uku.[30]

At Ani Udo, Edini also prospered. He became the father of Eze-keke, Ezekeke the father of Umuokpala, Umuokpala the father of Umuodogwu, Umuodogwu the father of Achoshia, Achoshia the father of Odogwu. Oral historians believe that many of the Ogboli clans that dot Anioma today were formerly the inhabitants of the original Ogboli community that was founded by Edini in Ani Udo. They also believe that the Benin-Anioma wars played a major role in dispersing the original residents of the Ogboli community, forcing them to abandon their homes at Ani Udo. Some moved closer to Igbuzo, where their new settlement became known as Ogboli-Igbuzo. Some moved to Issele-Ukwu to occupy the Ogboli-Issele-Ukwu quarters. Many more moved to Atuma and Akwukwu, while a large party fled across the Niger river to settle in Ogboli-Onitsha. Till this day, these Anioma communities still boast that they are *umu Nshi,* that is, the children of Nri.[31]

IGBUZO

"Our great-grandfather was Umejei, the son of Ikenga, the king of Isu," recalled an Igbuzo elder.[32] According to oral tradition, Umejei left Isu because he committed an offense against his people. It seems that Umejei's wife had a lover, and when Umejei heard of this distressing rumor, he questioned her several times about it, but on each of those occasions the woman denied the story. Umejei then nicknamed her *Ishinta anago,* that is, "Ishinta who is always denying." Both Ishinta and her lover soon ran out of luck and were caught by Umejei. Overwhelmed with an uncontrollable rage, Umejei killed the man.

The people of Isu gathered to discuss these acts of adultery and murder. Even though they agreed that Umejei had been wronged, they could not overturn the customary law which stipulated that any man who killed another would hang or go into exile. In a different version of the Igbuzo traditions, Umejei supposedly killed a man during a wrestling contest, and never nursed any ill feelings toward him.[33] Regardless which of the traditions is more accurate, to the people of Isu, killing, whether wilful or accidental, was a serious transgression against the earth goddess, *ani.* No one ever got away with murder in Isu.

Umejei's father was greatly disturbed when he learned of the tragedy. He gathered together his entire household and vowed not to watch his son die a disgraceful death. He also stated that "the son of a king never dies in his father's presence." He asked Umejei and Umejei's senior sister, Onuoha, to prepare to go into exile. He prepared a pot of medicine and asked Onuoha to carry it on her head. The party was instructed to travel across the Niger River and settle down wherever the pot miraculously fell off Onuoha's head.

Onuoha's husband, Anyala Obum, volunteered to accompany his wife and Umejei. Umejei's younger brother Abala, joined the group. Oko, Ishiagwu, and Ewulu also accompanied the exiles. The king of Isu gave each of these volunteers a pot of medicine and asked each of them to settle down anywhere his pot fell.[34]

Early the next morning, before the first crow of the cock, the party set out for the unknown. They headed west, but soon after crossing the Niger River, the pots of the travellers fell, one after the other, and each brother cleared the bush and built his settlement as he had been instructed. It was at Omeze in the present-day Igbuzo that Onuoha's pot fell. Here Umejei, together with his sister and her husband, founded the nucleus of the town that became known as Igbuzo.[35]

After some years' stay at Igbuzo, Umejei fathered three sons. The first was named Onuma, meaning that it was out of anger that Umejei had killed a man at Isu. The second son was called Oshe-Ukwu, meaning that it was due to the palaver of the great ones that he had to leave his father's house. The third son was called Oshe-Nta, meaning that Umejei had become so small that no one now asked about him. The people of present-day Igbuzo believe that the nine maximal lineages of their town sprang from the children of Umejei.[36]

These oral narratives might be inaccurate in detail, but they are reliable in outline. For instance, while it is plausible that Umejei was the founder of Igbuzo and that he had come from an eastern Igbo town called Isu, it is doubtful that the other Anioma towns of Abala, Oko, Ishiagwu, and Ewulu were founded contemporaneously with Igbuzo by the men who accompanied Umejei. Second, no one can say whether Umejei's father was the sole ruler of Isu or one of the titled chiefs, *ndi ozo*, of Isu. Third, there are many settlements in Igboland with the name Isu. It is not possible to identify the very one from where Umejei started his journey. One other problem with the Igbuzo, Ogboli, and Ogwashi-Ukwu oral narratives has to do with their claims that the major actors in these "migrations" were exiles, carrying pots of medicine. However, even if these accounts are inaccurate in detail, at least they point to the roles of religion and ritual sanctions in directing early Igbo "migrations." In other words, the early Igbo diffusion cannot be explained in material terms alone.

Whether the first known occupants of Anioma were beckoned by psychological circumstances or not, the overwhelming evidence is that they were Igbo-speaking. The evidence further suggest that these early Igbo-speaking settlers were later joined by other immigrants from other places, as illustrated by the story of Asaba.

ASABA

Most Anioma traditions speak of migrations into Anioma, not out of it, suggesting that there was always enough land for newcomers. We have no evidence of wars resulting from land disputes; instead, we know that many communities admitted people of diverse origins. The growth of Asaba illustrates the way in which newcomers were welcomed and incorporated into existing Anioma communities. Asaba traditions recall that the first settlers in Asaba were Ezeanyanwu and his descendants. Not much is known about the provenance of Ezeanyanwu but his name suggests that he was Igbo and must have come from eastern Igboland. He may have been one of those Igbo men who, as previously discussed, crossed the Niger into Anioma in the earlier centuries in search of fertile lands, meat, and elephant tusks. Several generations later, the descendants of Ezeanyanwu were joined at Asaba by the parents of Nnebisi. Nnebisi's father was Ikenga, an Igala man, and his mother, whose name oral historians have forgotten, was an Igbo woman from Nteje, near Awka.[37]

As time went on, many more immigrants entered Asaba. Among the newcomers were some Ishan-speaking farmers, traders, and craftsmen. On arrival, the people of Asaba provided them with farmlands and wives. Oral traditions state that the Umunkwo quarters of the Umuezei lineage of Asaba were founded by Nkwo, who had come from an Ishan town. Nkwo, it is said, married Onyebuchi, a daughter of Ezenei, and it was from this union that the present-day people of Umunkwo sprang. However, because Nkwo was a stranger and Onyebuchi a female, the people of Umunkwo could not produce a *diokpa* (the most senior elder and custodian of ancestral shrines) in Asaba, not even in Umuezei.[38] Like the people of Umunkwo, the occupants of the Ogbe-Ochele quarters of Asaba descended from another immigrant from Ishanland, while the founders of the Idumojei and Umuokwubata lineages came from Osamala and Igalaland, respectively. Finally, the Ogbilo section of the Umuonaje lineage was founded by immigrants from Ijoland.[39] Thus Asaba exhibited what one might describe as disjointed migration and settlement patterns.

It must be stated that a number of Anioma communities claimed origin from existing Anioma settlements, while a few claimed that they had always occupied their present sites and that their ancestors did not come from any of the places listed above. Some informants cited strange and doubtful traditions that maintained that their founding fathers dropped from the sky with boxes or shells containing sand. At the time of their arrival, they said, these supermen and women from the sky perched on the branches of trees because the land was covered with water, but when sprinkled with sand, it became dry. Such traditions were meant to explain and legitimize the settlers' claims to the lands they occupied. Perhaps these communities might have occupied their present settlements for so long that they forgot the provenance of their founding fathers and, for political reasons, had to invent new traditions or conceal the old ones.

In any case, large numbers of Anioma people are certain of the origins of the first men and women who founded their settlements. As we have seen, many have identified some particular towns in eastern Igboland as the original hometowns of these founding ancestors. As would be expected, most of these towns are within close proximity of Nri and Awka, that is, in the old Onitsha Province, which had experienced a population explosion along with soil deterioration in the earlier centuries. Names like *Nteje, Isu, Achala, Okuzu, Nri, Ogidi* and *Awka* feature prominently in these traditions. On the other hand, the Anioma groups with traditions that link them up with the Nri-Awka area include communities within Asaba, Okpanam, Igbuzo, Ogboli, Ogwashi-Ukwu, Illah, Abala, Atuma, Akwukwu, Ute-Okpu, Owa, Abbi, Obiarukwu, Amai, and others. Put another way, insofar as many Anioma groups claim to have come from eastern Igboland, their ancestral homes can be traced to an area situated within a radius of fifty miles from Nri, that is, within the area that is usually associated with the immediate Nri culture complex.

The foregoing claims are confirmed, not only by oral traditions, but also by the sheer fact of proximity, and by the realization that the Nri-Awka cultural influences are widespread in Anioma. A close look at the ethnographic patterns of these societies would convince the observer that the foundations of Anioma cultures are strongly linked to the Nri-Awka. Traces of these cultural traits are clearly borne out in the Anioma language, as well as in title associations, the instruments and symbols of leadership and authority, yam cults and festivals, dances, music, the Igbo market days, and the democratic and small-scale nature of these groups' political institutions. It is not surprising, therefore, that Anioma people should show a clear evidence of closer relationship to the "Onitsha Igbo" than they should to the Bini, Igala, Yoruba, or even to the other Igbo groups in the Nsukka, Abakiliki, Aro, Orlu, Owerri, Afikpo, and Ikwerre districts.

It would appear that most Anioma movements were inspired by the search for material wealth and spiritual freedom. Most founding fathers have been described as exiles, hunters, or travelling ritual specialists. We have seen that while the founding fathers of Ogwashi-Ukwu, Igbuzo and Ogboli were religious fugitives who had been implicated in cases of law-breaking, Nnebisi, a co-founder of Asaba, was a hunter from Nteje. Also, the founders of the Umuakpanshi and Umutei quarters of Illah have been described as travelling ritual specialists from Nri, while Kanagba, the founder of Obamkpa, whose travels took him as far as to Benin City, was a practicing herbalist from Ogidi.

If we accept that these traditions are reliable, why then did these fugitives, hunters, and ritual specialists from the Nri-Awka region direct their migrations toward Anioma? The stories of medicine-pot-carrying exiles notwithstanding, the more persuasive explanation would appear to be largely economic. The present vegetation of the Nri-Awka area is open palm forest although in the distant past it was rain forest. This transformation was due partly to over-cultivation and partly to the fact that the soils suffered from heavy leaching and surface erosion. Onwuejeogwu has suggested that it is for these reasons that the present-day people of Nri have taken more and more to trading, to the relative neglect of farming. It was probably for the same reasons that Nri men travelled widely as itinerant ritual specialists, since agriculture alone could not support the population.[40]

It is difficult to determine precisely when the population density of the Nri-Awka area began to strain the available natural resources. Thurstan Shaw has suggested that at least a thousand years ago the economy of the area was based partly on agriculture and partly on a wide range of commercial contacts with the outside world.[41] The economy also derived much of its sustenance from a high level of artistic craftsmanship that produced bronze objects, such as those that were unearthed at Igbo-Ukwu, and metal products, such as those of Awka smiths. These vocations presupposed trade, and trade meant contact. Thus, the search for fertile land, raw materials, and commerce must have impelled the Nri-Awka men to diffuse among their neighbors.

Naturally, any such diffusion must have begun with contiguous districts if these were rich in natural resources or favorable for trade. We have already observed that a thousand years ago there was enough land in Anioma for newcomers and that the soils were rich. The Niger River, which traversed this part of Igboland, was the most important trade route in West Africa. In addition, the distance from Nri or Awka to Asaba was only about twenty-five miles. This distance could have been covered in one day, and with convenient stops at Enugwu-Ukwu and Ogidi, a round trip on foot would have taken only two days. Also, a journey from Nri or Awka to Agbor with stops at Abagana, Asaba, Ogwashi-Ukwu, and Ubulu-Ukwu would have taken about four days to complete. These estimates were confirmed in 1906 when a colonial administrator, accompanied by a force of troops, marched from Asaba to Umunede (near Agbor), a distance of forty miles, in twenty-one hours.[42] In fact, Nri-Awka migrations into Anioma confirm the view that groups like the Igbo, the Ibibio, and the Efik were essentially autochthonous, and that when they moved, they moved into contiguous districts.

One other factor to consider in examining the diffusion of Igbo-speaking peoples is trade. Elephants were abundant in Anioma and ivory was very much coveted by Nri and Awka men. These men needed ivory with which to pay for their copper, lead, and, possibly, iron, as these metals were not mined locally. Ivory was also used for the manufacture of bangles and trumpets. Since Anioma was near at hand and elephants were abundant there, the Nri-Awka men could have acquired their ivory either by trade or by hunting for elephants. Oral traditions collected at Agukwu Nri confirm that Nri men obtained their ivory in Anioma by both methods. They also obtained fish and a number of agricultural products, which they paid for with bronze objects (such as bells), beads, specially designed cloth called *akwa akanka,* ritual knives, ritual spears, staffs for titled men, red caps, rings, anklets, and amulets.[43] Also, Awka smiths and traders sold, made, or repaired metal pots, hoes, knives, guns, powder, and a number of household utensils in Anioma. Over the years, some of these traders, hunters, smiths and ritual specialists must have decided either to settle among their hosts or to establish new settlements nearby, as there was enough land for everyone.[44]

Equally interesting is the fact that until the activities of Nri ritual specialists were proscribed by the colonial administration in 1911, Nri men continued to travel extensively in Anioma, carrying Nri culture with them. They were also the representatives of Eze Nri. Whenever they visited Anioma, they expected and received all the diplomatic privileges and courtesies they enjoyed in the east. A representative of Eze Nri was usually present during the taking of the *eze* or *ozo* title. On such occasions he offered the desired prayers and tied the ankle cords on new initiates. The travelling Nri ritual specialists cleansed polluted homes, set standards of moral conduct, and defined acts of abomination. As Richard Henderson has pointed out, the people of Nri acquired these rights because their divine king, Eze Nri, was "a mythological participant" in the creation of the earth. Since his sacrificed children were the first persons to bear the marks of ritual identity purification, Nri gained the right to confer certain emblems of such ritual purification, and since he was the first to develop a ritual relationship to the land, his people gained the right of spiritually cleansing every community of any sins committed against the land (nso-ani or alu).[45]

Most Nri men visiting Anioma were treated as diviners, and so, in addition to cleansing the communities of any sins committed against the land, they offered public prayers at public ceremonies, and private prayers in private homes. An Akwukwu elder who witnessed the activities of these travelling Nri ritual specialists at the turn of the century recalled that when they stopped over in a settlement, they were requested to offer prayers (igo ofo) and to remove misfortunes (ajahu), for which activities they received fees or gifts.[46] They also explained the causes of worries and perplexities (nsogbu uwa) to those who cared to find out, invoked certain powers that would prevent their recurrence, and then prepared the right charms and medicines to protect the users from some malignant, invisible forces. Since the travelling Nri were also fortune-tellers, they elaborated for those who paid the right fees what was going to befall them in the future, whether good or bad.

The unique position which the people of Nri occupied among the Igbo is clearly recorded by Major Arthur G. Leonard, who worked among the Anioma and other Igbo groups in the early twentieth century: "The street of the Nri family is the street of the gods, through which all who die in other parts of Igboland pass to the Land of the Spirits."[47] Also, Father Duhaze, who encountered these people in 1906, noted that the Umunri travelled widely in Igboland and influenced the cultures of their host communities. He observed that "the religious influence of Nri once extended over the whole of igbo country. The Nris were the high priests of the idols, and from their hands the chiefs loved to receive the insignia of office. They regulated even the building of huts for fetishes."[48]

Whereas the activities of Nri ritual specialists were terminated by a colonial enactment in 1911, those of Awka smiths were curtailed by both European commercial competition and Western technology. With the arrival of the steamboat came such mass-produced European hardware as hoes, knives, cutlasses, cooking pots, and even coins. For a while, Awka smiths held on, but after the first few decades of the twentieth century, when their products could no longer compete with imported European goods, they slowly recoiled to their hometown where they occupied themselves largely with the manufacture of a few ritual objects, highly decorated iron gates, and "home-made" guns.

The foregoing discussion suggests several conclusions. First, the most ancient Anioma towns were founded by immigrants from eastern Igboland. Second, these immigrants came from a number of towns situated around Nri and Awka. Third, until recently, a strong cultural link was maintained between the Anioma communities and the eastern Igbo people in the immediate vicinity of Nri-Awka.

It should not be assumed, however, that every Anioma settlement was founded by fresh immigrants from eastern Igboland. The available evidence is that many Anioma settlements were founded or enlarged by immigrants from already established towns and villages of Anioma. Examples of these are communities within Ubulu-Ukwu, Obiarukwu, Amai, Utagba-Ogbe (Kwale), Owa, Owa-Alero, and many others. Let us next examine the traditions of origin of some of these communities.

UBULU-UKWU

Ubulu-Ukwu is said to have been founded by immigrants from Afor, a town in the Kwale district. Tradition claims that two brothers, Ezemu and Aniobodo, left Afor to settle at Ubulu-Uno, where they disputed over who would rule the land, a dispute which persuaded Ezemu to leave. He travelled north and founded the town of Ubulu-Ukwu.

Ubulu-Ukwu later emulated many of the elements of Benin political institutions. Most of its titles—*Onishe, Iyase, Ojunwa, Ojiba* and *Ozoma*—were derived from Benin. Nevertheless, the present-day people of Ubulu-Ukwu still remember that their Obis did not have to receive their investiture from Benin. As an Ubulu-Ukwu elder put it, "Our Kings have never been crowned by the Obas of Benin. Although we had certain things in common with the Edos, we were never compelled to obtain permission from them before we did anything."[49]

OBIARUKWU AND THE UMU AKASHIADA CONFEDERACY

The traditions of origin of the Ukwuani groups suggest that these people are historically among the most recent settlers in Anioma. This suggestion stems from the fact that most of them claim origin from such existing Igbo settlements as Asaba, Aboh, Onitsha, and Ubulu-Ukwu. On the other hand, only a few of the Ukwuani communities, like Ogume, Okpai, and Ase, make mention of Benin in their traditions of origin, but even so, they do not seem to be anxious to trace their origins to Chima or Essumai.

Obiarukwu is an important Ukwuani town and its early history illustrates the fact that most Ukwuani settlements claim origin from existing Anioma settlements. Obiarukwu is called an inland town. Its inhabitants say that their ancestors arrived at different times, having been attracted to that spot by the clear water of the principal stream and by the very fertile nature of the soil. They also point out that their ancestral homes were only a few miles away.

Obiarukwu is a member of the Akashiada confederacy, whose other members are Umusume, Okuzu, Umuedede, Umuebu, Ezionum, and Eziokpo. The latter is believed to be the senior member of the confederacy, a belief that would seem to be confirmed by the fact that its elders are the keepers of the confederacy's major shrines. They also have the prerogative to officiate at the major ritual ceremonies of the clan. For instance, the common ritual of *ichi-okpala* is supervised by the *okpala ukwu* (most senior elder) of Eziokpo.[50] During the annual sacrifice to the eponymous ancestor, Akashiada, the whole clan meets at Eziokpo for the sacrifice, and the ceremony is led by the *okpala ukwu* of Eziokpo. The Abraka, who formerly belonged to the Akashiada confederacy but who later adopted the Urhobo language and customs, have since been excluded from these ceremonies. Moreover, it would appear that neither the Umu Akashiada nor the Abraka seem to harbor any strong desire for a reunion.[51]

Parts of these traditions have been contested, however. Some oral historians have stated that the first immigrants to Obiarukwu were inhabitants from Okuzu quarters, a "quarter" being a term used by British colonial officials to refer to the *ogbe,* a sociopolitical unit based on lineage. The Okuzu residents of Obiarukwu claim that their ancestors had left Okuzu, in eastern Igboland, to settle in Aboh and later moved on to take up residence at Umuebu. At Umuebu they felt dissatisfied with their share of the land and decided to move into an uninhabited area now known as Obiarukwu because the land there was better and larger than the land of Umuebu.[52] It would appear that in the course of time some of the relatives whom the people of Okuzu had left behind at Aboh also joined their kindred at Obiarukwu. These were the people of Umuedede. As time went on, some other lineages also left Umuebu to join the earlier settlers of Obiarukwu.

On the other hand, the people of Umuebu claim that their ancestors came from Ebu (an Anioma community), while the ancestors of those of Ezionum came from Asaba and Utchi.

However complicated the traditions of the these Anioma people may appear, one thing is borne out clearly, namely, that all the quarters of Obiarukwu and the Akashiada confederacy derived from existing Igbo settlements. It is also significant that their institutions and rituals are typically Igbo in character, as illustrated by the ritual authority of the functionary known as *Okpala ukwu* (the most senior elder), and the absence of a paramount chief (or royal family or Obi) and the observance of *ifejioku* (the yam cult). Moreover, there is a complete absence of Benin titles at Obiarukwu.[53]

ABBI

Abbi was founded by an Igbo hunter named Amacha, whose original hometown was Achala in eastern Igboland.[54] He is believed to have crossed over to the west bank of the river during one of his hunting expeditions and decided to stay on rather than return to Achala. According to one version of the Abbi traditions, Amacha first stopped at Aboh, where he was welcomed by the inhabitants, who spoke his language. At Aboh, Amacha fathered several children, among whom were Ogwazi, Aninta, and Okolo. After staying at Aboh for many years, however, Amacha decided to move further inland. Accompanied by his sons, he left Aboh and made brief stops at Umuolu, Ashaka, and Utchi and finally arrived at the present site of Abbi. According to this tradition, Abbi is the shortened form of the Igbo expression, *kanyi bili nebeni,* meaning "now let us settle down here (after much wandering)."[55]

Amacha became the common ancestor of the maximal lineages of Elovie and Umia while the common ancestor of the Okwere maximal lineage was Udu, a native of Ubulu-Ukwu who had joined Amacha and his family at Abbi. In addition, there sprang up small settlements scattered about on the outskirts of the town.[56]

As already pointed out, the traditions of origin of many of the Ukwuani towns suggest that their most ancient founding fathers came from some already established Igbo settlements, some from east and others from the west of the Niger; these first settlers were later joined by immigrants from Benin, Idah, Ijo, and Urhoboland. Utagba-Ogbe (Kwale), for instance, was founded by immigrants from Utagba-Uno, the latter being twenty-two miles from the former. Amai was founded by immigrants from Aboh and Ubulu-Ukwu, while Emu was an offshoot of Onicha. Onicha, on the other hand, is said to have been related both to Utagba Uno and Utagba Ogbe. Obikwere was founded by immigrants from Onya, a town in the Ase district. Afoh (between Ashaka and Iselegu) is an Ukwuani town of eight quarters. One of these, Obodigbo, is said to be the original village that was at the site of Afor before immigrants from Benin arrived.[57] Like Akwukwu and Asaba, the Ukwuani are a broad mix.

HOW DO THE ANIOMA PEOPLE PERCEIVE THEMSELVES?

To this day, not all Igbo-speaking people perceive themselves as Igbo. The Aro, for instance, would say they are not Igbo but the children of God (*Chukwu*), while the Anioma would point to all the Igbo groups who live on the eastern side of the Niger as *ndi igbo* (Igbo people). The people of Onitsha, Atani, Osamala, and Aboh say that they are not *ndi Igbo,* and so do the group of towns in the Agukwu Nri area. A British official report of the early colonial period stated that "these Umundzi [Umunri] declare they are not Ibo [Igbo] in origin though they speak to-day the Ibo language. They declare that they and the Igara [Igala] are the same cultural stock."[58]

Though there is enough evidence in the traditions to confirm that the founding fathers of many Anioma communities hailed from eastern Igboland, most of them would prefer to be identified as Enu-ani or Aniocha (from the Asaba hinterlands), or Ika (from the Agbor district), or Ukwu-ani (from the Kwale district), or Odiani (from around Ukwunzu). Their objection to the name *ndi Igbo* has nothing to do with recent Nigerian experiences but arises simply because until a few decades ago, hardly any group, east or west of the Niger, accepted the name *ndi Igbo* (Igbo people). This is understandable because the word Igbo, which simply must have meant a "community of people" or "the people," was corrupted to mean "forest dwellers," "bush men," "slave," or even "backwardness"—terms usually applied to outsiders or to certain sanctioned conducts. It is interesting, however, that today, the cry *"Igbo kwenu!,"* is used by the Igbos in Nigeria and overseas to rally all Igbo speakers together for a common cause. Virtually all their gatherings are declared open by this solidarity cry.

Somewhat paradoxically, it was only after the formation of the Igbo State Union in the 1940s that the Igbos seemed to have become conscious of their identity, that is, as a people with a common interest and destiny. Thus, until an Igbo national consciousness was forged in the second half of the colonial period, nearly all the Igbo clans continued to reject the expression *ndi Igbo*. If the Onitsha, the Nri, the Ogbaru, the Aro, and the Ikwerre rejected the term *ndi Igbo*, it is not surprising that the Anioma people should not have thought of themselves as Igbo, either.

Furthermore, even though most Anioma people would resist the term *ndi Igbo*, many of them would agree that their founding fathers were Igbo. An Ogwashi-Ukwu chief told me that his people were not *ndi Igbo*, but found no contradiction in his claim when he boasted that Odaigbo, the founding father of Ogwashi-Ukwu, was *nwa Eze Nshi* (the son of Eze Nri), an Igbo man from eastern Igboland. One would wonder if the act of crossing the Niger River was sufficient to wash off an ethnic identity.

At least part of the denial of Igbo identity emanates from the tendency to confuse a language with its various dialects. Whereas there is only one Igbo language spoken by all the people in the Igbo culture area, there are perhaps more than a dozen major sub-dialects and endless variations of them. For instance, Anioma people, who number about a million, speak three major dialects, (Ndokwa, Ika, and Aniocha), and at least twelve sub-dialects. It is important to mention that the conception of the term dialect is not precise and can be broadened or narrowed according to the user's view.

One reason the Igbo people spoke so many different dialects is that until the last hundred years, the vast majority of them did not travel very far from home. Most people therefore learned to speak only their own dialects. Mutual group intercourse, which would have helped to level out dialectical differences, was therefore removed.

A second factor sustaining the large array of Igbo dialects is the extent of various groups' isolation. H. L. M. Butcher has observed that if a man travelled a distance of forty miles in Igboland, he might find the greatest difficulty in making himself understood, largely because most clans were separated from one another by dense forest. Under these circumstances, he said, local variations in speech tended to develop in small areas.[59] These variations were also responsible for the fragmentation of the Igbo political and social structures. We now sometimes speak of "Igbo cultures" rather than "an Igbo culture" because these local variations, coupled with other external influences, have modified the original Igbo culture. Among such external influences were the language, belief systems, and political organizations of the neighbors of the Igbo people. For instance, the Nzam of northern Igboland have been influenced greatly by their Igala neighbors in much the same way as the Agbor of Anioma have been influenced by their

Edo neighbors. In both places the original Igbo culture has been infiltrated markedly by the Igala and Edo cultures, respectively. Thus, the Nzam differ slightly in culture, political structures, and dialect from the Agbor, just as the Aro culture differs from that of the Ikwerre.

Nevertheless, despite these differences, all Igbo groups speak a fundamentally common language, have similar political and social institutions, and share a common cultural heritage. These commonalities are the products of internal dynamics and the outcome of their interactions with the human and physical environments in which they found themselves. It is historically inaccurate to attribute the Igbo people to some foreign origins—to Israel, Egypt, or North Africa, for example. Most Igbo people have always been where we find them today. The vast majority of the people of Anioma are Igbo in origin even though their customs and political structures have been modified by contacts with and settlement of non-Igbo-speaking people in the western part of the Igbo culture area. In the next two chapters we shall examine the results of the Anioma people's contacts with their non-Igbo-speaking neighbors, beginning with the Bini.

NOTES

1. Simon Ottenberg, *Leadership and Authority in an African Society: Afikpo Village-Group* (Seattle and London: Univ. of Washington Press, 1971), xi.

2. Basil Davidson, *The African Genius* (Boston: Little, Brown: 1970), 57.

3. Thurstan Shaw, *Ibgo-Ukwu: An Account of Archaeological Discoveries in Eastern Nigeria* (Evanston: Northwestern Univ. Press, 1970), 2: 171–85.

4. Ibid., 159.

5. Shaw, *Igbo-Ukwu*; Michael A. Onwuejeogwu, *An Igbo Civilization: Nri Kingdom and Hegemony.* (London: Ethnographica, 1981); Adiele E. Afigbo, *Ropes of Sand* (Ibadan: Ibadan Univ. Press, 1981).

6. Elizabeth Isichei, *A History of the Igbo People.* (London: Macmillan, 1976), 3.

7. George T. Basden, *Niger Ibos* (London: Seeley, 1966), 411–23.

8. Ibid., 417.

9. Percy Amuray Talbot, *The Peoples of Southern Nigeria,* Vol 2. (London: Frank Cass, 1969), 43.

10. Discussed in Austin J. Shelton, *The Igbo-Igala Borderland: Religion and Social Control in Indigenous African Colonialism* (Albany: State Univ. of New York Press, 1971), 5.

11. Olaudah Equiano, *The Interesting Narrative of the Life of Olaudah Equiano,* abridged and ed. Paul Edwards (London: Hakluyt Society, 1967); James A. Horton, *West African Countries and Peoples* (Edinburgh: Edinburgh Univ. Press, 1968).

12. Horton, *West African Countries,* 167–71.

13. Simon Ottenberg, "The Present State of Ibo Studies," *Journal of the*

Historical Society of Nigeria, 2, no. 2 (December 1961): 211–30; Adiele E. Afigbo, "Igbo Historians and Igbo History," duplicated paper, University of Nigeria, Nsukka, 1972.

14. Afigbo, *Ropes of Sand,* 2.

15. Shelton, *The Igbo-Igala Borderland,* xvi.

16. Charles G. Seligman, *Races of Africa* (1930), 96.

17. Hugh Trevor-Roper, *The Rise of Christian Europe* (London, 1965), 1.

18. Vivant Denon, *Travels in Upper and Lower Egypt* (London: Longman and Rees, 1803).

19. Seligman, *Races of Africa,* 96.

20. Edith R. Sanders, "The Hamitic Hypothesis; Its Origin and Functions in Time Perspective," *Journal of African History,* 10, no. 4(1960): 521–32.

21. Francis N. Anozie, "Archaeology of Igboland," paper presented at a workshop on the Foundations of Igbo Civilization, University of Nigeria, Nsukka, May 20–22, 1980.

22. Ibid.

23. Personal interviews with Francis Anozie and Vincent Chikwendu, University of Nigeria, Nsukka, February 1981.

24. Ibid.

25. Donald D. Hartle, "Archaeology in Eastern Nigeria," *The West African Archaeological Newsletter,* no. 5(November 1966): 13–17; Vincent E. Chikwendu, "Recent Archaeological Discoveries in Igboland," paper presented at a workshop on the Foundations of Igbo Civilization, University of Nigeria, Nsukka, May 20–22, 1980.

26. Hartle, "An Archaeological Survey of Eastern Nigeria," *The West African Archaeological Newsletter,* no. 2(May 1965), 4–5; Hartle, "Bronze Objects From Ezira, Eastern Nigeria," *The West African Journal of Archaeology,* 10 and 11 (1980–81): 83–102; Hartle, "Archaeology In Eastern Nigeria," *Nigeria Magazine,* no. 93(June 1967), 134–44.

27. Ottenberg, *Leadership and Authority,* 23–25.

28. Ibid., 24–25.

29. Michael A. Onwuejeogwu, "An Outline Account of the Dawn of Igbo Civilization in the Igbo Culture Area." *Odinani: The Journal of Odinani Museum, Nri.* 1, no. 1(March, 1972): 15–55.

30. Chief Iheaza of Ogwashi-Ukwu, titled man, interviewed at Ogwashi-Ukwu on August 4, 1974.

31. Obi Patrick Okonkwo of Umueze Ogboli, Igbuzo, an *eze* man, interviewed at Ogboli, Igbuzo on July 16, 1974.

32. Obi Udita of Ogbe-Ogwugwu, Igbuzo, an *eze* man, interviewed at Igbuzo on September 2, 1974.

33. Nosike Ikpo of Umuodafe, Igbuzo, a titled man and member of the Obi-in council, interviewed on September 2, 1974.

34. L. N. Ashikodi of Igbuzo, interviewed in Lagos on July 7, 1974.

35. A second oral tradition makes no mention of Umejei's sister and her husband. Instead of the sister carrying the pot, Umejei himself bears his burden. The instruction from his father is simple: "Wherever this pot of medicine falls from your head will be your new home." Ashinze of Umuodafe, Igbuzo, a titled man, age c. 77, interviewed on September 9, 1974.

36. Thomas Ohadike of Umuodafe, Igbuzo, a titled man, interviewed at Igbuzo on September 1, 1974.

37. Obi Nna Monye of Ugbomanta, Asaba, titled chief, interviewed on August 11, 1979 by Nkechi Onianwa, in "Nkechi Onianwa Collection," in *Western Igbo*, ed. Don C. Ohadike and Rick N. Shain, *Jos Oral History and Literature Texts*, vol. 6 (Jos: Univ. of Jos, 1988), 189–90.

38. A. C. Okolo of Idumodikpe, Umuezei in Asaba, interviewed by Elizabeth Isichei, "The Elizabeth Isichei Collection," in *Western Igbo*, ed. Ohadike and Shain, 1–2.

39. Ibid., 1–3.

40. Onwuejeogwu, "An Outline Account," 41–42.

41. Shaw, *Igbo-Ukwu*.

42. PRO, CO 520/54, Confidential, "Report on the Operations in the Agbor District," June–August 1906.

43. B. A. Akunne, interviewed at Nri, July 6, 1974.

44. Don C. Ohadike, "Nri and the Foundations of Western Igbo Civilization," paper presented at a Workshop on the Foundations of Igbo Civilization, Institute of African Studies, University of Nigeria, Nsukka, May 20–22, 1980.

45. Richard N. Henderson, *The King in Every Man*, (New Haven: Yale Univ. Press, 1972), 60–61.

46. Odafe Ikenweaju, interviewed at Ogbeani, Akwukwu, December 26, 1974.

47. Quoted in NAI, Kwale Dist., 10/8, "Taking of Eze and Ozo Titles in the Awka Division."

48. Quoted in Shelton, *Igbo-Igala Borderland*, 12.

49. Sylverus Onochie, interviewed at Idumu-Ishionum, Ubulu-Ukwu, March 23, 1978.

50. Chief I. O. Dafikpaku, interviewed at Obiarukwu on March 16, 1978.

51. NAI, CSO 26, File no. 29300, "Intelligence Report on the Kwale-Ibo Clans, Warri Province."

52. Chief Egwali, interviewed at Obiarukwu on March 15, 1978.

53. Onyimika Ozoka and Chief Joseph Opene, interviewed at Obi-Igbe Quarters, Obiarukwu, March 15, 1978.

54. S. O. Omoh, interviewed at Echala Quarters, Abbi, on March 20, 1978.

55. Chief P. I. Nwosa, interviewed at Okwere Quarters, Abbi, June 20, 1978.

56. S. I. Nwoseh, interviewed at Umia Quarters, Abbi, March 20, 1978.

57. NAI, CSO 26, File no. 29300, "Intelligence Report on the Kwale-Ibo Clans, Warri Province."

58. NAI, Kwale Dist., 10/8, "Taking of Eze and Ozo Titles in the Awka Division."

59. H. L. M. Butcher, "The Ika-Ibo People of the Benin Province, Southern Nigeria," dissertation for the diploma of anthropology, Cambridge University, 1931 (courtesy of Rhodes House Library, Oxford University, Oxford).

2
≈≈≈

BENIN-IGBO WARS AND THE SETTLEMENT OF EDO AND YORUBA-SPEAKING PEOPLE IN ANIOMA

WAR AND DIPLOMACY AMONG THE IGBO

IN THE PRECEDING CHAPTER, we found that the Igbo homelands, situated on both sides of the lower Niger River, had one of the highest rural population densities in Africa. We also saw that the people experienced a thousand years of social transformations that were linked with food production, trade, and craft manufacture. These transformations were accompanied by persistent outward movements from the Igbo core area into fertile agricultural lands on the periphery. Economic considerations, therefore, must have been the primary underlying reason for this early diffusion. Because of the problems associated with soil depletion and overpopulation, the Igbo in the core area made conscious and successful attempts to escape into more agriculturally favorable areas.

Like most sedentary agricultural societies, the ancient Igbo communities concerned themselves mostly with production and exchange and remained conscious of the fact that peace and interclan cooperation were vital for healthy trade. Nonetheless, the oral traditions of the Igbo people make mention of conflicts that ranged from small-scale skirmishes to large-scale wars whose regularity remains a matter of speculation. There is every indication, however, that until the demands of the Atlantic slave trade generated widespread social violence in the seventeenth, eighteenth, and nineteenth centuries in the Aro-dominated trading enclaves, most armed conflicts in the Igbo heartland were waged between neighboring towns, and deliberate efforts were made to keep the number of casualties to the barest minimum. It was unusual for many towns or clans to combine their military forces to battle a common enemy, and the social organization of the Igbo did not permit the existence of a standing army. Instead, every man was a warrior and when called upon, fought a particular battle and then returned to his usual tasks. Some communities might have produced mercenary soldiers, but their use was not widespread. It was not uncommon to encounter in each town a few restless young men who sometimes paraded themselves as warriors, or "strong heads" (*isi ike*) or "killers" (*ogbu*). They were at the same time valued and feared even though their numbers were extremely small. In times of war, they were the first to rise in defense of their towns, but their reckless conduct sometimes provoked unnecessary interclan clashes. Such reckless young men were numerous in Ogwashi-Ukwu, where they combined patriotism with brigandage.

In Igboland, east of the Niger, the social organization of certain clans instigated the reproduction of generations of "headhunters." Motivated not by material but by social considerations, the young men of Abam, Ohafia, Abiriba, and Edda were expected to return home with trophies of human heads after wars that were usually provoked for the purpose of proving they were brave men, deserving of the exalted title of *ufiem*. Those men who could not accomplish this feat were treated as cowards, *ujo;* they were laughed at and denied certain rights and privileges. N. Uka, who made a detailed study of these communities, reported that the primary reason for making these ancient wars was "the compelling desire for heads in battle in order to rid oneself of the odium of *ujo* [coward] status, which was worse than that of a slave. Heads of victims were, as a result, in great demand as trophies and as qualification for membership of the *ufiem* club. The man-slayer was saluted publicly as *ogbu madu* (he kills man)"[1] Uka further stated that

> the non-*ufiem* title holder, is often taunted with name-calling by all and sundry including people of younger age-grades and slaves who are non-*ufiem* title-holders. The worst teasing group are members of his own age-grade. In season and out of season they will taunt him with the name of *ujonta otula akoro* (coward with the dry buttocks). His property can be looted at will and his wife is often rendered naked in public places should she dare to

dress up in pretty clothes. He is denied all forms of yam titles.
. . . Society usually provides him with no avenue for redress
and he can only terminate his plight by taking the *ufiem* title."[2]

Headhunting was not an accepted moral conduct of the Igbo people, however, since the taking of life was everywhere regarded as a serious abomination. Therefore, those communities that practiced it committed a serious crime against *ala* or *ani* (mother earth), and were thus loathed by their neighbors, who viewed them as people with deviant dispositions. Even among the headhunting communities themselves, the public made sure that headhunters atoned for their heinous crime of murder by demanding that they thoroughly cleansed themselves. As explained by Uka,

> On return, the warriors who had secured heads of victims were made to undergo vigorous purification rites before rejoining their families and moving about freely once again in the community. For this purpose the warrior was given a bowl of water in an earthenware vessel, *nja,* to wash his hands and face, after which ritual he would break the vessel into two before entering his house. Then for eight days he fed out of the broken vessel and was not permitted to bathe. At the end of this period of atonement, he washed himself very thoroughly and put on his best clothes. . . . This purification rite shows the sacredness with which human life was held by the people and goes to prove that the killings were not motivated by sheer blood lust and wickedness but by compelling social pressure at home.[3]

Headhunting was not an organic part of the Igbo social organization but a recent invention whose origin can be traced to the expansion of the Aro trading activities in the era of the Atlantic slave trade. True, every known society honored its heroes, but to assume that the Abam, Ohafia, Abiriba, and Edda started wars purely to prove that they were heroes, masks the fundamental reasons for initiating aggression. In the first place, these people were borderland Igbos who were compelled by their geocultural circumstances to develop strong military traditions to contain the possible aggression of their non-Igbo neighbors until the Aro, responding to the demands of the Atlantic slave trade, turned them against other potentially less aggressive Igbos. Thus, even though youths everywhere in the world would try, whenever possible, to distinguish themselves in battle, headhunting among the Abam and their allies should be seen as a euphemism for slave-raiding, especially when one considers its close association with the slaving activities of the Aro.

John N. Oriji is in agreement with Uka that "the Aro exploited to their own advantage the desire of Abam youths to distinguish themselves in battle." He said that when there was any fighting to be done, the Aro gave gifts to Abam chiefs, who then enticed "prospective warriors" or the *ujo* (those who had not yet distinguished themselves as man killers) "to join the Aro in invading the offending community."[4] Oriji pointed out that Abam raids were intensified in the eighteenth and nineteenth centuries, when the demand for slaves from the hinterland increased, and explained that when "the Abam swooped on a community by surprise in the early morning hours and quickly withdrew to their base," the Aro took advantage of the confusion to capture as many people as they could for enslavement while the Abam beheaded as many as they could, possibly those too weak or too old to fetch good sums of money in the slave markets.[5] Thus, even if headhunting was part of the social organization of these borderland Igbo groups, the available evidence confirms that this uncommon pastime increased during the era of the Atlantic slave trade and should therefore be included in the checklist of the evils of the trade.

To the vast majority of the Igbo, however, the shedding of blood remained an abomination. To kill a kinsman or kinswoman was to commit a crime against the earth deity; the offender might be required to go into exile or to hang. As we have seen, the traditions of origin of the Igbuzo people recall that Umejei, a son of Eze Isu, killed his opponent during a wrestling contest but rather than hang himself or be hanged, he opted for exile and founded Igbuzo in the process.[6] Most Igbo groups made no fine distinctions between murder and manslaughter; both crimes received the same punishment. In Oko, for example, the punishment for murder or manslaughter, whether accidental or not, was hanging.[7]

Since homicide was a transgression against mother earth, *ala* or *ani*, every effort was made to discourage it. Eze Nri, the divine Igbo king who received the gift of yams from *Chi Okike*, the supreme being, is believed to have turned the instruments of war into the instruments of peace. According to Michael Onwuejeogwu, "Blacksmiths around [Nri] made spears and cutlasses and in later dates dane guns. But these primitive instruments of naked force were transformed into ritual objects. Thus spears were used as the staff of peace (Otonsi), and as the staff of political office (Alo). The club was used as the staff of ritual-political authority (Ofo), and cutlasses as objects of [the] yam cult (Ifejioku). There was no incentive for militarism."[8]

Like many Igbos, the Nri were "conservative" and would not encourage "militarism." It would also appear that the entire Igbo communities recognized the pacific nature of the Nri and reciprocated accordingly. An Nri man, woman, or child, bearing his or her scarified face, *ichi,* travelled the length and breath of Igboland without fear of molestation. This immunity from harm was expressed in the song and saying:

> *Igbu nwa Nri adiro olu*
> *Kama nife anezelu Nri*
> *bu baka ofo*

which means, "to kill a child of Nri is not difficult but the consequences may be too great."[9] It was believed that if an Nri person was harmed, Eze Nri would withdraw Nri religious specialists from the offending community, "leaving it in a state of ritual blockade and siege" until it sued for peace.[10]

Some Igbo groups pursued peace almost to a fault. During certain days in the growing season these people thought it was *alu,* forbidden, for people to quarrel or speak in loud voices. It was also forbidden to declare war during the planting season, as this would offend the goddess of fertility, who would respond by bringing defeat and humiliation on the aggressor. Unless attacked, these groups would not wage war during the growing season; wars might be declared only after crops had been harvested and stored away. In 1910, a British intelligence officer notified the provincial commissioner of the preparation of the Ogwashi-Ukwu clan to declare war against the British soon after the crops had been gathered. He warned that preparations were being made for an outbreak in October, that gunpowder and iron bars for bullets were being freely distributed, that "the amount of yams and other foodstuffs under cultivation far exceeded the needs of the country and the talk had been fairly open that the white man was now going to be driven back into the sea immediately after the yams were in about October next."[11] The British, who had become acquainted with the patterns of traditional Igbo warfare, promptly responded to this useful intelligence by attacking the people of Ogwashi-Ukwu before they could gather their yams, setting fire to their farms and razing their villages.[12] This was particularly painful to the people of Ogwashi-Ukwu because it was the period when crops were about to be gathered and the people were least prepared to fight, as this would destroy a whole year's labor and usher in a year of famine.

On the whole, many Igbo groups considered intergroup conflicts undesirable. Not only their abhorrence of bloodshed, but also their refusal to fight large-scale wars kept their political structures small and fragmented well into the twentieth century. Thus, despite their dense population, the Igbo could only organize themselves into town and village republics, a reflection of their philosophical, political and agricultural preferences. The Igbo have never been empire builders.

WARS ON THE BORDERLANDS

Full-scale wars did occur in the borderlands, however, where the Igbo could not regulate the dispositions of their non-Igbo neighbors. Once the movement out of the core area had begun, it continued, filling up all available space, until the Igbo people came into contact with other ethnic groups. As we have seen, the Igbos encountered the Tiv, Igala, and Idoma in the north, the numerous ethnic groups of the Cross River valley in the east, and the Ogoni and Ijo in the south. Crossing the Niger to the west and occupying what is today known as Anioma brought the Igbos within close proximity of Benin City, the Edo capital.

Oral traditions confirm that the arrival of each Igbo-speaking group was contested by its neighbors, the result of each struggle being determined by the strength of the indigenous inhabitants' opposition. In the Igbo-Igala borderlands, for example, the Nsukka Igbo battled the Igala for centuries and remained, for some time, at least, vassals of the Attah Igala. Austin J. Shelton has stated that the Igala conquest of Nsukka resulted in some substitution of Igbo religious practices by the Igala Attama and the addition of Igala lineages and priests to Igbo clans and villages.[13] In fact, the whole conflict between the Igala and the Igbo in the Nsukka district revolved around the legendary figure, Onojo Oboni, who was believed to have been anxious to extend Igala imperial domination over the northern Igbos and capture the trade routes that had been dominated by the Aros.[14] These wars must have occurred in the eighteenth and nineteenth centuries when, according to Samson Ukpabi, the Igala empire was in its golden age. For it was at this time that the Igala soldiers invaded Nsukka and built fortifications that stretched from the north (around Eta) and the Nsukka-Udi scarp down to Opi and then to Anambra.[15] One could infer, however, that the Igbo and the Igala must have clashed during earlier centuries, for as Shelton has suggested, Igala control over Nsukka villages must have been gained in successive conquests even though Onojo Oboni attained prominence probably because his conquest was among the last.[16]

In general, the most warlike Igbos were those who lived in the borderlands. Our concern in this chapter is specifically with the Igbos who occupied the western part of the Igbo culture area, that is, the people of Anioma, who developed strong military traditions, strong enough to contain the aggression of their equally warlike enemies—the Edo, Urhobo, and Ijo. Both oral and written records state that the Obi of Aboh derived much of his prestige from the fact that he protected the outlying settlements from marauding bands of Ijo who had developed the bad habit of raiding the riverside communities.[17] Only the Aboh were sufficiently powerful on the water to prevent these raids, and as the price of protection the villages had to acknowledge the Obi's overlordship.[18] The Obi and the warrior chiefs of Aboh also maintained war canoes with which they protected their spheres of trade and influence on the lower stretches of the Niger. Apart from keeping the military powers of Idah, Akassa, Brass, Patani, and Opobo in check, the Obi was able to collect tributes from the traders who ventured into Aboh territories.[19] Obi Ossai boasted in 1841, "When other chiefs quarrel with me and make war, I take all I can as slaves."[20] But this statement, which simply emphasized the obvious, should not be interpreted to mean that the Aboh waged wars only to harvest slaves. The militarism of Aboh was developed, not for headhunting nor for slave raiding, but to cope with the aggressive dispositions of the merchant princes of the Niger and the Delta, most of them slave traders, who plied the distributaries with fleets of war canoes that were equipped with canons and manned by restless musketeers.

Further inland, the Utagba people of the Ukwuani district developed strong military institutions that were designed to keep the Urhobo in check. There was among the Utagba a warrior age-grade named *Otu Odogwu*. The members of this age-grade were specially selected and trained by an extra-executive body known as *Eze-emenjo* to act as scouts and advance guards in wartime. They were required to fight the enemy and must never retreat but instead "win or die where they stood." Anyone who retreated was expelled from the *Otu Odogwu* in disgrace. The Utagba used this Spartan-type military tradition as a counter-force against the Urhobo, who sometimes took advantage of the difficulties of intervillage communication to attack the clans living between Emu and Onicha.[21]

While the people of Anioma trained to contain the military strength of their non-Igbo neighbors, they tried as much as possible to maintain friendly relationships with the other Anioma communities. For example, the Agbor, according to J. Macrea Simpson, kept up with Benin an intermittent warfare which met with varying success, but on their eastern boundaries, "peace reigned" with the Issele-Ukwu clan, which "ripened into a warm friendship" that lasted into the colonial period.[22]

One can infer that before Benin was transformed into an imperial power, the Edo and the Igbo might have lived like good neighbors, for, as predominantly sedentary agricultural communities, they might not have had any need for wars. But soon after the Obas embarked upon a career of territorial expansion in the fifteenth century, the Edo-Igbo borderland became the scene of violent political clashes which set in motion population movements and changes in the ethnic composition and political development of Anioma. The people of Anioma as a whole battled the Bini for over three hundred years during which some of them, especially those who had settled within close proximity of Benin City, retraced their steps toward the Igbo heartland. Some crossed the Niger and settled in what became present-day Onitsha. Others moved farther south and settled among the Ogbaru, Ukwuani, and Aboh. To fully comprehend the impact of the Benin-Igbo wars on settlement patterns in Anioma, it is important to examine the transformations that took place in Edoland at the end of the Ogiso period.

THE RISE OF MILITARISTIC BENIN

The Edo political institutions, as Alan Ryder has observed, were similar to those of the Igbo, and were based on village settlements where the male populations were organized in age-grades, each grade representing a different level of political and economic authority. "In all likelihood," Ryder wrote, "agricultural village communities with these features of social and political organization characterized early Edo settlements, and such compact communities, largely autonomous in their political and economic life, still exist among them, especially in the north-western area."[23] In other words, before the rise of Benin, most Edo communities must have been organized like most Igbo communities, and in their cultural traits, resembled the Igbo. If so, at what moment in time, and under what circumstances, did the Edo political structures assume a different character from the Igbo? What turned Benin (the Edo capital) into an aggressive expansionist kingdom? How did the transformation of Benin into an empire affect the social history of Anioma?

The manner by which Benin developed from a mini-state into a large empire is still a puzzle. In fact, opinions are still divided on the origins of the state in West Africa. While some scholars strongly hold that such West African grassland empires as Ghana, Mali, Songhai, and Oyo owed their rise to long-distance trade, others attribute state formation in certain regions to an intensive use of slave labor. Emanuel Terray, a strong proponent of the latter view, has stressed that in most African formations, "it was the command over men—and so the possibility of organizing their co-operation on a large scale—that was the key to economic power."[24] Arguing strongly against Catherine Coquery-Vidrovitch, Samir Amin, Maurice Godelier, Yves Person, and others, Terray stated that any thesis that emphasized the importance of long-distance trade in state formation in Africa would be unsatisfactory. Using the Abrong Kingdom of Gyaman as his case study, Terray noted that although trade was important in the state, the basis of its strength lay in the production of gold, whose extraction depended on slave labor. The local mines, he said, were owned by the local aristocracies and their wealth was accumulated from the surplus labor they extracted from the servile classes who produced goods that were channelled into long-distance trade. Terray further stated that the ruling classes were not traders but military aristocracies, and state wars continued to be the primary means of procuring captives. He argued that "since the relations of captivity were the dominant element in the social formation," it was "these slave relations which evoked the formation of a state as the condition of their functioning and reproduction." He therefore dismissed Coquery-Vidrovitch, Person, and others "for mistaking the primacy of trade over production."[25]

Although Terray's thesis is attractive, it cannot be applied to more than a handful of precolonial African social formations. In fact, what Terray emphasized was the growth or expansion of a kingdom and not its origin. The use of slave labor was widespread in Africa, but, as Coquery-Vidrovitch has warned, exchange and states functioned only with the help of limited slavery, which "cannot be compared with a real Slave Mode of Production." She explained that tributes levied by some highly organized despots, like the kings of Dahomey, were not necessarily meant to support the state since they were "immediately distributed" in annual festivals.[26]

In the forest belt of West Africa, a number of kingdoms and empires emerged but scholars have not been able to adequately account for their origins and development. In fact, scholars are still confused about the roles that long-distance trade and/or slavery played in their evolution. This confusion prompted Robert M. Wren to declare:

> It is only with great difficulty that historians account for such states as Ife and Benin. . . . Traditions and archaeology together

attest to wealthy civil complexes several centuries before Portuguese ships reached West Africa and stimulated the formation of trade centers. Igbo-Ukwu does not appear to be associated with a "state," if Ife and Benin are taken to be the models. Instead . . . Igbo-Ukwu seems to have power without warfare, wealth without trade, and an apparent "royal" art without kings.[27]

Perhaps it was with the same bizarre feeling about kings without kingdoms, wealth without enterprise, and peace without law and order that David Northrup wrote his illustrious book, *Trade Without Rulers: Pre-Colonial Economic Development in South Eastern Nigeria.*[28]

Although R. E. Bradbury spoke of the hereditary chiefs of Benin, the Uzomo, who acquired great wealth "through fief-holding, control of political patronage, long-distance trade, and participation in war and slave raiding,"[29] it is doubtful that Benin, during its formative stages, was particularly involved in any meaningful long-distance trade or made use of slave labor on a large scale. In fact one cannot categorically state that Benin owed its rise and sustenance to slavery. In the first place, pre-empire Benin was organized on strict kinship lines, and societies with such social organizations had limited use for slave labor. Slavery was neither an economic necessity nor a vital component of the entire social and political life of the society. In the second place, even after the rise of Benin as a large kingdom, its involvement in slavery was limited. Ryder has demonstrated that Benin's participation in the Atlantic slave trade or the European trade generally was minimal.[30] Ryder's thesis is confirmed by the fact that the Edo political structures were not particularly affected by the European trade as was the case with Dahomey and the Gold Coast.[31] Under the circumstances, therefore, we must search for the rise of Benin, not in material conditions, but in a number of sociological and other nonmaterial circumstances prevailing in Edoland in pre-empire Benin.

It has been observed that, perhaps, Benin was fundamentally like any of the 130 or more political units in the Edo country which it later outstripped in importance, eventually establishing an effective political authority over them.[32] Adé Ubayemi analyzed the methods by which this transformation must have been achieved and suggested that Benin illustrates the basic patterns of social organization from which most great states must have developed.[33] He argued that this basic organization could be represented by a building-block known as the patrilineage, headed by a lineage head who acquired the position by virtue of his age. The various lineages that formed the mini-state (or community) might or might not have been related to a common ancestor; nevertheless, life in such a community was regulated by cross-cutting institutions. Obayemi went on to identify two alternative processes by which a large state could have been born, suggesting that the need for defense could have compelled the mini-states to come together without necessarily resulting in an increase in political concentration. Alternatively, the formation of a large state could have been initiated when many communities clustered around one mini-state. Obayemi strongly believed that the rise of Benin could have been initiated by one or both of these processes.[34]

However, by the twelfth century A.D., many Edo polities had begun to amalgamate. This amalgamation process was accompanied by a population build-up and the emergence of strong personalities who were able to enlist the cooperation of men and women on a large scale to build a complex network of walls whose purpose was less for defense than to show the boundaries of the land belonging to each of the various federating communities.[35] Historians and archaeologists believe that these earthworks, whose ruins are still visible in Benin today, were built during the Ogiso period, and that each of the dozen or so villages that were enclosed within them was ruled by a village head.[36] Some scholars have also suggested that the ambition of these village heads to inflate their powers must have contributed to the rapid termination of the Ogiso period. Perhaps the Edo people were appalled by the despotic tendencies of their rulers and therefore carried out a revolution.

The last ruler of the Ogiso period was Owodo, whose misrule resulted in a palace coup after which Evian, a man who had served the people well, was requested to look after the affairs of the state until such time that an acceptable governing arrangement could be worked out. But when Evian made an attempt to install his family as the new ruling dynasty, the Edo got rid of him and appealed to Oba Oduduwa at Ile-Ife to give them a king. The request was favorably considered and the prince, Oranya (Oraminiyan), was sent to Benin.[37]

Oranya spent only a brief period of time in Edoland, however, for when he could no longer stomach the habitual feuding of the Edo people (hence *ibinu*, or bickering) he quietly returned to his father's court at Ile-Ife. Eweka, who was born to him by an Edo woman, was left behind in Benin, however.[38] Tradition maintains that it was Eweka, the son of Oranya, the grandson of Oduduwa, who gave to the Edo people the dynasty which rules in Benin till this day. Jacob Egharevba, the Benin historian, proudly dedicated his *Short History of Benin* to "the Memory of His Highness, Eweka II, The First Oba of Benin in the third period of its empire."[39]

Not only did the arrival of Oranya from Ile-Ife mark the beginning of a new dynasty, but it also opened up a new phase in Benin political and social history; this was the period of "constitutional and ritual development accompanied by territorial expansion."[40] According to Obayemi, "Thus with Eweka we see the effective establishment of a dynasty in Benin and, even if it was a 'foreign' one in its origin, it had already grafted itself onto the basic Edo sociological framework, to work within the cultural milieu in the elevation of the kingdom whose fortune became inextricably bound up with the central institution of the Obaship."[41]

These events must have taken place in the thirteenth century and must have been marked by the liquidation of some of the more important chiefs and office holders, the reorganization of the central administration, and the strengthening of the powers of the Oba. Ryder has warned, however, that despite these bold moves, no further significant changes appeared to have been effected in the balance of power within the state.[42] Thus for two more centuries (c. 1250-1440), and until Oba Ewuare the Great ascended the throne about 1440, Benin remained a small political unit, embracing no more than the capital—Benin City—and a few scattered villages within a radius of about fifteen miles.[43] It was only about 1440 that the Obas of Benin embarked upon a career of territorial expansion—by warfare.

Five Obas of this period are still remembered for their contributions to the expansion of Benin. These were Ewuare the Great (c. 1440-73), Ozolua (1481-1504), Esigie (1504-50), Orhogbua (1550-78) and Ehengbuda (1578-1606).[44] This period of ascendancy lasted for two centuries. It was also during this period that the Oba welcomed the first European visitors to Benin.[45] However, after the reign of these five powerful rulers, the fortunes of the empire began to turn. Certainly by the end of the first half of the seventeenth century the empire had entered a period of decline from which it never quite recovered.

THE FIRST ANIOMA-BENIN ENCOUNTERS

The transformation of Benin from a city-state into the metropolitan capital of an empire of the same name was not achieved without great pains, first to the Edos themselves, and subsequently to their neighbors. Alan Ryder has shown that the immediate consequence of Benin's attempt to subjugate and extract tributes from the village-based communities around it was to induce an exodus of some of their inhabitants away from the places of greatest political and religious persecution. Some groups moved into the outer districts of the Edo country where they "now trace their origin to Benin-City, often through some eponymous ancestors."[46] Some groups moved into the Niger Delta and others into Igboland where their descendants are still found today. This chapter is concerned with the groups who moved into Igboland, and I have classified them into three sub-groups. The first consists of some people who evacuated their homelands as a result of political or religious persecution in the Edo region and sought refuge in the western part of the Igbo culture area. The second group includes a number of non-Igbo-speaking people who participated in Benin wars as soldiers or mercenaries; some were Edo and others Ishan and Yoruba. These wars, generally referred to in Anioma and Onitsha as *aya Idu* (Benin Wars), lasted for about three hundred years (c. 1440–1750) albeit intermittently, and were marked by a general movement of peoples and cultures eastward from the direction of Benin City toward the Igbo heartland. The third class of emigrants consists of the followers of Eze Chima, Oraeze, Esumai-Ukwu, and others who also fled eastward as a result of these wars. While it is conceivable that the first two groups were Edo- and Yoruba-speaking, the ethnic origin of the third group is not certain and has sparked a controversy we shall presently examine.

Within Benin itself one major problem was the series of civil wars that destabilized the empire. The capital was torn apart as the ruling houses contested for the throne. Unfortunately for Benin, the Obas who reigned after Ehengbuda proved incapable of putting down the civil wars. Nyendael, Smith, and other European travellers who visited Benin in the eighteenth century remarked that the city was half ruined by civil wars and that the power of the Oba was minimal.[47] Two Obas of the eighteenth and nineteenth centuries were removed outright from the throne shortly after they occupied it and were replaced by their brothers.[48] In fact, after the reign of Oba Ewuare the Great, only one Oba of Benin, Obanosa, ascended the throne without a major succession dispute.[49] The instability that characterized the empire during these centuries lasted into the closing decades of the nineteenth century, confirming that the hierarchy of the state was crumbling and that power rested, not entirely in the hands of the Oba, but largely with the powerful chiefs and kingmakers. In 1897, for example, the Oba who reigned in Benin when the British expedition of 1897 took place could not exercise effective authority over his subordinate chiefs.[50] In that case the real power rested with the chiefs, who could ignore the Oba and take independent action against a group of British adventurers who had embarked on an uninvited visit to Benin and were ambushed. "When the king heard this," an eyewitness reported, "he got vexed and made a big palaver with all the chiefs and told them he was going to leave the city so that if the whitemen bring another war they could fight for themselves; but they begged him so much that he did not go anywhere. The people who killed the whitemen were turned back to the bush to fight the war that the whitemen would bring."[51]

It has been necessary to go into such detail in order to facilitate our understanding of the early history of the Igbo-speaking people who claimed Benin origin. It should be expected that each successive change within the Benin empire would trigger certain vital changes in Edo-Igbo relationships. A period of wars of territorial expansion eastward would be marked by population movements into and within the Igbo culture area as people attempted to escape from the ravages of war. In fact, oral traditions attribute the dispersal of Ogboli settlements in Anioma to *aya Idu*. In addition, a period of civil war in the vicinity of Benin itself would be marked by the flight of Edo citizens, some seeking refuge in the neighboring Igbo culture area.

THE FIRST EDO IMMIGRANTS INTO THE IGBO CULTURE AREA

The determination of the rulers of Benin to subjugate and extract tributes from the neighboring communities provoked an exodus of some inhabitants away from the places of greatest political and religious turbulence. Some Edo refugees who moved into Igboland can still be found in the Ikelike quarters of Ogwashi-Ukwu, the Ukwumaga quarters of Illah, and the Opu quarters of Akwukwu. Traditions of origin claim that the ancestors of these communities left Benin City after their failure to capture the Oba's throne.

One of these traditions insists that Ikelike, a segment of Ogwashi-Ukwu, was founded by immigrants from Benin. The elders of the Ikelike lineage say that their founding fathers left Benin City several hundred years ago because of a succession dispute. They travelled east, spent some time at a place called Ashama, and finally stopped at Ogwashi-Ukwu. Sometime after their arrival, they met a man called Odaigbo (or, perhaps, one of his descendants), whose original home was Nri. The immigrants from both Nri and Benin lived peacefully as neighbors in Ogwashi-Ukwu and evolved strong cross-cutting ties. Among these was the agreement that the immigrants from Benin would maintain the position of *okpala-ani* (the most senior elder), while those from Nri kept the institution of obiship (paramount chieftain). However, to validate the obiship, the incumbent had to be confirmed by the Ikelike elders. In later years, the Ikelike tradition claims, when Ogwashi-Ukwu fell under the sway of Benin, the Ikelike elders assumed the added responsibility of leading the obis of Ogwashi-Ukwu to the obas of Benin for the traditional investiture of office.[52]

A similar tradition was recorded at Akwukwu. According to this tradition, the Opu lineage of Akwukwu was founded by Opu, a Bini man who was excluded from the line of succession because he had only nine fingers instead of ten. Opu contested his disqualification in the battlefield but lost. Fearing a reprisal, he and his supporters fled eastward and were pursued by the Oba's soldiers. Luckily for the fugitives, their foot-prints were concealed by the civet cat, *edi*, which walked on their trail. This, it is said, explains why the people of the Opu quarters of Akwukwu do not eat the civet cat to this day.

This oral tradition maintained that Opu and his followers founded Akwukwu and were later joined by other immigrants from Nshi (Nri). Later still, some immigrants came from Ogboli-Igbuzo and settled in the Ogbe Ani quarters of Akwukwu; these people of Ogboli descent had escaped from the ravages of war. Soon afterwards, the people of Achala came, also from Igbuzo, and founded the present Achala lineage of Akwukwu. Then, Umolum people came from Umolum-uno, and were followed by a group who came from Ebu. Shortly afterwards, the people of Umuokeke arrived from Okpanam, and the people of Ogbeobi from Mgboke.[53] Like the inhabitants of Asaba, the people of Akwukwu were a broad mix.

The people of Illah have an oral tradition that claims that the founding father of one section of the town left Benin City as a result of a succession dispute. According to this tradition, some of the original inhabitants of Ala (Illah) were the Omoka. As a result of constant harassment from some river pirates, possibly Igala or Nzam (the Nzam being a mixture of both Igbo and Igala), the Omoka moved away from the original site of Illah, which was on the right bank of the Niger, and founded a new settlement further inland. But this withdrawal was useless, as the pirates continued to make periodic incursions into their new settlement until a Benin warrior, Edaiken, arrived from Benin and helped them destroy the river pirates.[54]

This oral tradition goes on to state that Edaiken, who had only recently lost the Benin throne, was anxious to resume his journey to Onitsha to join his brother, Oraeze, who had migrated with the Eze Chima party and had been installed the Obi of Onitsha. The people of Illah feared that Edaiken's departure would rob them of a valuable ally, so they offered him a wife and a large piece of land. Moved by these friendly gestures, Edaiken agreed to stay. He spent the rest of his life in Illah as the head of Ukwumaga, one of the major lineages of the town. The present residents of the Ukwumaga quarters of Illah still recount with pride that they descended from Edaiken, the Benin prince who saved the Omoka of Illah from the Igala river pirates.[55]

Largely because of its location on the Niger, Illah also attracted immigrants from other places. Oral traditions recall that the Ukpologwu and Umuasaga lineages came from Igalaland, that the Onya lineage came from Osamala, and that the Umuogwu who occupy a section of the Umuagwu lineage came from Awka.[56] The other lineages of Illah are Umutei, Umutei-Edem, Umuagwu, Ezenokwe, and Azanoma.

OLUKUNMI: A YORUBA COMMUNITY IN THE IGBO CULTURE AREA

The early Igbo settlers in Anioma were also joined by a large population of Yoruba immigrants. Some were traders and hunters, but the vast majority were Yoruba mercenaries under the service of the rulers of Benin. The latter had been recruited from the conquered regions of Yorubaland and were used against the people of Anioma. However, after each expedition, a few mercenaries refused to return to Benin or Yorubaland, preferring to remain among the Anioma people they had come to fight. Some married Anioma women, learned the Igbo language, and then founded their own settlements or joined existing ones. The descendants of these people can still be found in the Anioma towns of Ugbodu, Ukwunzu, and Ubulubu where they are called *Olukunmi*, a word which has been translated as "we have come as friends" or "we are friends."

What the word, Olukunmi, originally stood for is not clear. Robin Law recognized it as a term applied to Yoruba-speakers in modern-day Cuba and in Western Igboland (Anioma).[57] The words *Ulkami, Lucamee, Licomin, Ulcuim,* and other variants were used by some early European writers like Dapper, and judging from the context in which they were used, Law suggested that they referred to Oyo.[58]

Whatever *Olukunmi* might mean, the fact remains that some Anioma people who claim origin from Yorubaland bear this name. According to an oral tradition I have heard, the Odiani community of Anioma (Ugbodu, Ukwunzu, Ubulubu, Idumu Ogo, Ugboba, Anioma, and Ogodo) came from Ile-Ife. This tradition stated that the original founders of these towns had formed a part of the entourage whom, as we have seen, Oba Oduduwa had sent to Benin at the end of the Ogiso period to teach the Edo people how to install their own chiefs. When Oranya, the leader of this entourage, disagreed with the Bini and then decided to return to Ile-Ife, some of his followers, rather than accompany him, migrated eastward and settled in Anioma. This oral tradition insisted that the Olukunmi community of Anioma was founded during the days of Oranya by certain Yoruba men who had personally been chosen by Oba Oduduwa himself and then sent to Benin to protect Oranya. It also stated that this Olukunmi community was founded before the rise of Benin as a kingdom and that most of the subsequent immigrants from the direction of Benin and Yorubaland stopped over here before resuming their journey eastward.[59] To this day, members of the Olukunmi community of Anioma speak Igbo and Yoruba dialects.[60]

The original Olukunmi community continued to welcome Yoruba immigrants, especially traders and ritual specialists, and was able to retain the Yoruba language, which may help to explain why the Olukunmi could still speak "Yoruba" while numerous communities who claim Benin origin, like the Umu Ezechima and Aboh clans, cannot remember a word of Edo. In other words, we have, at least, linguistic evidence of the Olukunmi's claim to Yoruba ancestry.

THE WAR BETWEEN BENIN AND UBULU-UKWU (1750)

As already mentioned, the power and glory of Benin began to decline after 1650, but during the subsequent two and a half centuries (1650-1897) the Obas of Benin managed to wage wars in Yorubaland and in Anioma, although with lesser frequency. The available evidence suggests that some of these wars were provoked by nonmaterial reasons, as is illustrated by the conflict between Benin and Ubulu-Ukwu. In 1750 the Obi of Ubulu-Ukwu and the Oba of Benin went to war over the death of Adesua, a Benin woman who may have been the Oba's daughter or favorite. This notable Edo woman had been murdered in Ubulu-Ukwu, a crime in which the paramount chief was implicated.[61]

Adesua's death was received with shock and indignation in Benin City and the Oba sent his troops, composed mostly of Bini, Ishan, and Yorubas, to punish the Obi of Ubulu-Ukwu. Armed with charms and muskets, the Oba's soldiers sacked the Anioma towns of Obior and Ubulu-Ukwu, but were disappointed to find out that their residents had disappeared. Thinking that they had fled to Asaba via the Ogwashi-

Ukwu road, the Oba's troops gave chase and, in quick succession, ransacked Ogwashi-Ukwu, Igbuzo, and Asaba, but could not find the Obi of Ubulu-Ukwu, the prime object of their mission. As these Benin warriors retreated from Asaba, they were opposed and subsequently defeated by the people of Igbuzo, near their principal stream, Oboshi.[62]

Meanwhile, a contingent of the Edo warriors had built a war camp at Ubulu-Ukwu, where they awaited the return of their advance guard, which never arrived. The years passed and the people of Ubulu-Ukwu reoccupied their town. The remnants of the Benin soldiers finally acquiesced to the situation and turned their war camp into one of the lineages of Ubulu-Ukwu. This quarter was called Onije or Idumu Idu. Tradition has it that most of the Benin soldiers who built this war camp had been drawn from the Onije quarters of Benin City. It is further said that even today the people of Idumu Idu observe certain customs that are uncharacteristic of Ubulu-Ukwu.[63]

THE EZECHIMA FLIGHT

The largest amount of evidence of Igbo-Benin wars is contained within the traditions of the Umu Ezechima clan, whose settlements can still be found in Anioma and in Onitsha. These communities claim descent from Ezechima, a man whose identity and place of origin have sparked off much discussion in recent years. Who was Ezechima? Was he Edo or Igbo? From where did he start his flight, Edoland or Igboland?

It is fairly easy to show that Ezechima was an Igbo man. The name and its prefix (*Eze and Chima*) are Igbo, not Edo; so also are the names of most of his followers and descendants, among them Ora-eze, Ifite, Onicha, Eze-chi, Ezi-uno, Obi-oma, and Azubuike. Given this fact, it would be strange if Benin men should have taken Igbo names even before leaving their home town of Benin. It is also curious that the Bini should found new settlements and give them Igbo names and Igbo prefixes rather than Edo.

While it is clear that Ezechima was Igbo, his original home is not clear. Some observers have suggested that Ezechima and his people lived in Benin City proper, some say in the Edo-Igbo borderlands, and others say in one of the large towns ruled by Benin. Victor C. Uchendu has warned that Onitsha, Oguta, and the Ezechima group of villages could not have come from Benin: "Their eponymous ancestor Chima—an Igbo name—conclusively demonstrates that these Ezechima people were not Benin but Igbo-speaking people once under the political denomination of Benin Kingdom."[64]

We have argued in the previous chapter that the westward migration of the Igbo people as farmers, traders, craftpersons and ritual specialists had taken them across the Niger to within close proximity of Benin City. When Benin became a large metropolitan center, many non-Bini, including Igbos, Ishans, and Yorubas, may have settled in that city until they were expelled in the sixteenth century, and the Ezechima people could have been included. They may also have lived in some of the vassal states of Benin, only to be chased off when these communities were sacked by the Oba's soldiers. One of such states could have been Udo, which Oba Esigie destroyed in the sixteenth century. Charles K. Meek noted that when Udo was destroyed, many of its residents fled eastward towards the Niger.[65] The Ezechima people could have been some of them.

On the other hand, a number of scholars believe that Ezechima and his people lived, not in Benin City proper, but in the vicinity. Arthur G. Leonard has observed that "Onitsha-Mili . . . along with the towns of Onitsha-Olona, Onitsha-Ukwu, Onitsha-Ugbo, and Onitsha-Ukwuani, migrated or were driven out, presumably between two or three hundred years ago, from the vicinity of Benin City, which they speak of as Ado-n-Idu."[66] Peter Obue has also remarked that Ezechima was an Igbo man who led his people in a war of resistance against Benin's eastward expansion, but when overwhelmed, he and his followers fled eastward. They first settled at Agbor but "the news got to the Oba who threatened to deal with Ezechima."[67] Obue noted that Ezechima himself did not feel safe living so near the Oba so he left Agbor and moved farther east, accompanied by nine renowned warriors whom he recruited from the different quarters of Agbor.

Richard N. Henderson observed that one major concept of origin among the Onitsha is the "children of King Chima" (umu-eze-Chima) legend, which held that Onitsha people lived originally in a community called "Ado and Idu," Idu referring to Benin City and Ado referring (as far as Henderson could determine) to a general country of the Edo-speaking people bordering the western Igbo country.[68]

King Chima is said to have ruled over this country (Ado and Idu) which was tributary to Benin, and which, according to Northcote Thomas, was somewhere near Igbodo on the uplands, west of Asaba. Thomas also suggested that the origin of the Ezechima group of Igbos should be found in areas other than Benin. In his view, the original homes of these people were in the vicinity of Onicha-Ugbo and Igbodo. He, too, suggested that these people may have been driven off by a Benin expeditionary force.[69]

Kingsley Ogedengbe has warned against the tendency to interpret emigration from "Benin" literally. He cautioned that even though Ezechima, Esumai, and the other putative fathers of the Igbo communities that claim Benin origin came from the direction of Benin City, evidence that they were Benin citizens in the narrowest definition of the term is by no means conclusive. He said that even though traditions are vague as to whether these founding fathers were citizens of Benin who had been forced by internal strife to emigrate, or the residents of separate settlements in the neighborhood of Benin, the tendency has been to interpret emigration from "Benin" literally.[70]

Even if these people lived in Benin City, they did not have to be Edo. Benin City was the capital of a large kingdom and, like most metropolitan capitals, it would have admitted a wide range of immigrants. It would, therefore, appear that the more reliable traditions are those that trace the origins of the Ezechima clan to an area that was on the Edo-Igbo borderlands, which came under the political domination of Benin, rather than to Benin itself. This view is supported by Jacob Egharevba's disclosure that soon after the accession of Oba Ozolua (c. A.D. 1481) "he set himself to the task of subduing the rebellious and hostile peoples. He fought many desperate battles and waged war upon war with this or that town and village. In fact, his chief desire was to get plenty of fighting."[71] From this story one may infer that Ozolua inherited disturbances from the vassal states of Benin, and that there were many migrations from Benin itself during this period. In 1504 Osawe was crowned Oba of Benin with the title of Esigie. But Esigie squabbled with his brother, Aruanran, Chief of Udo, a man of giant stature. Esigie sent an expedition. Udo was attacked and destroyed and its inhabitants fled.[72] Egharevba's account does not tell us what sort of people inhabited Udo during the reign of Esigie, but other traditions say that it was during the reign of this Oba that Onitsha was founded by people who migrated from Benin. In fact, the entire reign of Oba Esigie, like that of Oba Ozolua before him, was rife with wars and rumors of wars. It is said that the flight of Ezechima lasted for a whole lifetime, that Ezechima bore many children during this period, and that it was not he but some of his followers who founded most of the towns of the Ezechima clan.[73] Of all the oral traditions so far collected, both in Onitsha and Anioma, it would appear that it is those from Obamkpa that provide the best clues to the original hometowns of the Umuezechima and the other Anioma groups who had had early contacts with Benin.

OBAMKPA

An oral tradition recorded by Kunirum Osia stated that Obampka was founded by a man called Kanagbana-Ogidi, meaning, "the one who was born while we were running away to Ogidi." It was in keeping with the well-established Igbo custom of naming children after the major event occurring at the time of their birth that he was given this name, for his mother was fleeing to Ogidi to escape the war between the Oze people and his father's hometown when Kanagbana Ogidi was born. His father was from a town situated within the immediate vicinity of Onitsha; his mother was from Ogidi, ten miles away. As the boy grew to adulthood, he became simply known by the shortened name of Anagba or Kanagba.[74]

Kanagba was a gifted child. He quickly mastered the medicinal properties of herbs and, even though he was born into a family of diviners, his parents believed he was much more talented in this art than his brothers and sisters. He became so proficient in his herbal and oracular practices that he was sought after as a top healer and soothsayer. As a young man, Kanagba travelled far and wide as an itinerant spiritual specialist. He eventually settled down in Benin City where he acted as a special herbal consultant to the Oba of Benin. But his fame and distinction in medicine soon provoked the wrath of other medicine men in Edoland. He may have already been contemplating leaving Benin City when the Ezechima flight began and therefore had no difficulty in joining it.

Kanagba stayed with and moved about from place to place in the company of the Ezechima people, acting as their guide and providing them with the necessary spiritual guidance. It is believed that Kanagba had no intention of founding a separate settlement from those of the Ezechima people, and that he had, in fact, planned to return to his father's hometown near Onitsha, or to his mother's place at Ogidi, but was forced by circumstances to found the Anioma settlement which we now call Obamkpa. According to the account given by one informant, Kunirum Osia, one day Kanagba accompanied his pregnant wife into the bush to collect materials for a hut they were building. While thus occupied, the woman went into labor and delivered a male child. Kanagba considered this a good omen and decided to settle there. This child was called Obamkpa, meaning, "a child born when we were collecting reeds" and so was the settlement which subsequently sprang up there. It is not certain whether this child lived, but it is known that Kanagba had two other sons, Ado and Ona, whose descendants were, and still are, commonly referred to as *Umu Ado na Umu Ona.*

As the years rolled by, Obamkpa attracted many immigrants. It grew in size but remained under constant threat of attack. To ward off hostilities from the Obas of Benin who remained determined to extend their suzerainty over the entire Anioma region, Kanagba established shrines as sentinels to guard all the entrances to the town. These shrines were Iru Afa, Iru Obinabu, and Iru Oraeze. Iru Afa still holds a primary position among these shrines for it was the first established. To this day, it serves as the main gateway to and from Obampka. Kanagba also named certain streams after persons and objects dear to his heart, in this order: Iyi Nmem Agadi, Iyi Ukwu, Iyi Ako, Iyi Ojiokpa, Iyi Ugo, Iyi Ocha, Iyi Ikolo, Iyi Enene, Iyi Odo, Iyi Nkpukpa, and Owuwu, which forms the confluence and tributary of the Ojiokpa, the biggest stream. Today, Obamkpa is divided into four quarters or major lineages, namely, Ogbe Obi, Ogbe Onoi, Ukpatu, and Ugboba. Obamkpa is still noted as the best place in Anioma to obtain the strongest medicine.

Kunirum Osia, from whom this account came, insisted that the Obamkpa people never traced their origins to Benin but to Ogidi through Anagba and Ezechima. He also emphasized that Kanagba, together with Ezechima and his children, only sojourned in Benin and were never Benin people as some historians have tended to suggest. Osia challenged historians to take a close look at the oral traditions and insisted they would find that the Obamkpa and the Umuezechima clans were Igbo-speaking people and not Edo.[75]

The uncertainties that surround the provenance of these clans have been exacerbated by some oral historians and politicians who have embellished their accounts. In their desire to inflate their importance *viz a viz* that of their hosts, the Ezechima people have sometimes distorted their own traditional history. For instance, during a leadership dispute which occurred in the early 1940s between the people of Onicha-Ugbo and Issele-Ukwu, the representatives of the former wondered why the people of Issele-Ukwu should assume leadership over the Umu Ezechima clan, since they were the lowest in the Ezechima hierarchy. Part of the petition addressed to His Highness, Oba Akenzua II, the Oba of Benin, read:

> Ado-Ezechima emigrated from Benin-city during the old tribal wars and settled at a place now known as Onicha-Ugbo. He had four issues—two daughters and two sons. His first-born child was Obioma or Obior (a daughter), the second Onicha-Ezechi or

Onicha-Ugbo (the eldest son), the third Ifite (the younger daughter) and the fourth Oligbo or Issele-Ukwu (the younger son). Onicha-Olona, Onicha-Mili and Onicha-Ukwu sprang from Onicha-Ugbo, and all are one. Ifite delivered Ezi-Uno and is the founder of Ezi. As a woman could not govern a kingdom, Obior, the first child, could not be trusted with the care of the house of Ado-Ezechima and hence it fell to the lot of Onicha-Ugbo (the first son). When Ezechima was emigrating from Benin, the then Oba of Benin handed him a majestic "Ada" to make him a king which Ezechima in turn bequeathed to his children as a heritage and hence our Obis are possessed of "Adas." There was never a time when the Obi of Issele-Ukwu received any special title from the Oba of Benin and he had never had the privilege of seeing the Oba of Benin face to face without being led by his senior brotherly towns."[76]

Three crucial issues are raised in this narrative. The first is that Ezechima fled his original place of abode as a result of wars; this is most likely accurate. The second is that he left Benin City as a result of these wars. This could be true or false; he could have left from any other town. The third is that when Ezechima was emigrating from Benin City, the Oba of Benin handed him a royal insignia, or *ada*, to make him a king wherever he went. This is clearly false. Kings do not give emblems of royalty to escaping rebels. In any case, why the flight and pursuit?

The claim that Ezechima came from Benin City could have several important explanations. E. J. Alagoa has observed that where a group no longer remembered its place of origin, it was likely to choose one that was both powerful and distant enough.[77] This could be said of the Ezechima clan, but the events that led to their dispersal occurred fairly recently in oral historic times and could not have been forgotten so quickly and so completely. Perhaps their claim to Benin origin is an example of what Alan Ryder has described as "the product of hankering after prestige institutions or simply the adoption of the most likely story, given the canons of traditional historiography."[78] Onwuejeogwu has also warned that, "Considering all other evidence available, the Onitsha claim to Benin origin is no more than a prestige claim and a safety device not uncommon in the history of people faced by the imminent invasion of their territory by powerful invaders."[79]

These views do not necessarily contradict one another, but one might also add that the claim to Benin origin could have been an attempt by some Igbo people to conceal the uncomfortable memory of defeat or subjugation, for it is not difficult to see that after Benin had overrun parts of Anioma, the vanquished groups must have been made to accept Benin overlordship. In due course, however, they might have decided to explain their vassalage in terms of blood ties. Moreover, even when the Edo menace was no longer apparent, some Anioma people still journeyed to Benin to solicit the Oba's recognition and support by accepting from him their staffs of office. Trips to Benin City must have been more frequently undertaken in times of succession disputes. Certainly, some Anioma communities must have thought it prestigious to pay homage to the Oba of Benin even when the Oba exercised no authority over them. As we shall see, in 1878, that is, at a time when Benin no longer exercised any political authority in Anioma, Obi Nwadishi, the newly crowned king of Ubulu-Ukwu, sent messengers to Benin "to announce his coronation and to present the Oba of Benin with some gifts and to have his accession confirmed."[80] Ikenna Nzimiro has been fascinated by the accounts of Igbo chiefs who journeyed to Benin for this purpose and has described them as "ada chiefs."[81]

The manner by which some Anioma people used the exalted position of the Oba of Benin to legitimize their own authority or to feather their own nests, so to speak, is illustrated by an Anioma oral tradition which recalls that in the beginning, the people of Igbuzo had no chiefs or kings; rather, they organized themselves in patrilineages and were ruled by their elders, *ndi okpala*. One day, Ezechi, a man from the Umuogwo maximal lineage of Igbuzo, declared that he had just returned from Benin City as a special guest of the Royal Court. Brandishing an insignia of authority, or *ada,* he stated that the Oba of Benin had appointed him the paramount chief of Igbuzo. He then decreed that the people of this place should treat him in a manner befitting a man of his royal stature.[82] One version of the Igbuzo traditions claimed that Ezechi did not travel to Benin, nor did the Oba give him any insignia of authority, and that the object he brandished, was, in fact, something he had captured during a war he led against the Bini invaders of Igbuzo.[83]

How he got the insignia is important, but more important is the fact that the people of Igbuzo accepted his claims and treated him as a distinguished person. However, as the years passed, the people became more and more offended by Ezechi's alien and despotic rule. They plotted against him and carried out a successful ritual coup, forcing him, his family, and his followers to flee to Ejima where some of their descendants still live.

After the removal of Ezechi, the people of Igbuzo introduced the *eze* or *ozo* title system. Seven men were selected from the various maximal lineages and conferred with the *ozo* title. These men, according to Nosike Ikpo, were the first generation of *ndi eze* in Igbuzo.[84] Elders from the Ogboli lineage, whose ancestors had come from Agukwu Nri, officiated at these and the subsequent coronations at Igbuzo. They alone could tie the ankle cords on new initiates and lead them to Ani Udo where the necessary rituals connected to the *eze* title-taking were performed. In 1936, however, the elders of the Ogboli lineage sided with the elders of Ogwashi-Ukwu, their cousins, in a land dispute with Igbuzo and were relieved of the ancient position of king-makers of Igbuzo.

THE BENIN-AGBOR WARS

Agbor and the other Anioma clans of Umunede, Owa, Ute-Okpu, and Idumuase were situated on and around an ancient trail that ran from Asaba to Benin. These Ika communities were the most warlike of the Anioma clans, and for three or four centuries, they acted as a bulwark against the expansion of Benin rule into Igboland, bearing the greatest burden of resisting Edo military imperialism.

We do not know exactly when the Obas of Benin began to send their soldiers against Agbor and the other Anioma towns in the Ika district, but according to Jacob Egharevba, a man called Agban, who lived during the closing years of Oba Orhogbua, was a great warrior and a prosperous chief (Ezomo) of Benin. In 1577, Oba Orhogbua learned that the vassal chiefs (obis) of Eka (Ika) and other towns on the western side of the Niger River were in a state of rebellion; they refused to pay their usual tributes to Benin, and the Oba sent Agban "to teach them a severe lesson." Agban quickly went into action, but found himself and his troops drawn into a grim battle that lasted for two long years. In the end, however, Agban captured several Igbo towns. The first, Igidi, was, Egharevba reported, renamed Agban after the conqueror, but this was later corrupted to Agbor.[85]

This narrative suggests that before 1577, Agbor and some Anioma towns had been vassals of Benin and might have been in a state of rebellion during the reign of Oba Orhogbua; their refusal to pay the usual tributes warranted their reconquest. It also suggests that even though the Benin general, Agban, eventually succeeded in subjugating Agbor and the other Ika towns, a state of conflict reigned in the region because of the determination of the rulers of Benin to expand their influence eastward and extract tribute. While many Igbo groups, like the Ezechima clan, grew weary of the intimidation, packed their belongings, and fled east, the Ika remained behind, sometimes living uneasily under the Oba's domination, sometimes revolting against it.

Nonetheless, during the closing years of the nineteenth century, the

British had begun to conquer southern Nigeria, menacing Benin at the same time. Between 1879 and 1896, the British imperial forces attacked and destroyed Onitsha, Idah, Aboh, Asaba, Ijebu, Ebrohimi, and Brass, the neighbors of Benin. The Oba of Benin, Ovonramwen, was worried about his own safety, but rather than mobilize his forces against the British intruders, he decided to reconquer Agbor, which had rebelled against his authority by refusing to pay the customary tributes. "In 1896," wrote Egharevba, "the Oba built a war camp (*eko*) at a village called Obadan and ordered every town and village in his own domain to send him soldiers. Over ten thousand men were recruited and stationed at Obadan to be trained, so that they might be used in Agbor and other campaigns which he proposed to undertake."[86] Egharevba, the "father" of Benin history, did not say what happened to these recruits, but we are told that soon after their training was supposed to have started, Acting Consul-General J. R. Phillips decided to undertake a "peaceful expedition" to Benin but met with a tragic reception; he had been warned not to come to Benin at that time of the year, when the Edo were expected to be left entirely alone as they communed with their ancestors. Rather than heed the warning, Phillips stubbornly led a large contingent of soldiers and carriers into the road that led to Benin City, and they were ambushed and cut down by angry warriors. The British colonial government retaliated by sending a strong force which entered Benin City, sending Oba Ovonramwen himself, together with all his chiefs and warriors, into a hasty flight. The Oba later returned to Benin to face trumped-up charges, was found guilty on several counts, and was then exiled to Calabar.[87]

With the defeat of Benin City by the British in 1897, the people of Agbor might have hoped finally to consolidate their independence, but it was a futile hope. British colonial officials, partly through ignorance of local history and partly through their own inflated conception of the extent of the Benin kingdom, committed a political blunder when they imposed some Benin chiefs as the authority over the Ika peoples of Agbor, Umunede, Owa, and Ute-Okpu.[88] Worse yet, Sir Ralph Moor, who was the high commissioner of the protectorate of Southern Nigeria in 1900, fixed a small tribute which the Ika towns and villages were supposed to pay to these Benin chiefs for their services.

To the Ika people, the decision by the British colonial administration to allow Benin chiefs to overrule their decisions nullified their centuries-old struggle against Benin. It is therefore not surprising that, from the day when Sir Ralph Moor became the principal colonial agent in Southern Nigeria, Ika people registered their protest against the imposition of both British officials and Benin chiefs. A Public Record Office source stated that in 1902, Johnson, the district commissioner of Benin City, was fired at while passing through Agbor. In the same year, Chief Aiguobasimwin, son of Ovonramwen, the exiled king of Benin, resigned his appointment as the district head of Agbor, and was "frightened to go near the place."[89] Jacob Egharevba described the latter encounter in greater detail even though the date he furnished was one year earlier than the one provided by the Public Record Office. According to Egharevba, Aiguobasimwin, the son of Oba Ovonramwen, was made a warrant chief of Benin and district head for Agbor district, but in 1901 "the Agbors rose against him on the grounds that his father had been preparing to make war against them before the Expedition in 1897. They came on him with cudgels and he would have been pushed into a well if he had not jumped backwards. He warned his men not to strike a single blow, so his enemies calmed down and he was able to return to Benin City."[90]

Aiguobasimwin returned safely to Benin City but resigned his position as the district head of Agbor. The district commissioner, who did not consider the Ika people capable of looking after their own affairs, requested another Benin chief, Osula, to occupy the position vacated by Aiguobasimwin.[91] The colonial government stationed a strong military force in Agbor to protect Osula and enforce his appointment, and the Ika endured this imposition until 1906 when they rebelled, killing the new district officer, S. O. Crewe-Read, together with some Benin chiefs and private citizens.[92] After these killings, the head chief of Owa Oyibu commended the action of his people. He was reported to have boasted: "I have sent all the OEBOS [Owa Oyibus] to do that. We are all tired of the white man's work . . . I do not want any white or Benin man in my town again, only Lagos traders."[93]

These events culminated in the so-called Agbor expedition of 1906, during which the Ika people resisted British imperialism with unsurpassed bravery. Although their resistance was eventually crushed, it forced the colonial administration to abolish the policy which allowed officials to impose Benin chiefs on the Ika communities. Indeed, it was only in 1906 that the Ika finally regained their independence of Benin even if they remained the subjects of His Majesty, the King of England until 1960.[94]

As for the British colonial agents, their fear of the Ika remained real for some years to come. In 1910, the governor of Southern Nigeria, Sir Walter Egerton, while on a tour from Lagos to Calabar on a bicycle, wrote in his diary that he was "glad to get safely clear of Agbor where the attitude of the people was hostile and truculent."[95]

Egerton had every reason to fear for his life, for he still remembered that Crewe-Read, the former district commissioner of Agbor, who had been shot by Owa rifle-men during a tour of his district in 1906, had also been riding a bicycle.[96] This time, Egerton was mistaken, however. Once "pacified," the Ika would forgive and forget, exemplified by the fact that during the First World War (1914–18), the Ika cooperated with the British in the "war effort." They provided a considerable number of men who went from the Agbor district to serve in Cameroon and East Africa to preserve the British empire.[97] In one of those ironies of colonial relationships, the oppressed shed their own blood so that their oppressors might live.

THE HISTORICAL IMPORTANCE OF THE BENIN-ANIOMA WARS

Perhaps in no other part of southeastern Nigeria is there such interesting, if conflicting, evidence of a long period of military clashes between two neighboring ethnic groups. The Anioma-Benin wars, together with the civil wars that were fought in the Edo capital, caused many Bini to emigrate from a sparsely populated area into a relatively more densely populated Igbo culture area. These disturbances and migrations went on for several centuries, compelling the Anioma people to accept some measure of social discomfort, political dislocation, and economic readjustment. Some of the more noticeable changes took place in the political sphere where there was an acceptance of the Benin-type institution of kingship, or obiship, and in the settlement patterns of some Anioma communities where there was a tendency to congregate in compact settlements for purposes of defense. Many Anioma communities went further to organize their towns on a war footing, dividing them into sections with each placed under a non-hereditary war chief, fashioned after those of Benin and bearing such Edo-derived war titles as *Iyase, Onishe, Ezomo* and *Uwolo.* Perhaps it was the strong presence of these Edo elements in the Anioma culture that persuaded Daryll Ford and G. I. Jones to conclude that "The Western Ibo [Igbo] groups appear to be of diverse origins owing to influences from, and possible admixture with, the Edo-speaking peoples of the west. Some of these contacts probably antedate the rise of the Yoruba influence and the Edo state of Benin."[98]

In spite of inconsistencies in these traditions, we have a clear picture of how some Edo- and Yoruba-speaking peoples entered and settled in the Igbo culture area. We know, for instance, that they came in small numbers and that their arrival was spread over a period of three or four hundred years. With the exception of the Olukunmi, most of the immigrants eventually lost their language and rituals, for the available evidence confirms that none of the Igbo communities that claimed Benin origin retained the Edo language. Instead they spoke the Igbo language, talked in mature Igbo parables, and used Igbo expressions and idioms. Their major deities and emblems of worship had the same basic names and represented similar forces and concepts as those of the eastern Igbo people. They also performed certain rituals and took part in some religious ceremonies, such as the iwaji (the yam festival), which resembled those of the Igbo more than the Edo.

As we shall see in the next chapter, the *diokpa* or *diokpala* or *onyisi umunna* of the Anioma communities that claimed Benin origin performed the same functions as their counterparts in the other parts of Igboland. This position was nonhereditary and was occupied by the oldest man in a lineage. Even in Agbor, where the Obi was relatively powerful, the *diokpa* still acted as the spiritual, executive, and judicial head of the *umunna*.

Any account of the Anioma-Benin wars also sheds light on the early history of the Ezechima clan and the other Anioma communities that claimed Benin origin. We have seen that the migration of some eastern Igbo people across the Niger River was well under way before the rise of Benin and that some of these Igbo people were later repelled when the Edo began to expand their kingdom. If so, the timing of Ezechima's flight would be less puzzling than his ethnic origin. Most writers would date that movement to the reign of Asije (Oba Esigie, c. 1504–50). The period when the power of Benin was at its zenith was the fifteenth and sixteenth centuries, that is, during the reigns of such warrior Obas as Ewuare the Great (c. 1440–73) and Ozolua (c. 1481– 1504), followed by Esigie. By the sixteenth century the Lower Niger had increasingly become "a frontier of economic opportunity." From then on, the trade of the Niger increased rapidly as a result of the European presence in the coastal ports. Some communities or individuals on both sides of the Niger might have consciously moved toward this highway of commerce and contact. Among the groups who could have responded to such opportunities may have been the followers of Ezechima, the Igala, and the Nri-Awka traders and ritual specialists. This hypothesis is in keeping with the view expressed by Kenneth O. Dike that it was probably "the lure of the great commercial highway of the Niger valley itself which stimulated another migration within the hinterland and the hardy and adventurous people from Benin area once again established themselves at places on the river bank favorable to trade."[99]

The timing of the Ezechima flight has another historical importance. In the traditions of origin of some Anioma communities, mention is made of the first contact between the Ezechima people and their Igbo hosts. When the followers of Ezechima arrived at Onicha-Olona, they had no fire with which to prepare their meals. They therefore sent a female member of their group to Akwukwu, a nearby settlement, for fire which, when procured, was lit under an *olomina* tree, hence Onicha-Olomina or Onicha-Olona. One tradition claims that the tree was *ukpaka,* the oil bean tree.[100] Whether *olomina* or *ukpaka,* until recently the procurement of this historic fire and its lighting under the equally historic tree were recounted during annual festivals at Onicha-Olona. If we accept this tradition (and there is no reason to reject it), it would mean that the Ezechima flight must have begun after Akwukwu had been founded. The Akwukwu, on their part, claimed that the founder of the town was a man called Igbo who had come from Nshi (Nri) in the company of Odaigbo and Edini, the founders of Ogwashi-Ukwu and Ogboli-Igbuzo, respectively.

Traditions also make mention of other Igbo-speaking people whom the Benin immigrants met on arrival. "The town of Aboh," wrote Augustus F. Mockler-Ferryman, "belonged to the Akris, one of the numerous Ibo [Igbo] clans, the fore-fathers of the present inhabitants being natives of Idu."[101] Another tradition recalls that Onitsha was originally owned by the Oze, who were driven off when the Umueze-chima arrived.[102] Illah, as we have seen, was occupied by the Omoka before Edaiken came from Benin and founded the Ukumaga lineage.

From the foregoing discussion, one may conclude that the power and the extent of the Benin empire were not as wide and effective as they are often portrayed. While the period of Benin's glory was "clear and vigorous," even during the peak period of its fame it did not seem to have established any effective and enduring control over its vassal states, especially those located in the Igbo culture area. "Our subjection to the king of Benin," wrote Olaudah Equiano around the close of the eighteenth century, "was little more than nominal, for every transaction of the government, as far as my slender observation extended, was conducted by the chiefs or elders of the place."[103]

Alan Ryder has noted that the Benin empire had "a somewhat informal character" and that "only the central area within easy reach of the capital ever came under the permanent supervision of the Oba." Elsewhere, Ryder continued, some of the bonds which existed between

Benin and its vassal states were "as light as air, demanding little more than a formal acknowledgement of the Oba at the beginning of his reign and a friendly attitude thereafter."[104] We have seen how the Obi of Ubulu-Ukwu sent messengers to the Oba of Benin in 1876 to announce his coronation and to solicit the Oba's continued friendship. However, it has been traditional for historians to imagine that parts of the Igbo culture area, especially Anioma, had been brought under the effective domination of Benin. There might have been periods of effective control in certain locations, but because of the "informal character" of Benin's rule, the Obas could not have possibly exercised a long-lasting sovereignty over the conquered territories, hence the frequent charges of the vassal states' refusing "to pay the usual tributes." Thus historians may have assigned an undue importance to the concept of a clear-cut Benin conquest of these territories.

Indeed, many of the distortions about the power of Benin were initially fostered by the early European visitors to West Africa. Even the Encyclopaedia Britannica erroneously reported: "Europeans in the seventeenth century spoke of it as 'Great Benin.' Colonists from Benin founded the port of Lagos and Badagry. While the area of the kingdom was small (somewhat larger than Wales), its influence was very wide and it is said to have extended west as far as Sierra-Leone, and south to the Congo River."[105]

Notwithstanding the inconsistencies in the sources, the available evidence is that Benin was one of the most powerful kingdoms of the forest belt of West Africa. Its wars of expansion affected its neighbors in Yorubaland, Edoland, Igboland, and Urhoboland. The inhabitants of Owo, Akure, Lagos, Warri, Asaba, Onitsha, and Ubulu-Ukwu still recall that at one time or the other they came under the influence of Benin, even if that influence was "little more than nominal," as Olaudah Equiano might have testified.

NOTES

1. N. Uka, "A Note on the 'Abam' Warriors of Igboland," *Ikenga: Journal of African Studies* 1, no. 2(1972): 78.

2. Ibid.

3. Ibid., 80.

4. John N. Oriji, "The Slave Trade, Warfare and the Aro Expansion in the Igbo Hinterland," *Geneve-Afrique*, 24, 2(1986): 107.

5. Ibid., 107, 108.

6. Don C. Ohadike, "The Ohadike Collection," in *Western Igbo*, ed. Don C. Ohadike and Rick Shain, vol, 6, *Jos Oral History and Literature Texts* (Jos: University of Jos, 1988), 105–8.

7. NAI, CSO 26, File no. 31303, "Intelligence Report on the Oko Okwe Area of Asaba Division," 1935.

8. Onwuejeogwu, M. A. "An Outline Account of the Dawn of Igbo Civilization in the Igbo Culture Area." *Odinani: The Journal of Odinani Museum, Nri.* 1, no. 1(March, 1972): 50

9. Ohadike, "The Ohadike Collection," 69.

10. Onwuejeogwu, "An Outline Account," 48.

11. PRO, CO 520/93/18685 of June 18, 1910, enclosure in governor's dispatch to Colonial Office.

12. Ibid., enclosure no. 2, "Interim Report," A. Norton Harper, A.D.C. political officer, Ogwashi-Ukwu Patrol, May 18, 1910.

13. Austin J. Shelton, *The Igbo-Igala Borderland: Religion and Social Control in Indigenous African Colonialism* (Albany: State Univ. of New York Press, 1971). xii.

14. Ibid., 20.

15. Samson Ukpabi, discussed in Shelton, *The Igbo-Igala Borderland,* 20-7.

16. Ibid., 23.

17. Local Government Archives, Benin City, File no. 26769, E. A. Miller, "Intelligence Report on Abo," April 1931.

18. NAI, CSO 26/3, File no. 26769, vol. 1. G. B. Williams, "Intelligence Report on the Ibo-Speaking Clans of the Kwale Division, Warri Province," 1931.

19. MacGregor Laird and R. A. K. Oldfield, *Narrative of an Expedition into the Interior of Africa by the River Niger in 1832, 1833 and 1834* (London: Richard Bently, 1837), vol. 1: 97.

20. William Allen and T. R. H. Thomson, *A Narrative of the Expedition to the River Niger in 1841,* (London: Richard Bently, 1848), vol. 1. 218.

21. NAI, CSO 26 File no. 29300, H. Shelton, "Intelligence Report on the Kwale-Ibo Clan," 1933 (with an introduction by Mallison).

22. NAI, CSO 26/4, File no. 3038X, J. Macrea Simpson, "Intelligence Report on the Agbor, Oligie and Emuhu Clans, Agbor District," 1935.

23. Alan. F. C. Ryder, *Benin and the Europeans, 1485-1897* (New York: Humanities Press, 1969), 2.

24. Emanuel Terray, "Long-Distance Exchange and the State: The Case of the Abrong Kingdom of Gyaman," *Economy and Society* 3(1974): 331.

25. Ibid.

26. Catherine Coquery-Vidrovitch, "Research on an African Mode of Production," in *Perspectives on the African Past,* ed. G. W. Johnson and Martin Klein (Boston: Little, Brown, 1972), 33-51.

27. Robert M. Wren, "OZO in Achebe's Novels: The View from the Past," duplicated paper, University of Houston, 1980, 4.

28. David Northrup, *Trade Without Rulers: Pre-colonial Economic Development in South-eastern Nigeria* (Oxford: Clarendon Press), 1978.

29. R. E. Bradbury, "The Kingdom of Benin," in *West African Kingdoms in the Nineteenth Century,* ed. Daryll Forde and P. M. Kaberry (Oxford: Oxford Univ. Press, 1969), 17.

30. Ryder, *Benin and the Europeans,* 196-227.

31. I. A. Akinjogbin, "The Expansion of Oyo and the Rise of Dahomey,

1600-1800" in *History of West Africa,* ed. J. F. Ade Ajayi and Michael Crowder (London: Longman, 1976), 373-412. For the Gold Coast see Ivor Wilks, "The Mossi and Akan States," in Ibid. 413-55.

32. Bradbury, "The Kingdom of Benin," 17; Ryder, *Benin and the Europeans,* 196-227.

33. Ade Obayemi, "The Yoruba and Edo-speaking Peoples," in *History of West Africa,* ed. Ajayi and Crowder, 207-8.

34. Ibid., 208-29.

35. Ibid., 242-43.

36. Graham Connah, *The Archaeology of Benin: Excavations and other Researches in and around Benin City, Nigeria* (Oxford: Clarendon Press, 1975); Alan. F. C. Ryder, "The Benin Kingdom," in *Groundwork of Nigerian History,* ed. Obaro Ikime (London: Heinemann, 1980), 110.

37. Jacob Egharevba, *A Short History of Benin* (Ibadan: Ibadan Univ. Press, 1968). This version has been challenged by some more recent Benin writers.

38. Ibid., 6-7.

39. The third period of the Benin empire refers to the post-independence period of Benin, starting in 1914 when Oko Aiguobasimwin, the eldest son of the exiled Oba Ovonramwen, was installed as the new Oba of Benin with the title Eweka II; Egharevba, *A Short History,* 61

40. Obayemi, "The Yoruba and Edo-speaking Peoples," 247.

41. Ibid., 247.

42. Ryder, "The Benin Kingdom," 113.

43. Ibid., 113.

44. Egharevba, *A Short History of Benin,* 13-33.

45. Bradbury, "The Kingdom of Benin," 1; Ryder, *Benin and the Europeans,* 24-31.

46. Ryder, *Benin and the Europeans,* 2.

47. See for instance, Thomas Hodgkin, *Nigerian Perspectives, An Historical Anthology,* (London: Oxford Univ. Press, 1969), 152.

48. Bradbury, "The Kingdom of Benin," 31.

49. Egharevba, *A Short History,* 42.

50. Ryder, *Benin and the Europeans,* 288.

51. As quoted in ibid., 289.

52. Augustine Okafor, interviewed at Ikelike village, Ogwashi-Ukwu, August 29, 1974.

53. This account is from Otono Onweazim, a very old man. He saw the first white man to come to Akwukwu. He was a blacksmith but now blind. He was the oldest man in the Opu quarters and therefore the *diokpa* (most senior elder) of Opu.

54. *Edaiken* in Benin is a title reserved for the Oba's eldest son. We do not know the name of the Edaiken mentioned in these traditions.

55. Barnabas C. Agadah, "Migrations and Inter-group Relations," research project, Department of History and Archaeology, University of Nigeria, Nsukka, June 1974.

56. Elizabeth Isichei, ed., *Igbo Worlds: An Anthology of Oral Histories and Historical Descriptions,* (Philadelphia: Institute for the Study of Human Relations, 1978), 146.

57. Robin Law, *The Oyo Empire c. 1600–c. 1830: A West African Imperialism in the Era of the Atlantic Slave Trade.* (Oxford: Clarendon Press, 1977), 16–20.

58. Ibid., 219–21.

59. His Royal Highness, Obi Ogoh I, interviewed at Ogbeagidi, Ukwunzu, December 20, 1982.

60. I speak the Yoruba language and have observed that the language is spoken differently in many parts of Nigeria and that it is sometimes difficult for, say, a Lagosian to understand an Ekiti if the latter communicates in his or her native dialect.

61. Egharevba, *A Short History,* 40.

62. E. Ashinze, interviewed at Umuodafe quarters, Igbuzo, September 15, 1974. Also see Onwuejeogwu, "The Dawn of Igbo Civilization,"

63. Sylverus Onochie, interviewed at Idumu-Ishionum, Ubulu-Ukwu, March 23, 1978. In my own research, I was unable to confirm whether an Onije quarter existed in Benin City.

64. Victor C. Uchendu, *The Ibo of South Eastern Nigeria* (New York: Holt, Rinehart and Winston, 1965), 3.

65. Charles K. Meek, *Law and Authority in a Nigerian Tribe* (London, New York: Oxford Univ. Press, 1937) 11–12.

66. Arthur G. Leonard, *The Lower Niger and Its Tribes* (London: Frank Cass, 1968), 35.

67. Peter O. Obue, "Some Aspects of the Pre-colonial History of Agbor," research project, History Department, University of Jos, June 1980, 20.

68. Richard N. Henderson, *The King in Every Man,* (New Haven: Yale Univ. Press, 1972), 78.

69. Northcote Thomas, *Anthropological Report on the Ibo-Speaking People of Nigeria, Part 4: Law and Custom of the Ibo of Asaba District* (London: Harrison, 1914), 3.

70. Kingsley Ogedengbe, "The Aboh Kingdom of the Lower Niger, c. 1650–1900," Ph.D. diss., University of Wisconsin, 1971, 163.

71. Egharevba, *A Short History,* 6.

72. Ibid, 25.

73. Ohadike and Shain, ed. *Western Igbo, passim.*

74. Kunirum Osia, a written interview, October 4, 1992.

75. Ibid.

76. Local Government Archives, Benin, File no. A.D. 632/A. Ezechima Clan Administration, November 13, 1944.

77. E. J. Alagoa, "Ijo Origins and Migrations," *Nigeria Magazine* no. 9(December 1966). 279–88.

78. Ryder, *Benin and the Europeans,* 3.

79. Onwuejeogwu, "The Dawn of Igbo Civilization," 33.

80. *The Church Missionary Intelligencer* (1879), 239.

81. Ikenna Nzimiro, *Studies in Ibo Political Systems* (London: Frank Cass, 1972), 8. See also Ogedengbe, "The Aboh Kingdom," 154–76; Nnamdi Azikiwe, *My Odyssey* (London: C. Hurst, 1970), 11.

82. Ohadike, "The Ohadike Collections" in *Western Igbo,* ed. Ohadike and Shain, 118–24, 130–35.

83. Ibid., 121–24.

84. Ibid., 113–14.

85. Egharevba, *A Short History,* 32

86. Ibid., 49

87. Ryder, *Benin and the Europeans.*

88. PRO, CO 520/38, confidential enclosure, "Agbor District Rising," F. S. James, provincial commissioner, Central Province, Warri, to Colonial Office, December 12, 1906.

89. Ibid.

90. Egharevba, *A Short History,* 61.

91. Ibid.

92. PRO, CO 520/38, confidential enclosure, "Agbor District Rising," F. S. James, provincial commissioner, Central Province, Warri, to Colonial Office, December 12, 1906.

93. PRO, CO 5200/36 of August 28, 1906. Widenham Fosbery to Colonial Office, July 28, 1906. Confidential enclosure, statement by Omorege, a Benin man sent by the king of Abavo.

94. Don C. Ohadike, *The Ekumeku Movement: Western Igbo Resistance to the British Conquest of Nigeria, 1883–1914* (Athens: Ohio Univ. Press, 1991), 154–55

95. NAI, CSO 26/4, File no. 3038X. J. Macrea Simpson, "Intelligence Report on the Agbor, Oligie and Emuhu Clans, Agbor District," 1935.

96. Ohadike, *The Ekumeku Movement,* 151.

97. NAI, CSO 26/4, No. 3038X. J. Macrea Simpson, "Intelligence Report on the Agbor, Oligie and Emuhu clans, Agbor District," 1935.

98. Daryll Forde and G. I. Jones, *The Ibo and Ibibio-speaking Peoples of South Eastern Nigeria: Ethnographic Survey of Africa* (London, 1950), 46.

99. Kenneth O. Dike, *Trade and Politics in the Niger Delta* (Oxford: Clarendon Press, 1966), 25.

100. Nkemdilim L. Eneanya, "The Eneanya Collection", in *Western Igbo.,* ed. Ohadike and Shain.

101. Augustus F. Mockler-Ferryman, *Up the Niger: Narrative of Major Claude MacDonald's Mission to the Niger and Benue Rivers* (London: G. Philip, 1892), 234.

102. A. Nwabuisi, "The Nwabuisi Collection," in *Western Igbo,* ed. Ohadike and Shain, 242–43.

103. G. I. Jones, "Olaudah Equiano of the Niger Ibo," in *Africa Remembered: Narratives by West Africans from the Era of the Slave Trade,* ed. Philip D. Curtin (Madison: Univ. of Wisconsin Press, 1967), 70.

104. Ryder, *Benin and the Europeans,* 21.

105. From "Benin" in *Encyclopaedia Britannica,* 401–11, quoted in Egharevba, *A Short History,* 30.

3
~~~

SOCIAL AND POLITICAL STRUCTURES, A.D. 900–1900

SOCIAL AND POLITICAL INSTITUTIONS

DOWN THROUGH THE CENTURIES, and until the British invaded Nigeria in the 1800s, the people of Anioma organized themselves in lineages which were based on the concepts of *uno, umunna, idumu, ogbe,* and *obodo.* We have a fairly accurate description of how the political systems functioned on the eve of the British conquest of Nigeria, and there is reason to believe that what we found at that time was the outcome of the interactions between Anioma institutions and those of the Edo, Igala, Ishan, Urhobo, and Ijo.

The smallest social unit was the *uno.* This was conceived of as a natural family consisting of a man, his wife or wives, and their children. Such a unit hardly formed a separate territorial entity.

Next to the *uno* was the *umunna,* a form of joint family, composed of an elderly male (*onyisi* or oldest man), his wife or wives, his unmarried sons and daughters, together with his married sons and their children. This unit numbered anything from twenty to a hundred and, whenever possible, lived near one another since they were all closely related. It was unthinkable for a young man to form his own separate *umunna* from his father's.

A group of *umunna* formed an *idumu* or minimal lineage, and was headed by the *onyisi idumu,* the oldest male member of the group. The most important meetings of an *idumu* were held in the *obi* or *ogwa* (a meeting shed) of the *onyisi.* In a sense, an *idumu* can be described as a patrilineage that went further back in generation than an *umunna.*

A collection of *idumu* formed an *ogbe* or maximal lineage. (This was the unit often referred to as "quarters" in Colonial Office records.) The oldest member of the *ogbe* was also the head of this unit. Blood ties were not as strong among the members of an *ogbe* as they were with the *idumu.* Usually, it was at the level of *ogbe* that outsiders or people who could not trace their origins to the original founding ancestors of the *umunna* were admitted into existing communities. Michael Onwuejeogwu has described an *ogbe* (maximal lineage) as a political concept that transcended patrilineality, a "territorially organized group whose patrilineage components may or may not have a common male or female founder." Such a unit was identified by a name and members referred to themselves as belonging to it. It might have a common land and a common cult. They acted together as a political entity under a headman called *diokpa ogbe.*[1] Finally, a number of *ogbe* formed the *obodo,* a village or town.

For the sake of clarity, we shall adopt the following four classifications in the discussion that follows: *umunna* refers to joint family or lineage; *idumu* to minimal lineage; *ogbe* to maximal lineage or "quarter"; *obodo* to a town or compact village.

The *obodo* (town or compact village) was the highest territorially defined authority in Anioma. The oldest man in the *obodo* was its head. Relationships between towns were maintained by goodwill, mutual respect and diplomacy. Strictly speaking, however, political autonomy in Anioma was located not at the level of *obodo,* but with the *ogbe* (maximal lineage or quarter). Each ogbe was free to act independently in its relationships with outsiders or with other lineages and towns. The members of an *ogbe* could decide who to intermarry with or fight against. In the event of a war between two towns, an *ogbe* could dissociate itself from the conflict, claiming neutrality on the grounds of, say, marriage ties. As we shall see in chapter 6, when the British invaded Onicha-Olona in 1902, three out of the six ogbe of the town declared themselves friends of the British, while the other three declared war.[2] In fact, throughout the period of the Ekumeku wars, the British tried to make distinctions between those they described as friendly and hostile quarters or *ogbe.* It was not uncommon for some *ogbe* to have their own separate cults, deities, masks, and secret societies. In Illah, for example, the *nmo* society belonged only to the lineages that claimed Igala origin. It was also common for some *ogbe* to combine to produce their own separate *obi* (head chief), as in Akwukwu, and to refuse to recognize the head chiefs of the other *ogbe*. Sometimes, due to a serious quarrel, some *ogbe* might decide to exclude one or two *ogbe* from the general assembly of the town. This was the case in 1936 when the Ogboli lineage of Igbuzo was ostracized by the other nine *ogbe* of Igbuzo. These examples emphasize the democratic nature of the Igbo political systems, and to show that the real centers of political authority were located in the lineage heads and not necessarily in the chiefs or town assemblies.

Although we have used the word *onyisi* to describe the heads of these political units, most Anioma groups would prefer the term *diokpa* or *okpala*. Matters affecting a lineage were discussed at the meetings of the *ndi okpala* (plural) with the assistance of the adult members of the lineage. In inter-lineage disputes, elders from the affected lineages met to discuss solutions, the oldest man in the gathering presiding. There was hardly a formal concentration of power in a single individual or groups of individuals.

The authority of the head of the lineage derived from the acceptance of the community that he was the oldest living representative of the founding ancestors of the unit. He was the custodian of ancestral lands and the keeper of the lineage ritual objects which symbolized political authority. The lineage head commanded great respect because of his proven integrity, wisdom, and experience in the art of government. He was the group's spiritual and temporal head; he was also the intermediary between the members of his lineage and their ancestral spirits. An outsider was not recognized in the lineage organization because his or her origins could not be traced to the founder or cofounders of the lineage. To be admitted, a male stranger had to attach himself to a leading elder who would be prepared to accord him a fictive relationship. The elder would, however, be required to present this adopted outsider to the assembly of elders for screening. A female stranger had greater avenues for entering a lineage organization than a man, albeit through marriage. Strictly speaking, it would be this woman's offspring who would be admitted as full members of the lineage.

Occasionally, some members of a lineage would break away to form their own autonomous lineage but would remain tied to the parent lineage by "the principle of territorial proximity and functional interdependence."[3] But no matter how distant in time or space the separation might have occurred, the new lineage still remained politically attached to the old.

The search for better farmlands often caused lineages to break away but many are known to have sought separate existence for other reasons. For example, one version of the Igbuzo traditions of origin recalls that Osheukwu, one of the sons of Umejei, the founding father of Igbuzo, was a titled chief, and the father of many sons and daughters. He was also the chief priest of the Earth deity, *ani,* a position he acquired by virtue of the fact that he was Umejei's oldest son. When Osheukwu died, the members of his lineage could not raise all the money they required for his elaborate funeral rites. They eventually borrowed a large sum from a wealthy farmer at Okpanam to whom they pawned Agidi Onihe, the youngest son of the dead priest. While at Okpanam, Agidi Onihe hunted when he was not working for his creditor. One day he killed an elephant and from the sale of its tusks, he was able to raise all the money he needed for his redemption. He returned to Igbuzo, but rather than join his lineage, founded a new autonomous one, Umuehea.[4]

Lineages sometimes divided into two or more, following the principle of matrilineality. This was the situation at Igbuzo where the children of Ezebuogu split to form two autonomous lineages—Umuodafe and Idi-na-Isagba. In due course, however, Umuodafe also split into two lineages—Odukwu (or Umuodafe Ukwu) and Odanta (or Umuodafe Nta). Odukwu and Odanta were born of the same mother and so their separation could not follow the matrilineal principle but instead followed the principle of the autonomy of the minority group.[5] Thus, while it had been possible for each of Umuodafe and Idi-na-Isagba to lead a separate existence, Odukwu and Odanta could not do likewise because they were born of the same mother. They owned in common certain ritual objects, like *ogwugwu afo,* and some annual festivals, like *iwu,* which could not be divided. Although the population of Odanta later outstripped that of Odukwu, the former remained a "minority" or junior lineage. The common ancestral shrines of both lineages remained in the Odukwu territory where they had been located. Since Odukwu was the senior of the two lineages, their joint meetings were presided over by the *diokpa* of Odukwu and were held in his *ogwa* (a meeting place). In fact, it was only in the *ogwa* of the *diokpa* of Odukwu that any joint meeting of the elders of both Odukwu and Odanta could be held.

THE COUNCIL OF ELDERS AND THE AGE-GRADES

Jomo Kenyatta has observed that the history and legends of the Gikuyu of Kenya were explained and remembered according to the names given to the various age-groups.[6] Like the Gikuyu, the pre-colonial Igbo people remembered and explained their history and legends according to the names given to the various age-grades. This classification was determined by the period in which one was born (in the Igbo case) or initiated into adulthood after circumcision (in the Gikuyu case). All persons born or initiated within a general but well-defined period before or after a given year belonged together to one age-grade. The period was named after a major event, that is, each age-group was given a name which best described what was going on at the time of its members' birth, rebirth, or initiation. The Gikuyu still remember the age-grade called Syphilis. This was the period when, according to Kenyatta, the white men introduced this deadly disease into Kenya.[7] Though a tragic experience, it was an event which the Gikuyu did not wish to forget so quickly. Since the Igbo, like the Gikuyu, did not write down their history, they tried to remember major events in this way. Some Igbo groups have the Influenza age-grade, or *ogbo infelunza,* to remember when the influenza epidemic of 1918–19 killed many people. Others remember the *ogbo akpu nkono,* that is, when cassava (*foofoo* or *fufu*) was introduced in some specific towns.

The age-grade system is a form of relative dating method familiar to historians, anthropologists, and archaeologists. It enabled societies like the Igbo and Gikuyu to assign special duties and responsibilities to the different segments of the society in accordance with the principle of seniority. Everyone performed particular functions when he or she attained a particular age and gave them up when he or she entered another age-grade. The most junior age-grades did the most menial jobs; they cleaned the footpaths and swept the marketplaces. The middle age-grades formed the fighting force and cleared the bush at the beginning of each planting season. The most senior age-grades decided whether a town should go to war, when the various agricultural circles would open or close, when the various annual festivals would be held, and whether a criminal should be hanged or drowned. In most Anioma towns, the most senior age-grades, sometimes called *ndi okpala* or *ama-ala,* were responsible for judicial matters, while the middle age-grades acted as the executive arm of the government. In Agbor, for example, the *ikoro,* a middle age-grade, hanged condemned criminals, while in Asaba the *oturaza* age-grade drowned habitual criminals by binding them hand-and-foot and casting them into the Niger River to drown.[8] But the *oturaza* acted in this capacity for only ten years and then retired into a senior grade. The oldest member of the oturaza was usually sixty-six years of age and once he moved into the next senior grade, he never again took part in active service. He would join the *ichiokwa* grade, "the helpless elders" whose ages ranged from seventy-six to eighty-four. Next to the *ichiokwa* was the final age-grade, called *kandum*.[9] Only men and women who had attained the age of eighty-four were admitted into the *kandum* grade. These elderly people, who were greeted with the praise name, *kandum,* were highly respected and remained in this grade for the rest of their lives. The age-grade system as described here determined not only what specific roles people played in society, but also when they moved from one type of position to another and when they retired from active service. It is difficult to determine the exact age-span in an age-grade except at a few locations like Igbuzo, where the three-year interval operated.

The power and privileges of the elders, chiefs, and age-grades were limited and confined to the lineages and towns, however. There was no central Anioma political authority. Every town or village was autonomous. Each had its own sets of age-grades, secret societies, and religious cults, which acted as cross-cutting institutions. Even though the society was significantly stratified, every one enjoyed some measure of personal freedom. At the top of the social ladder were titled chiefs and elders, and at the bottom were untitled men, women, and children. Also, even though age and titles were the most important qualifications for office holding, no one was excluded from the great assemblies where important decisions affecting the lives of the citizens were made. Basil Davidson, a leading African historian, has rightly observed that if democracy meant participation, societies which were organized as the Igbos' were democratic, "even extremely so." Every Igbo man (and woman), he further observed, regarded his village assembly as "a birth right, the guarantee of his rights, his shield against oppression, the expression of his individualism and the means whereby the young and progressive impressed their views upon the old and conservative."[10] As J. Macrae Simpson has rightly observed, the *onyisi* or *diokpa* was *primus inter pares,* and would not act without having first obtained the approval of the village at a meeting. He was treated with respect because of his position as the religious, executive and judicial head of the village, but as a general rule, "nothing is done in any village until the matter has been fully ventilated at a village meeting."[11]

THE IMPACT OF BENIN ON THE PRECOLONIAL SOCIAL AND POLITICAL ORGANIZATIONS OF ANIOMA: THE IKA EXAMPLE

The basic political and social organizations of the Anioma people were affected by influences coming from the direction of Benin but, as already noted, this was more visible in the political sphere, that is, in the institution of obiship. We shall single out the Ika communities for a close examination, to demonstrate how the original organization of some Anioma communities might have been affected by contacts and conflicts with Benin. It will be shown also that despite the proximity to Benin and the existence of dual political structures, one hereditary and the other based on age, the Ika social and political systems remained fundamentally Igbo in character.

The Ika district is midway between Benin City and Asaba, with Agbor, the principal town, forty miles east of Benin City and forty miles west of Asaba. All Ika people are found in this district, which occupies an area of about 250 square miles. The western and northern neighbors are the Edo-speaking people while the eastern and southeastern neighbors are the Igbo-speaking people of Aniocha and Ndokwa. Ikaland occupies about one sixth the total surface area of Anioma (see map 2).

The available evidence suggests that the true Ika are among the oldest surviving Igbo groups in Anioma even though some of them appear not to be quite certain about their origin, as their conflicting traditions of origin attest. Some traditions link them with Benin, but these are mainly the traditions of the ruling families. A typical version of such traditions would say that the Obi of Agbor and the Oba of Benin were brothers, that both hailed from Ile-Ife, the original home of their great-grandfather, Oduduwa, but due to an accident of history the older brother was crowned the Obi at Agbor while his younger brother was installed at Benin.

However, while the ruling families would endeavor to trace their origin to Benin and Ile-Ife, the common people would simply say that they are Ika, that they are neither Edo nor Igbo, and that their great-grandfathers had occupied their present settlements from time out of mind.[12] J. Macrea Simpson, a former assistant district officer of Agbor, observed that certain communities in the Agbor district, such as Alizomo and Ozarra, "have forgotten, or do not care to remember their traditional story."[13] Simpson reported that these people spoke a language which differed from any other in the province, which suggests that they were perhaps the original inhabitants of the Ika district. Thus, the Ika may be among the earliest occupants of Anioma.

There is an erroneous tendency among some sources to describe all Anioma or Western Igbo people as Ika-Igbo. But Ika is neither a language nor an ethnic group; it is a dialect of the Igbo language, and the name of the people who live in the Agbor district and speak this dialect. As we have seen, prior to the 1940s hardly any Igbo group re-

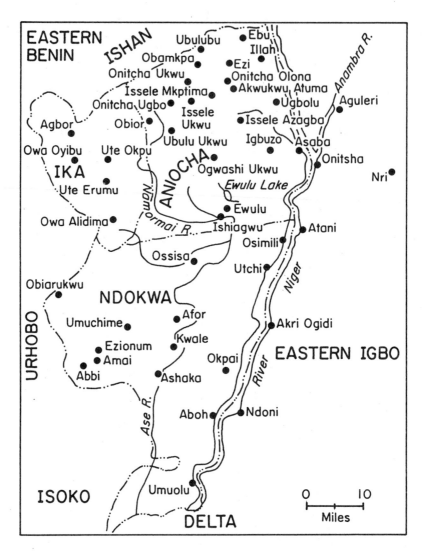

Map 2: Map of Anioma showing Aniocha, Ika, and Ndokwa—the Three Main Cultural Divisions

garded itself as Igbo. Thus, until then (and even to this day) most people living in the Agbor district identified themselves as Ika inasmuch as those living around Amai called themselves *ndi Ukwu-ani,* and those around Asaba, *ndi Aniocha* or *ndi Enuani.*

That the common people of Ika are more Igbo than Edo is clearly borne out by a number of ethnographic studies. To start with, it should be recognized that the Ika district lies in an important cultural crossroads, that is, between Edoland and Igboland. Under such circumstances, Ika people would be expected to exhibit some traces of both Edo and Igbo physical and cultural characteristics. However, if we isolate and carefully examine these traits we will find that the Ika are not only more closely related to the Igbo, but are also clearly derived from them.

Like the other Anioma groups, the Ika are of diverse origins and can be divided into three broad categories. The first includes some groups that have occupied their settlements for so long that it is almost impossible for anyone to account for their origins. For example, the inhabitants of the Ozarra and Alizomo speak a dialect which is almost unintelligible to the rest of the Ika, not to mention the Asaba or the Edo. It has therefore been suggested that the Ozarra and Alizomo must have been the remnants of what may have been the original inhabitants of this part of the district. They might have been to the Agbor what the Okala were to the Omoka of Illah, or what the Oze were to the Onitsha, or what the Akri were to the Aboh. Perhaps the true Ika are some of the surviving earliest Igbo occupants of Anioma whose cultural traits were modified by some ancient but unknown occupants of the district.

The second category includes certain lineages in some Ika settlements whose origins have been traced to Eastern Igboland. Some of the lineages, whose founding fathers are said to have come from Nhi (Nri), can be found in Owa Oyibu and Ute-Okpu. In the third category are a large number of Ika settlements, such as Akwukwu-Agbor, which trace their origins from a wide range of places, including Benin and Ishanland.

These diverse origins notwithstanding, the available evidence indicates that the dominant cultural and political traits of the Ika are more Igbo than Benin or Ishan. H. L. M. Butcher, a British colonial officer who carried out a painstaking study among the Anioma and Edo people in the 1930s, concluded that "Ethnologically the Eka [Ika] people are Ibo [Igbo] in character, but their history, involving them in contact with the Bini, has caused their tribal organization to be greatly modified from the present type." He further said that "in the 'obodo' [towns] more nearly affected by the Bini influence we have a very little trace of indigenous Ibo political organization today, while in others, on the side further removed from Benin, we get [the original] Ibo customs preponderating."[14]

Butcher's use of the name *Ika* is not clear, however. He might have been applying the term to the Ika or Agbor district properly or to the entire region of Anioma. He stated that according to a "very vague tradition the Ika country was first inhabited by an overflow of the Ibos from the Eastern side of the Niger," and that while some old men merely said that long ago their fathers lived at Asaba, others said that their origins could be traced to Benin. This could equally be said of many Anioma communities, such as the Umuezechima. Nevertheless, a number of colonial officials have made the more definite declaration that some Ika settlements were founded by immigrants from eastern Igboland. Daryll Forde and G. I. Jones, together with H. F. Marshall, J. Macrae Simpson and N. E. Whiting, were among the European investigators who listed Owa Oyibu and Ute-Okpu, near Agbor, as settlements that were founded by immigrants from Nri. These observations were confirmed during my own fieldwork among these Ika communities.

On the question of language, Butcher noted that Ika belonged to the Igbo family and was tonal. He said that a large number of Ika words were "purely Ibo, although the Eka [Ika] language has been so modified and affected by its neighboring Edo groups that it has assumed a character of its own, and is unintelligible to the Ibos of a few miles away." In accounting for the emergence of a distinct Ika dialect and the circumstances that might have differentiated it from the "pure Ibo," Butcher called attention to two crucial factors: isolation from the other Igbo speaking communities, and the influences coming from Edoland. The Ika district, said Butcher, "is an agglomeration of small self-contained units, separated in the past from their neighbours by dense bush," and under the circumstances, local variations tended to develop within small areas. He pointed out that a common feature of the Igbo dialects was their unintelligibility to those who lived just a few miles away. "In a radius of not more than thirty miles an Ibo will pass from one dialect to another, and find the greatest difficulty in making himself understood," Butcher insisted. The "Onitsha" Igbo, he said, would have difficulty in understanding Ika dialect because the Ika tones were markedly nasal and vowels were slurred over to a greater degree than the Onitsha Igbo. Butcher was therefore of the view that the difficulty of understanding dialects among the Igbos emanated from this type of local variation.

As for influences coming from Benin, Butcher noted that certain Edo words entered the Igbo language but were modified and absorbed by the host language. The result was that many words for objects, which were neither Igbo nor Edo, emerged. In the end, "Eka [Ika] was transformed into a hybrid language containing both Ibo [Igbo] and Edo elements, yet understood by neither Ibos nor Binis." But even so, he concluded, "both Eka and other Ibo dialects are similar in grammar and syntax. The order of words in Eka is the same in Ibo, likewise the system of counting, gender and pre-fixing."

Butcher was particularly fascinated by the political structures of the Ika people. He noted that both Benin and Igbo elements existed side-by-side and that the Ika political organization was fundamentally more Igbo than Edo. The unit of the Igbo community, he said, was the family or clan. A number of families formed an *umunna* and a collection of *umunna* formed a town. In a typical Igbo town or village there was no one head-chief because "the idea of one single head, uniting and symbolizing the tribe, is foreign to the Ibo mind." Matters affecting the clan were dealt with by the *ndi okpala* (the eldest members of the clan) with the assistance of the whole clan, no one of them having an absolute authority over the others.

Although Butcher made a sincere attempt to describe the basic social and political systems that he encountered on the Edo-Igbo borderlands, he seemed to understand the fundamental character of the Ika more than the Edo. He claimed that the Edo-speaking people were governed by hereditary monarchs who were assisted by a set of powerful chiefs, and that many Edo towns were governed by a hereditary nobility whose members were appointed mostly from Benin. This might be true, but Butcher's other assertion—that to the Edo, unlike the Igbo, the hereditary idea was fixed and the society was rigidly polarized, often with a "great gulf placed between the great nobles and commoners,"—was not an accurate characterization of the Edo notions of government. Butcher failed to realize that the Edo resisted arbitrary impositions, and, like the Igbo, they tried to organize their polities in the most democratic manner. The degree to which the ordinary Edo citizens succeeded in resisting such impositions depended, however, on the strength and determination of an Oba of Benin and his warrior chiefs to assume dominance. The civil wars that raged in Benin City during the earlier centuries could have started as protests against unpopular seizures of power.

Despite the inconsistencies, however, Butcher's investigations have helped to widen our perceptions of the political and social organizations of the Ika as they were at the turn of the century. His main thesis was that in the Ika district, the Edo and the Igbo forms of political and social organizations were brought into contact with each other, resulting in the formation of institutions that were sometimes Edo and sometimes Igbo in character. He identified four types of organizations. First, some towns were ruled by hereditary paramount chiefs (*ndi obi*), assisted by their nobility. In such places, royalty was passed down from father to son, or from a man to his brother if he died before producing a male heir. Second, some towns were ruled by paramount chiefs who did not inherit their positions directly from their fathers, but were chosen, in rotation, from among the members of certain families. The choice of each candidate ultimately rested on the community and not necessarily on the families who presented the candidates. During an election every member of the affected communities showed special interest in particular candidates. Third, some Ika towns were governed, not by paramount chiefs, but by elders and titled chiefs. And finally, some towns combined the system of paramount chieftaincy with the rule of elders and titled chiefs. The Ika political structures were complex indeed.

Butcher, warned that since the idea of hereditary succession to a position or title was not very common among the Igbo, it followed that in all the Ika towns where an obi or other type of head chiefs occurred, the chiefs nearly all owed their origin to some outside influences. "The advent of the virile Bini with all its traditions," Butcher wrote, "caused the Ibo method of government to be overshadowed by the Bini, although the Ibo customs were not entirely blotted out." The result was the emergence of what Butcher described as "a parallel organization" in the sense that even in the larger towns one sometimes found the rule of hereditary *ndi obi,* together with the rule of elders, title-holders, and other functionaries whose origins could be traced to either eastern Igboland or Edoland. Some of these title-holders and functionaries included *ndichie* (Igbo), *ndi nkpalo* (Igbo), *iyase* (Edo), and *onihe* (Edo). Butcher went on to add that despite the contradictions, "blood is thicker than water. No wonder when we have a sudden political crisis, and the feelings of the Eka are particularly stirred, we often find them going to their Okpalas and elders for help, rather than to the hereditary Obi. . . . This is an additional illustration of the theory that the system of hereditary chiefs has been imposed on the Eka [Ika] people from without, and is not an organic part of their constitution."

I have quoted extensively here from the work of Butcher who remained fascinated by the complexities of the Ika social and political organizations. Now let me turn to J. Macrae Simpson, another British colonial officer who studied the Ika people of Anioma in the 1930s. Simpson began by noting that the Ika were "a sub-tribe of the Ibo and speak a dialect of that language."[15] Apart from their language, Simpson continued, the Agbor clan exhibited features of social organization that confirmed their Igbo roots:

> The lowest unit found among the Ikas was the Umunna, consisting of a man, his wife or wives, and their children. . . . The lowest territorial unit usually found is the umu . . . The oldest man in the Umu, known as Onyisi Umu, is the spiritual, executive and judicial head of the Umu, the priest of the ancestor-cult and the law-giver. All orders from a higher authority are delivered to the Umu through him, all sacrifices to the ancestors are made through him as priest; in his Ogwa, or meeting-shed, are held the Umu meetings over which he presides, and where his pronouncements are authoritative.

From this report, one would conclude that it was upon the basic social unit, *umunna* that all Ika relationships were founded and around which all social and political functions revolved. In fact, this and a number of other ethnographic reports strongly suggest that the political systems of the Ika were similar to those of the other Anioma groups, including those whose origins have conclusively been traced to eastern Igboland, and that the contradictions that later characterized them derived from the role which the Ika region played as a receptacle of various waves of immigration from the direction of Benin. As already shown, most of these Edo immigrants were either refugees fleeing Edoland as the power of the Obas of Benin began to spill beyond the immediate confines of Benin City, or hunters, traders, and others who came to Anioma in search of economic opportunity. These immigrants were responsible for the importation of Edo culture and institutions, although the practice was escalated when the Obas of Benin began to impose their favorites as overlords on the various Ika communities.

An analysis of these European reports and the numerous testimonies that have been collected in this territory point conclusively to the fact that ethnographically, the Ika were Igbo in character but their social and political organizations were modified by contacts with and influences coming from Benin. An Agbor elder, who was interviewed in 1980 by Peter Obue, had no doubt in his mind that the people of Agbor were Igbo "in reality." When asked about the traditions which traced the origin of Agbor to Benin, the elder retorted, "We do not by any means come from Benin but being neighbours, we are bound to borrow from one another."[16] However, this elder did not disclose what Benin borrowed from Agbor, nor did he identify the exact place of origin of the people of Agbor.

We have already noted that Benin military assaults and political intransigence in the Ika district began in the fifteenth or sixteenth century and lasted intermittently until 1906. The consequences were far-reaching. First, Benin spread new ideas about chieftaincy and title systems. In places like Agbor, people of Benin origin were installed as overlords with titles that were based on the Benin hierarchy. In some communities where no foreign impositions were apparent, the people had to adopt titles that had some resemblance to the Benin title system. The tendency to accept Benin political institutions was great in Agbor, where Benin military incursions started very early and where Benin influence lasted for a very long time. It is therefore not surprising that after three or four hundred years of rowdy contacts with the Edo, the Ika would have had their political institutions modified. This phenomenon has been observed in many parts of Anioma and largely explains the contradictions and inconsistencies that still characterize Anioma political institutions. Unfortunately, ignoring the possibility of political diffusion, some observers have interpreted Benin political presence in Anioma as a confirmation of Benin origin.

THE IMPACT OF IGALA ON ANIOMA

Benin was not alone in modifying the ancient Anioma institutions. We have some evidence that the people of Anioma were in constant touch with the Igala, from whom they borrowed certain social and political institutions. While Benin influence spread over a wide area in Anioma, however, the impact of the Igala was restricted to a narrow strip of land along the Niger River. Even in Igboland east of the Niger, Igala influence would seem to have been felt only around Nsukka and the Anambra valley.

Some of the traditions recorded by M. D. Jeffreys and others claimed that the northern Umueri clan was founded by a man called Eri who had emigrated from the Igala country and settled at Aguleri in the Anambra valley. There he founded the Umueri lineage, which subsequently split into two—the northern group which centered around Aguleri, and the southern group around Nri (founded by the first son of Eri), thirty miles to the south. Aguleri, Nteje, Amanuke, and Igbariam were the principal towns of the northern section while Nri, Oreri, and Igbo-Ukwu belonged to the southern section.[17]

These traditions notwithstanding, the Igala do not appear to recognize the Umueri as their relatives. All they are sure of is that they have had some important historical connections with the Anambra region in which Aguleri was situated. Such connections were linked with the legendary Igala figure, Onojo Oboni, who lived at Ogurugu and who, from there, carried out periodic raids on the neighboring Igbo communities as far south as Nsukka, the Anambra valley, and the Niger.[18]

The Igala regarded several riverine towns as settlements that were originally founded by Igala men whose language and customs, they said, were formerly Igala but were later lost as they were absorbed by their Igbo neighbors. The towns mentioned include Aboh, Okpai, Umuolu, and Onya on the right bank, and Ndoni and Osamala on the left bank. Only a few traditions of the Igbo-speaking people inhabiting the Niger valley speak of Igala origin. Among these were Ebu, Illah, Onya, Oko, Umuolu, Okpai, and Osamala. Elsewhere, the riverside communities recall early contacts with Igala traders and fishermen whom their founding fathers met on their arrival.[19] At Onitsha, for instance, it is said that the early settlers who migrated across the river to found this town were assisted, when crossing the river, by Igala water-men.

When Igala power extended down the River Niger, it is claimed, such towns as Okpai and Oko were subject to the Attah who lived in the lower Igala country near the Anam flood plains. Further, Onojo Oboni is remembered by certain communities as a warrior who hunted elephants and slaves and who terrorized them and once occupied Asaba. Another tradition claims that Nnebisi of Asaba took a wife from the house of the Attah Igala, a woman who had been betrothed to Ika, by whom she had had a son called Ala, the founder of Illah. Some elders point to this tradition and its several variants as evidence that the people of Illah and Asaba were relatives.[20] But despite the apparent relationship between Asaba, Illah, and Idah, the popular belief is that Asaba was founded or enlarged by immigrants from Nteje—at a point where the outposts of the Igala and Aboh domains converged. This location, points out H. Vaux, "afforded Asaba the opportunity to develop pure Igbo characteristics uninfluenced by either."[21]

However unsatisfactory these traditions may appear, they point to earlier Igala-Anioma contacts. Unfortunately, evidence of Igala cultural and political influences in Anioma is scanty, nor has the evidence been sufficiently researched. We know, however, that certain Anioma communities, such as Illah, Ebu, Umuolu, and Onya, have strong cultural ties with the Igala, and might have derived from them. Igala-Illah relationships are evident in the Illah *nmo* society. According to Barnabas Agadah, some of the Illah lineages that claim Igala origin formed a unit of political institution with the *nmo* or Igala mask as the unifying factor. "This *nmo* society," said Agadah, "has been entrenched into the social fabric of Illah." The concept, according to him, was imported from Igala and those who wore the mask did not speak Igbo but Igala. He suggested that the ease with which they spoke and sang in the Igala language reflected a long relationship.[22]

The institution of Obi Illah is also believed to have had its origin from Idah rather than Benin. This is why in the past, Agadah continued, whenever an obi was to be installed at Illah, emissaries were sent to the Attah of Idah to organize the ceremony. The affair is said to have started with Obi Igbo, the first Obi of Illah who is said to have copied the process of his installation from the Attah of Idah.[23]

This tradition of receiving obiship from Idah would seem to reflect recent developments, however. For, as we have seen, some of the earliest settlers of Illah were eastern Igbo people from the Anambra valley, possibly Nri. They were later followed by the Edo and then the Igala. Furthermore, the people of Illah have such Umunri-derived titles as *nkpalo* (*ichie*), and, according to some Illah traditions, it was the prerogative of *umunshi* (the representatives of Eze Nri) to confer the eze title on Illah citizens who wished to take it.[24] The occurrence of the institution of obiship would then suggest a later borrowing from Benin, since obiship belonged, not to Igala, but to the Benin cultural complex. If emissaries were sent to the Attah of Igala to organize the ceremony, it would reflect a later state of borrowing or even domination. The earliest immigrants to Illah must have brought with them the Nri title system, and then after the rise of Benin and the arrival of Edaiken to Illah, probably in the sixteenth century, the institution of obiship was introduced (see chapter 2). However, when the Igala influence reached Illah and Benin was no longer a potent force, emissaries had to be sent to the Attah of Igala, rather than to the Oba of Benin, on the occasion of the coronation of the Obi of Illah.

In fact, it is not difficult to see how Igala cultural and political systems could have been brought to Illah, Ebu, and Onya. The Igala were traders whose canoes plied up and down the Niger. The Attah of Igala, whose capital was at Idah, is said to have imposed his rule over many fishing and trading villages on the Niger, as far south as Asaba. But this influence did not penetrate inland; it was also more commercial than political. Michael Onwuejeogwu has warned that "just as the influence of Benin on the Lower Niger Basin might be described as more cultural than political, so also the influence of Igala might be described as more economic than political."[25] Be that as it may, Illah has a triple heritage; it witnessed the blending of the Igbo, Edo, and Igala cultural and political systems.

Throughout Anioma, strangers were welcomed and incorporated into the society as free men and women, but the arrival of large numbers of strangers must have caused further changes in the political organization of the communities. The available evidence suggests that there were increasing opportunities for strangers to gain full acceptance in society. The rise of the Atlantic slave trade in the sixteenth and seventeenth centuries stimulated the arrival of new adventurers from Benin, Yorubaland, Igalaland, Ijoland, and Ishanland, eager to participate in the new trade. We are told that Obi Igweli, a leading chief of Asaba in the mid-nineteenth century, originally was not a native of Asaba. He had come from Ishanland and was admitted into Asaba as a full citizen. A very enterprising man who emulated the Igbo work ethics, he quickly amassed wealth, took several wives, and purchased the *eze* title, all of which facilitated his flight up the social ladder. When the Europeans arrived in the mid-nineteenth century, they found Obi Igweli an invaluable ally. He encouraged the introduction of Christianity and European trade; it was from him that the agents of the Church Missionary Society (CMS) purchased their first piece of land at Asaba in 1873. He was a friend of Bishop Samuel Ajayi Crowther, to whom he gave much support and encouragement, but he remained faithful to the traditional religion of Asaba. When he died, he left behind over forty slaves, together with many wives and children.[26]

By the end of the eighteenth century, however, the major waves of migration into Anioma had come to an end as most lands had been effectively occupied. New immigrants like Obi Igweli could no longer form new settlements, but could only seek refuge in already existing towns where they were made to conform to the cultural etiquette of their hosts.

THE PRECOLONIAL SOCIAL CLASSES OF ANIOMA

Some scholars have been tempted to romanticize the Igbo past, describing it as egalitarian or classless. On the contrary, classes did exist among the Igbo, especially the Anioma Igbo, even though most people had many avenues to social mobility. Because of their obsession for wealth, the society was broadly divided into the rich, the not-so-rich and the poor. The rich were those who had acquired the highest titles, like *obi, eze,* or *ozo;* the not-so-rich were those who had purchased the junior titles like *alo,* and were on their way to securing the higher ones. The poor were men and women without titles. As in most societies, the poor were the majority even though a sudden upward turn in trade or an unexpected good harvest could turn many poor into rich. As we shall presently see, this was the case when the palm oil trade of the second half of the nineteenth century pulled many men and women above the poverty line. In any case, because the lines between the rich and not-so-rich were so thin and arbitrary, we shall, for the purposes of analysis, regard the Anioma society as more appropriately falling into four social classes, namely, the paramount chiefs (*obi*), the non-hereditary titled men and women (like *ndi eze* and *ndi omu*), the untitled men and women, and, finally, the slaves.

PARAMOUNT CHIEFS: OBI

The highest social class of the Anioma was the obi but not every Anioma town had one. Strictly speaking, an obi was a paramount chief, and only one person could occupy the position at any given time. An obi was a very rich man because, at least in theory, all land was vested in him. He also received tributes from his community and was the final court of appeals in judicial matters. Obiship was acquired by inheritance, as in Agbor, but sometimes it rotated among certain families, as in Ogwashi-Ukwu. In Aboh, on the other hand, the position was conferred on the wealthiest and most popular candidate who emerged after an election. The Ogwashi-Ukwu and Aboh systems often sparked heated rivalries. For example, war broke out in Ogwashi-Ukwu in 1909 between the rival factions led by Nzekwe and Okonjo. The conflict, which opened the way for British colonial government intervention, was provoked by a dispute over who would occupy the throne of Ogwashi-Ukwu after the death of older Nzekwe in 1907.[27] Also in Aboh, following the death of Obi Ossai in 1854, the throne remained vacant for nearly ten years during which the warring factions had a free rein. In the end, Olise, the son of a previous ruler of Aboh, was elected while Aje, the son of Obi Ossai, was rejected.[28]

Some title-holders of Anioma are sometimes wrongly called obi; such men must not be confused with paramount chiefs. An *ozo* or *eze* titled man is not a paramount chief and should not be called *obi*. The institution of obiship had its origin from Benin; it is a strong feature of those communities that claim Benin origin, though not always so. For example, the people of Ogwashi-Ukwu claim origin from eastern

Igboland but have a strong affinity for the institution of obiship. One important distinction is that only one person can occupy the position of obi at any particular time in a given town or lineage. The *ozo* title, on the other hand, had its origin from eastern Igboland and there is no limit to the number of men qualified to purchase it. The obis carry the sword of office, *ada,* while *ozo* men carry *otonsi,* a different type of staff of office.

The institution of obiship seems to have been best developed in Agbor, possibly because of its proximity to Benin and probably because the royal household was an extraction from Benin. Obiship was based on a hierarchy of power, birth, and wealth. The wealthiest and most influential men of Agbor were the obi and the *idibodei.* The *idibodei* were the descendants of previous obis and the personal advisors of the obi. They formed the obi's personal council.[29] Much of their wealth derived from their share in the presents given to the obi by persons who wanted titles or some other favors. Next to the obi and the *idibodei* were the three powerful titled groups of *uzama, eghaivi,* and *ifiokpo.* The *uzama* represented the "conservative opinion" of the clan, while the *eghaivi* symbolized the more "liberal opinion." The *ifiokpo,* who were also the "repository of tradition," represented the "religious view" and were "the most reactionary members of the obi's council."[30] The obi and these titled chiefs exercised great power in Agbor, not only because they earned their positions by inheritance, but also because they were the heads of the major lineages in Agbor. Thus, whereas any wealthy man of Asaba or Okpanam, for instance, could purchase the *ozo* or *eze* title and become a member of the ruling council of chiefs, in Agbor only certain select people, born into the royal families or appointed by them, could ever hope to be members of the obi's ruling council. Despite its attractions, the institution of obiship contradicts the whole Igbo notion of leadership and authority, which, as Simon Ottenberg has made clear, centered around local autonomy, a deep mistrust for centralized institutions, and a strong emphasis on an open status system, with few ascribed positions and considerable status mobility.[31]

THE TITLED CHIEFS: *NDI EZE OR NDI OZO*

Many of the Anioma towns that did not have the Benin-derived institution of obiship had the *eze* or *ozo* title system. As a male child grew from infancy toward adulthood, he acquired certain titles which enabled him to climb the social ladder. Adult males who could not progress beyond the most junior title of *nkpisi* were regarded as men without status and were treated as boys. In Illah, for example, they were taunted, *isi igwu,* "lice breeders" or "heads full of lice."

The *eze* title was acquired by purchase. To qualify for the *eze* title, a man must have purchased the junior titles of *nkpisi* and *alo,* satisfactorily discharged all the duties normally assigned to the members of the junior title groups, accumulated enough wealth, and completed all the ceremonies connected with the second burial of his father. The last of these requirements was particularly important and derived from the belief that no man could attain a status that might equal his father's; in other words, a man could not be a king while his father lived and functioned with a lower title within the group.

Movements from the junior toward the higher titles were the preliminaries that would eventually lead to the acquisition of the *eze* title. The final ceremony involved a ritual death and resurrection, without which immortality could not be attained. The entire process of *eze*-taking must of necessity be consummated by this ritual death and resurrection. Men who were able to complete the process were called *ndi ichie,* "the immortals"; to take the *ozo* or *eze* title and receive the gift of immortality transformed the recipient from the status of an ordinary human to that of a god. The Igbo also believed that as immortality could not be inherited, so could a title not be passed down from father to son or daughter. Immortality, the Igbo would say, had to be achieved or acquired through a process of title taking called *ichi-echichi,* that is, to secure the breath of life, to attain immortality or godship. As Jeffreys has rightly observed, the Igbo word chi represented invisible forces, spirits, and personal gods; it was the root of such words as *Chineke,* the Creator, *Chukwu,* the Great God, *ichie,* a titled man, and *ndi ichie,* titled men.[32]

Status attainment was clearly linked to the acquisition of wealth through hard work. The taking of the *eze* title was very expensive, demanding elaborate feasting, the offering of animal sacrifices, and the paying of very high initiation fees. In times of prosperity due to successive years of good harvests or profitable trade, for example, the number of men aspiring to the position of *eze* could rise astronomically because Igbo men invested their surplus wealth in titles, as was the case during the second half of the nineteenth century, when the palm oil boom enriched many Igbo. In 1888, Asaba, with an estimated population of five thousand, had between three hundred and five hundred titled chiefs, whereas fifty years earlier, there were not more than a dozen.[33] Both oral and written sources confirm a marked expansion of the corporate titles among the lower Niger Igbo people, including Onitsha, in the nineteenth century. A Christian Missionary Society agent resident in Asaba in the 1870s was so thrilled by the large number of *eze* titled chiefs he encountered there that he described the town as a land of kings. "Every man is a king, or nearly so," he declared.[34]

The *eze* title system belonged to the Umunri kingship system, an institution widespread in the areas close to the Niger.[35] Some Igbo believed that Eze Nri was the first man to take this title, and his representatives therefore reserved the right to invest the title on any Igbo man who wished to purchase it. At least one representative was expected to be present at a coronation to tie the traditional ankle cords on the newly crowned. A representative of Eze Nri was either a man or woman from Nri or anyone who could trace his descent to Nri. There were at least thirteen Nri-related communities in Anioma and everyone born therein claimed to be a representative of Eze Nri. Until a dispute arose between the people of Igbuzo and Ogboli-Igbuzo in 1936, the citizens of the Ogboli section of Igbuzo reserved the right to confer the *eze* title on Igbuzo candidates. The Ogboli claimed this right on the grounds that they had emigrated from Nshi (Nri).

Some scholars have argued that the *eze* or *ozo* title system was not of Igbo origin, and must instead have diffused into Igboland, possibly from Igalaland. They claimed that the title system was based on divine monarchy and therefore was not consistent with the Igbo political organization which was rooted in the concepts of *umunna* and *ndi okpala*. This diffusionist view has been challenged by some scholars who argued that the institution of *ozo* was a legacy of the Umunri culture complex and could have been invented independently in Igboland.[36]

Whatever its origin, every Niger Igbo man coveted the *eze* title (or some of its variants, *alo* or *ichie*) because it guaranteed its holder a seat in the governing council of his town. It also entitled him to certain portions of livestock slaughtered in his lineage, together with portions of all fees paid by new initiates into the title association. Furthermore, the title exempted its holder from all manual labor. His red cap, decorated with eagle feathers, and his staff of office, *otonsi*, were immediately recognized anywhere he went. He was greeted with the salutation, "igwe" (His Highness), and anyone who troubled him or failed to give him the respect he deserved was made to pay a heavy fine. It was perilous to cause an *eze* man bodily harm. These chiefs constituted the privileged, non-laboring, ruling class.

All in all, Anioma communities, like the Igbo communities east of the Niger, were ruled by their elders in association with title-holders and age-grades. Every man tried to purchase some titles because it was by so doing that one quickly elevated himself to higher positions on the social ladder. A man without a title was like a child without a face and without a name. When he died, he was not mourned with much grieving, nor was his corpse buried with dignity. His *ikenga,* a carved wooden object which symbolized his strength and spirituality, was not preserved but split in two with a cutlass and then thrown into the bush, like ordinary trash. The Igbo believed that a man who died before acquiring the higher titles had failed to secure immortality and therefore would not join the ancestors, nor would he reincarnate to dwell with the living. Instead, his spirit would roam the universe, aimlessly, sometimes causing mischief and pain to the living. To purchase the highest title was, therefore, to be born again, to be admitted into the community of rulers, *otu ochichi,* and to be initiated into the cult of the ancestors, *otu ndi ichie.* A titled man's *ikenga* was never thrown away but preserved and added to the "congregation" of *ndi ikenga* of departed ancestors. Should a male child be born to a family soon after the death of a titled man, it was a sign that the man just departed had "returned" from his temporary abode in the land of the ancestors. The male child might be given the name *Nnamdi,* "father is still alive" or "father is back."

The obis and *ndi eze* were the wealthiest and the most politically active members of the Anioma society. In the nineteenth century, they were virtually the final decision makers in important political matters. They represented their respective towns in their dealings with European traders, missionaries, and the agents of European governments.

WOMEN'S TITLES

Generally, women belonged in the same social classes as their husbands. Since this was the case, some successful women traders and farmers advanced their not-so-rich husbands the cash with which to purchase the highest titles. Women did not have to tie their own success to that of their husbands, however. Some women gained status by amassing wealth through trading, farming, or weaving, and were treated as *ogalanya.* Some occupied important religious positions; women were dominant in the religious sphere and controlled many of the traditional cults and shrines. For example, since the majority of Anioma traders were women, it was only natural that a woman should play the role of the priestess of the marketplace.

These apart, Anioma women had their own titles, the most important being the *omu*.[37] In Asaba, Igbuzo, and Ogwashi-Ukwu, for instance, the position of *omu* was elective.[38] The successful candidate headed the council of women called *otu omu* (the *omu* society). Any woman who had enough wealth to pay for her initiation ceremonies could be admitted into the *otu omu*, whose members controlled local trading, the marketplace and the cult of the marketplace. They acted as a pressure group in political matters and reserved the right to impose fines on men and women who disturbed the peace of the marketplace. They also punished those who broke certain traditional taboos like incest and adultery.

The leaders of the *otu omu* were required to be present at the meetings of the councils of chiefs and elders, where important decisions affecting the welfare of the citizens were being discussed. Though they would not themselves take part in wars, these women could decide when to urge the male warriors to start one. Onwuejeogwu has recalled one such instance, when the *omu* of Igbuzo and her female supporters mocked the warrior chiefs of Igbuzo for their delay in recapturing a section of their town that had been occupied by Benin soldiers during one of the Edo-Anioma wars of the earlier centuries. Shamed by their inaction, the warrior chiefs of Igbuzo moved into battle and drove away the occupying Benin forces.[39]

Although most Anioma towns had the *omu* association, the role it played in each town differed. In Ogwashi-Ukwu where the institution of a paramount chief was well established, the *omu* was the obi's counterpart.[40] In Asaba, the *omu* was the counterpart of the *asagba*. But in towns like Igbuzo and Okpanam, where there were no paramount chiefs, the *omu's* position was somewhat ambivalent, for she could not be the counterpart of anyone. Whatever the contradictions, the *omu* association, like the *otu umu ada* and *otu inyeme di* (two other important women's associations), acted as part of the checks and balances in the social and political organization of the Anioma. The *otu umu ada* was an association of women born to a lineage or town, while *otu inyeme di* was an association of women married to the men of a lineage or town. In theory, every married woman belonged to both associations, while an unmarried woman belonged only to *otu umu ada*. These associations enabled women to exercise influence in the politics of both their hometowns (no matter the distance) and the towns where they might have been married. It was perilous for any man, no matter his age, wealth, or influence, to wilfully provoke the anger of any of these women's associations. The *otu omu*, together with the *otu umu ada* and *otu inyeme di*, ensured that gender balance and equality, as enshrined in the traditions of the society, were upheld. Their political and social activities were sometimes oppositional yet constructive at the same time.

SLAVES

At the very bottom of the social ladder were slaves, *ohu*, of various classifications. Generally, slaves were acquired outsiders, having been captured or purchased and then accorded the minimum levels of acculturation. Their treatment was regulated by the dominant ideologies of their owners' communities, which varied from place to place. Their most common disability was their limited access to resources. They owned no farmlands, and must grow crops only on the pieces of land made available to them by their owners, sometimes as "share-croppers." Slaves could not marry into the "freeborn" families unless they were set free and then made to undergo a rigorous process of acculturation and assimilation. Apart from these major restrictions, most slaves were allowed to lead unmolested lives, provided they observed all taboos and performed the usual tasks demanded by their owners. They were regarded as kinless dependents whose daily activities did not differ very significantly from those performed by the members of the host communities. One can therefore make clear distinctions between freeborn and slave in Anioma. The freeborn (*nwamadi* or *nwamadu*) claimed origin from the founding fathers of the clan, whereas slaves, *ohu*, were adopted outsiders. There were also pawns (*nvunvu ego*), debtors or their representatives who pledged to work for their creditors until the debt was discharged. The labor they rendered was the customary substitute for interest. They were treated as collateral for the sum of money borrowed; they regained their freedom immediately after their debt was repaid.

The people of Anioma had no cult slaves, *osu*, or persons dedicated to the service of a deity. *Osu* were not slaves in the ordinary sense of the word because, once dedicated to a deity, they could neither be bought nor sold and could move about freely. The main restrictions they suffered were that they could marry only other osu; they could not belong to the clubs of the freeborn; when they died their corpses could be buried only by other cult slaves in places reserved for them. But despite this apparent freedom, some Igbo believe osu were inferior to ordinary slaves (*ohu*) because an *osu* could never hope to attain the status of a freeborn, whereas the *ohu* could.[41]

Equally important is the fact that slaves could not acquire immortality through title taking. They were regarded by the communities that held them captive as men, women, and children of different ethnic, clan and family backgrounds with no known common ancestors. They could not take the *alo* and *eze* titles and thus become *ndi ichie* because no one knew whether the ancestors they might represent took the titles, and if so, when and where. Because they were outsiders, no freeborn would lend them the *ofo*, a symbol of authority given only to tested men, to present to the council of titled elders as a testimony that their fathers or fathers' fathers took the higher titles. In other words, since they were strangers, no one might have been present to witness when their fathers or fathers' fathers took the higher titles.

Thus, even though the Anioma polities were democratic, they were also stratified. The distinctions between the various social classes were exhibited everywhere, especially during certain annual festivals. In Igbuzo, for instance, the annual yam festival, *ifejioku,* was celebrated differently and on different days by the four different social classes of *ndi eze, ndi-nkpalo, ndi-ngbankpisi,* and *ndi ohu.* Thus, there were the *ifejioku ndi eze, ifejioku ndi-nkpalo, ifejioku ndi-ngbankpisi* and *ifejioku ndi-akankolo.* (*Akankolo* and *ugwule,* along with *ohu* were names by which slaves were known in Anioma.) Women celebrated on the days when their husbands or fathers celebrated. The *otu omu,* together with the *otu umuada* and *otu inyeme di,* had no special *ifejioku* set aside for them.

I have shown in two other works that the people of Anioma received large numbers of slaves in the nineteenth century, partly because of the British effort to abolish the overseas slave trade and partly because of the Islamic reform movements which continued to generate slaves in the northern and middle-belt regions of Nigeria at a time when the Atlantic slave trade had become history. Captives who would have been shipped abroad were now channelled into the internal African trade, resulting in an unprecedented fall in price. To cope with the sudden influx of strangers into Anioma, the chiefs and elders adjusted the ideologies that regulated the treatment of slaves.[42] Because of their large numbers, the vast majority of Anioma slaves could not live in the compounds of their owners and were therefore consigned to large slave villages called *ugwule,* a social unit established and controlled by the slave owners. There, the *ohu* led their own lives undisturbed, except when required to work for their owners.

Everywhere in Anioma, owners recognized that it was in their best class interest to treat their slaves humanely and, in fact, custom demanded it. Slaves realized that they owed their entire existence to their owners and that since they owned no separate farmlands, their own happiness depended on the success of their owners. The people of Anioma encouraged but did not insist on the rapid acculturation of outsiders. Slaves, on their part, recognized that a swift acculturation accelerated their movement from the margins of society toward a greater incorporation into the host society. The nineteenth century was on the whole a prosperous period for the ruling class of chiefs who succeeded in establishing strong relations of domination over a large number of outsiders from whom they extracted surplus labor. Deprived of any cross-cutting ties and confined to the different slave villages, Anioma slaves remained politically weak and could not rebel against their owners. In chapter 7 of this book, we shall see how British colonial rule enabled slaves to regain their freedom and access to resources, how they acquired western education and farmlands, even before freeborn women, and how their emancipation impoverished their former owners. Here we have another paradox of colonial rule. For now, however, we turn our attention from social and political institutions to religious institutions and the conflicts they engendered in Anioma.

NOTES

1. Michael A. Onwuejeogwu, *The Traditional Political System of Ibusa* (Ibadan: Odinani, 1972), 18.

2. PRO, CO 520/18/7937 of February 29, 1903, Widenham Fosbery to High Commissioner.

3. Onwuejeogwu, *The Traditional Political System*, 16.

4. Ibid., 16–17.

5. Ibid., 17.

6. Jomo Kenyatta, *Facing Mount Kenya.* (New York: Vintage, 1965), 129.

7. Ibid., 129

8. On hanging criminals see NAI, CSO 26/4, File no. 3038X, J. Macrea Simpson, "Intelligence Report on the Agbor, Oligie and Emuhu Clans, Agbor District, Asaba Division, 1935; for thinning villages see NAI, CSO 26 File no. 30927, H. Vaux, "Intelligence Report on the Asaba Clan," 1936.

9. Elizabeth Isichei, ed., *Igbo Worlds: An Anthology of Oral Histories and Historical Descriptions* (Philadelphia: Institute for the Study of Human Issues, 1978), 183.

10. Basil Davidson, *The African Genius* (Boston: Little, Brown, 1969), 91, 92–93

11. NAI, CSO 26/4, File no. 3038X, J. Macrea Simpson, "Intelligence Report on the Agbor, Oligie and Emuhu Clans."

12. During my interview with His Highness, Obi Aku Aghulor of Ute-

Okpu, on August 17, 1974, he and about fifteen of his elders whom he had summoned to meet with me, insisted that the founder of their town came from nowhere; "Okpu has always been here—from the beginning of time," they maintained.

13. NAI, CSO 26/4, File no. 3038X, Simpson, "Intelligence Report on the Agbor, Oligie and Emuhu Clans."

14. H. L. M. Butcher, "The Ika-Ibo People of the Benin Province, Southern Nigeria," Dissertation for the Diploma of Anthropology, Cambridge University, 1931. (By Courtesy of Rhodes House Library, Oxford University, Oxford). All references to Butcher in the ensuing discussion are to this source.

15. NAI, CSO. 26/4, File no. 3038X, Simpson, "Intelligence Report on the Agbor, Oligie and Emuhu Clans." Ensuing references to Simpson are to this source.

16. Peter Obue, "The Peter Obue Collection," in *Western Igbo*, ed. Don C. Ohadike and Rick N. Shain, vol. 6, *Jos Oral History and Literature Texts* (Jos: Univ. of Jos, 1988), 219.

17. M. D. Jeffreys, "The Divine Umundri Kings," *Africa* no. 8(1935): 350.

18. J. S. Boston, "Notes on Contact between the Igala and the Igbo," *Journal of the Historical Society of Nigeria* 2, no. 1(December 1960): 55.

19. Richard N. Henderson, *The King in Every Man* (New Haven: Yale Univ. Press, 1972), 68.

20. Nkechi Onianwa, "The Onianwa Collection" in *Western Igbo*, 191–93.

21. NAI, CSO/26, File no. 30927, H. Vaux, "Intelligence Report on the Asaba Clan," 1936.

22. Barnabas Agadah, "Migrations and Inter-group Relationships at Illah," research project, Department of History and Archaeology, University of Nigeria, Nsukka, 1974, 27.

23. Ibid.

24. O. Egbuchiem, interviewed at Umuakpa-Nshi, Illah, December 19, 1974.

25. Michael A. Onwuejeogwu, "An Outline Account of The Dawn of Igbo Civilization in the Igbo Culture Area," *Odinani: The Journal of Odinani Museum* 1 no. 1(1972): 34.

26. Elizabeth Isichei, *The Ibo People and the Europeans,* (London: Faber and Faber, 1973), 170.

27. PRO, CO 520/93/17110 of June 6, 1910, Lt. Col. H. C. Moorhouse to the Governor of Southern Nigeria, April 24, 1910.

28. Kingsley Ogedengbe, "The Aboh Kingdom of the Lower Niger, c. 1650–1900," Ph.D. diss., University of Wisconsin, 1971, 341.

29. NAI, CSO 26/4, File no. 3038X, Simpson, "Intelligence Report on the Agbor, Oligie and Emuhu Clans."

30. Ibid.

31. Simon Ottenberg, *Leadership and Authority in an African Society; Afikpo Village-Group* (Seattle: Univ. of Washington Press, 1971), xii–xii.

32. NAI, Kwale Dist. 10/8, "Taking of the Eze and Ozo Titles in the Awka Division."

33. CMS, CA3/A3/1888/48, reports by Rev. Johnson, May 21, 1988; Elizabeth Isichei, *A History of the Igbo People* (London: Macmillan, 1976), 100.

34. CMS, CA3/031, from the annual letters of Edward Phillips, August 31, 1880.

35. Northcote Thomas, *Anthropological Report on the Ibo-Speaking People of Nigeria, Part 4: Law and Custom of the Ibo of Asaba District* (London: Harrison, 1914), 54. See also Jeffreys, "The Divine Umundri Kings," 346.

36. Boston, "Notes on Contact." 52-58.

37. Felicia Ekejuba has described an *omu* as a queen. See Felicia Ekejuba, "Omu Okwei: The Merchant Queen of Ossomari," *Nigeria Magazine* no. 90(September, 1966): 213-20.

38. NAI, CSO 26, File no. 30927, H. Vaux, "Intelligence Report on the Asaba Clan," 1936.

39. Onwuejeogwu, *The Traditional Political System*, 23-39.

40. Kamene Okonjo, "The Dual-Sex Political System in Operation: Igbo Women and Community Politics in Midwestern Nigeria," in *Women in Africa: Studies in Social and Economic Change*, eds. Nancy J. Hafkin and Edna G. Bay (Stanford: Stanford Univ. Press, 1976): 44-58.

41. Don C. Ohadike, "The Decline of Slavery Among the Igbo People." in *The End of Slavery in Africa*, ed. Suzanne Miers and Richard Roberts (Madison: Univ. of Wisconsin Press, 1988): 439.

42. Ibid., 441.

4

≋

THE ANCESTORS CONFRONT THE ANGLICAN CHURCH

ASPECTS OF ANIOMA TRADITIONAL RELIGIONS

THE PEOPLE OF ANIOMA organized themselves in the manner described
in the preceding chapters until the last quarter of the nineteenth century, when they were confronted by European-trained Christian missionaries, traders, and colonial agents. That contact initiated the
undermining of the social, political, and economic institutions of
Anioma. In this chapter we shall consider the nature of the presence of
the Church Missionary Society (CMS) and its conflicts with the traditional religions of Anioma. It would be difficult to discuss all aspects
of Anioma traditional religions in this work, but to gain an insight
into the causes of the religious conflicts that raged in this region for
half a century, I begin here with an examination of the main features
of the Anioma religious beliefs and practices.

Rev. Julius Spencer, George T. Basden and many other Christian
missionaries observed in Onitsha, Okpanam, Asaba, Ubulu-Ukwu,
and the other towns on the Lower Niger that each time they preached
against certain indigenous practices the people often responded, "It is
the custom of our ancestors and we their children will be regarded as
degenerated ones if we should either swerve or depart from that which
was being done from countless ages back."[1] What were those customs
which they received from their ancestors and were reluctant to give
up? Another missionary, Samuel Ajayi Crowther warned that these
people were frequently "occupied either in feasting and dancing, and

have no time or inclination for spiritual things."[2] Is this an accurate assessment of the spiritual condition of the people of Anioma?

Anioma culture was a religious culture; life outside this culture was unthinkable for the Igbo. Their religion was the hub of their entire being. To remain faithful to their religion was to lead a worthy life, to live in peace with the ancestors, to enjoy good health, and to have many children and good harvests. To break religious taboos or to dissociate oneself from the religious practices of one's community was to incur the wrath of the higher beings. Indeed, the people of Anioma were very religious; their world was defined by a hierarchy of invisible forces from which they could not easily escape. These forces ranged from the personal spirit, *chi,* to the almighty creator, *Chukwu.*

Chi was conceived as a personal god, the equivalent of the Christian guardian angel. A man's *chi* followed him all the days of his life, and could be benevolent or malignant. A man with a good *chi, (onye chi oma),* was always successful in his endeavors, while a man with a bad *chi* was, generally speaking, an unfortunate man, *onye ajahu,* who often labored without reaping. He might even become a "ne'er-do-well," *akalogoli.* But the people of Anioma did not believe that a man's destiny was entirely conditioned by his *chi.* Instead, they were convinced that no matter how "good" a person's *chi* was, he would not achieve success if he did not work hard and lead an upright life. The importance of hard work was emphasized in the saying, *"Onye kwe, chiya ekwe,"* literally meaning, "If a person says 'yes,' that person's *chi* says 'yes'." In addition, the Igbo believed that the diviners and other medicine men and women could intervene on behalf of a potentially unfortunate person to change his malignant *chi* into a benevolent one. Most private prayers, sacrifices, and invocations were directed toward chasing off misfortune and keeping oneself in a state of harmony with one's *chi.*

The people of Anioma believed that *Chukwu,* or *Chi-Ukwu,* the Great Creator, lived far away in the sky but took direct and indirect interest in the activities of humans. *Chukwu* was the origin of all things and knew all things, hence the Igbo often named their children *Chukwuma* (He who knows everything). They believed that God watched everyone's footsteps, so that another common name for children was *Chukwudumebi* (He leads and protects me). They also knew that God's time was the best, so they named their children, *Amaoge Chukwu* (God's time is the best). A man may name his child *Chukwukelu* or *Chukwuneke* (God is the creator), or *Chukwunyelu* (God gave me), or *Ifeanyichukwu* (nothing is impossible with God), or *Ngozichukwu* (God's blessing), or *Ikechukwu* (God's will). Apart from the names they gave to their children, Anioma proverbs, folk tales and incantations testified to their belief in the existence of God. Since nothing happened by chance, except by the will of God, everything, be it good health, illness, fortune, and misfortune, was attributed to Him. Even a malevolent *chi* was created by the almighty *Chukwu*, for it was believed that *Chukwu* gave every person his or her own *chi* at conception.

The people of Anioma had no symbols of *Chukwu* because no one knew what he looked like. With the exception of a few communities in the Agbor district, the people of Anioma kept no special altars and shrines for the worship of *Chukwu* since he was perceived to be everywhere at one and the same time. Some believed that the sky was his natural abode, from where he kept a constant and watchful eye over the universe. They believed that every act of transgression was an offense against *Chukwu* and that a person did not fall sick without breaking certain taboos. But because no one exactly knew God's wish (*onyema uche Chukwu*), they constantly prayed that evil be removed from their path. They also asked that those transgressions which they might unknowingly commit be forgiven them. The people of Anioma nursed a deep reverence for the mysterious nature of *Chukwu* and were not too sure how to approach him. They knew, however, that *Chukwu* was a spirit and that those who worshiped him must do so in spirit. They therefore communed with him through the major spirits and ancestors.

Anioma religious concepts were uniform but the methods of communicating with the invisible forces differed greatly from town to town. These differences were reflected in the countless religious intermediaries and religious practices. For instance, as Percy Amuray Talbot has rightly observed, whereas specific sacrifices were made at the two yam festivals, *ifejioku* and *iwaji*, in the event of a sickness, certain deities required special objects for sacrifice which could be determined only by certain doctors. Talbot, who made a survey of the religious practices of the Anioma people, testified that almost every family possessed a shrine for household worship; though special priests were appointed for the principal lodges or temples and often also for the town shrines, as well as for those of important chiefs, as a rule it was the oldest man in a family, and in a quarter, the *ogbe*, who performed the ceremony. Talbot was particularly struck by the near absence of priestcraft among the Anioma people, where most religious ceremonies were led by the oldest men in a family.[3] As we have already seen, the *diokpala* (elder) of each household was its chief priest and the custodian of ancestral shrines (See chapter 3).

The religions of Anioma involved three main activities, namely, propitiation, supplication and atonement. When a person felt disturbed by some unseen forces, for example, he might approach a diviner who might recommend that the unseen forces be propitiated. A scapegoat, in the form of a chicken or other animals, might be used. Should a person want special favors from the higher beings, the supplicant would make some sacrificial offerings, accompanied by the right prayers. During the periodic "national" festivals, the entire community, under the leadership of the chief priests and elders, would offer sacrifices, asking the higher forces for bountiful harvests, good health, good luck, many offspring and long life.

Percy A. Talbot, Felix Ekechi, Francis Arinze, E. Ikenga Metuh, and other scholars who studied the Igbo traditional religion and society have commented on the importance of sacrifice in Igbo religious ceremony. They stated that it formed an essential part of every religious ceremony; without it, the protection of the superior forces could not be guaranteed. "Sacrifice," wrote Arinze, "is the soul of the Ibo [Igbo] cult. If it is removed, Ibo traditional religion is almost emptied of its content."[4] The chief element in sacrifice, according to Talbot, is the desire to show gratitude to the gods or spirits for past blessings and others to come. A religious ceremony could be expiatory, that is, it could atone for or extinguish the guilt incurred by a person or persons, or it could be "the expression of regret for past wrongs" together with "the plea that punishment for these ill-deeds rest as lightly as possible on the offender." A sacramental feast signified the intention of the supplicant to "enter into communion with the deities, to become one with them . . . so that grace might flow into them."[5] Many sacrifices were intended to ask the superior powers for protection against enemies. When an animal was slaughtered for any of these purposes, only a small portion of it was reserved for the gods, the main part being eaten by the supplicant and his family, and by the priest if one was present.[6] In the case of a personal sacrifice, the supplicant and his priest were the only ones who could determine what victims suited the supplicant's need and means. Chukwu rarely received sacrifices, even though he was recognized as the ultimate recipient of the animal victims offered to the different deities.

The people of Anioma had a wide range of spirit symbols which often took the form of natural phenomena. Among these were spirits of the rivers, hills, lightning, iron, rain, the farm, the earth, strength, fertility, and witchcraft. One of the chief deities of the precolonial Anioma society was *ani,* the earth deity, or the great mother goddess who was also the spirit of fertility, "the nearest and dearest of the deities," and the most revered in the Anioma pantheon. She induced fertility, not only among humans, but also in plants and domestic animals. Sacrifices were offered to her, especially at the beginning of the planting season to ask her to reward the hard-working men and women with a good harvest. She was also remembered when the first fruits appeared and later during harvest. Because of her role in the reproductive process, every village and, indeed, every homestead had a shrine dedicated to her.

Ani had her own priestesses who were among the most important religious functionaries and who played a leading role in many aspects of community life. They reserved the right to declare when the goddess needed special propitiations. They officiated during all religious ceremonies that concerned *ani,* and presided over all matters involving crime against the earth force. Their presence was vital when matters concerning incest, birth, death and burial were being discussed.

The goddess, *ani,* was also respected by men. Before any man drank his palm wine, he asked for *ani's* blessing by pouring a little to the ground and saying, *"ani la manya,"* "Mother earth, partake of this wine." Also, when a man broke a kola nut, he gave a piece to ani saying, *"ani toji"* "Mother earth, accept this kola nut." When men gathered to discuss an important judicial, ritual, or political matter, no one was allowed to eat or drink before *ani* had been properly invoked and given her fair share of all the refreshments that were available.

Furthermore, if a person committed an unprovoked attack against another person, the latter could curse the former by uttering the expression, *"Ani ga tu gi,"* meaning, "May the earth deity overwhelm you with her wrath." It was considered very perilous to embark on a journey with such a curse hanging on one's back. These are only a few illustrations of the fear and respect with which the earth goddess was held among the people of Anioma.

Olokun was a god of the sea whose origin has been traced to Benin and Yorubaland. *Olokun* might have been a male, but was usually represented by the clay image of a woman, which was kept in a little shrine in front of a compound. *Olokun* was mostly worshipped by women, and most of his priests were women.[7]

There was also the *Igbe* cult, worshiped mostly by women. The *Igbe* cult must have entered Anioma from the western Niger Delta, as it was and still is a favorite deity of the Urhobo, Itsekiri, Isoko, and Edo. The *Igbe* cult members were distinguished by the red attire which formed a part of the regalia.

Apart from the *nmo* Igala, there does not appear to be any major religious influence coming from Igalaland. And apart from *ani* and *olokun,* which were widely worshipped, the vast majority of the Anioma religious cults were fundamentally Igbo in character. In addition to the aforementioned cults, every town had a principal deity that was recognized by every person in the town. For example, in Issele-Ukwu, the central and the most powerful deity was *mkpitima.* Anyone who swore falsely to it was supposed to die. Should anyone offend *mkpitima* and die, his or her property was deposited at her shrine, and anyone who took away from, or ate anything belonging to a person killed by *mkpitima* was also expected to die.[8]

At Igbuzo, the diety *oboshi* was recognized by every person. She was the goddess of the principal stream, also known as Oboshi. All the fish that lived in the stream were her children; it was an abomination to fish or to eat a fish caught therein. *Ohene* was the main priest of the goddess, *oboshi.* An *ohene* could be male or female. "May *oboshi* take away your life" was a common curse among the people of Igbuzo. Also, the cry, "*Oboshi mbah,*" which means, "Protect me, oh, Oboshi," was a common prayer usually said in moments of crisis. To swear falsely in the name of *oboshi* was to incur the wrath of the goddess.

Finally, every lineage and every household had its own sets of gods or forces which were not worshipped by the members of other lineages and households. These gods or forces are too numerous to be discussed here, but mention will be made of *ikenga,* the personification of a man's strength, and *ofo,* a symbol of authority and truth and a representation of the departed ancestors. As we shall see in a later chapter, only men who owned or acted as custodians of the ancestral *ofo* sticks qualified for the highest titles of the land.

Many practices, taboos, ceremonies, and festivals were rooted strongly in religion. For example, a titled man ate his meals in isolation since no one was allowed to see his mouth. Moreover, no menstruating woman was allowed to enter his kitchen or prepare his meals. To ensure that these restrictions were strictly observed, a titled man's wife was required to change her clothing often, for the garments might have been worn at one time or other during menstruation. To be on the safe side, the titled man may demand that a woman borrow a man's clothes before preparing his meal.[9] Also, it was an abomination for any menstruating woman to enter the *obi* where a titled man kept his major ritual objects, or sit on his *isi ukpo,* an elevated mud seat or bed where he often sat or slept.

Some belief systems derived their rationale from the concept of reincarnation. In fact, the entire religious system of these people revolved around the concept of birth, death, and reincarnation. The idea of resurrecting after death, on or before the day of judgment, only to proceed again to hell or heaven did not exist. Instead, the inhabitants of Anioma believed that when elders died, they usually did not go away for good, but lurked unseen, looking after the welfare of the living members of the lineage. Before a living elder ate his meal, or drank his palm wine, or ate his kola nut, he gave some to his departed forebears, asking for their protection and guidance. Animal sacrifices were also offered in the name of the departed ancestors. If a baby boy was born soon after the death of his grandfather, this child could have been no other person than the old man, reincarnated, and might be named *Nnamdi* or *Nnadi*, "father is back." Likewise, if a baby girl was born soon after the death of a paternal grandmother, she might be named *Nnena*, "father's mother is back." But not all dead people could reincarnate. Among those who could not were persons who died a "bad death" (say, by suicide), childless persons, people with violent and criminal dispositions, strangers, and all people with doubtful origins.

The people of Anioma believed that infants could also reincarnate, but these were usually babies who had put their parents through unnecessary pain. These babies often died soon after birth only to come back again to the same parents, on account of which they were called *ogbanje*, meaning, those who "come and go." Some women were known to have lost up to eight children, none of them living long enough to witness the birth of the next child. However, if the right diviner was consulted, in good time, the *ogbanje* could be stripped of its power to return to the world of the dead.

At this juncture, it is possible to group the Anioma belief systems under three heads. First, are those beliefs and religious practices which were uniform throughout the region, as illustrated by the belief in *Chukwu, chi, ani, ifejioku, iwaji, olokun, igbe,* and *ogbanje*. Second, some beliefs and practices were peculiar only to particular towns and were not exactly represented elsewhere, examples being the *mkpitima* deity of Issele-Ukwu or the *oboshi* of Igbuzo, together with such festivals as *ine, iwu,* and iwaji, which were widespread but based in the individual towns. Third, were the numerous deities, beliefs and religious practices which, even though they were familiar to everyone in Anioma, were confined only to particular families. Among these were the *ofo* and *ikenga*.

On the whole, like their political institutions, the Anioma religious practices were highly decentralized and autonomous. Every town had its own set of beliefs, rituals, and ceremonies. More important is the fact that all the religions and cults of Anioma showed "a friendliness to one another." Commenting generally on African traditional religions, Talbot noted that "Consideration towards the convictions of others and respect for their sacred symbols are expected from strangers and are naturally accorded by these. This tolerance in religious matters is one of the negroes' most attractive qualities."[10] This was a strong feature of the African traditional religions which the European-trained missionaries of the nineteenth century grossly misunderstood and cared so little to study. It was these misunderstandings that sparked the inter-religious conflicts that we shall presently examine.

THE CHURCH MISSIONARY SOCIETY, 1841–1907

It was almost inevitable that the people of Anioma would clash with the early Christian missionaries who entered the region with preconceived notions about African "barbarism" and lack of religion. Both oral and written records attest to the fact that no European ever visited Anioma until 1830 when two British explorers, John and Richard Lander, got to Asaba by canoe from the direction of Lokoja. They were captured by Aboh traders who took them to Aboh, where the Obi sold them to a Brass trader who took them to the coast, hoping to make a profit from the transaction. The Brass trader was, however, disappointed when the British trader to whom he had presented the Lander brothers sailed away without paying the agreed sum. After this brief encounter, however, no European came to Anioma until 1841, when an officially British-backed expedition sailed up the Niger with the aim of establishing trade and Christianity in the Niger valley. The members of this expedition included British government agents, traders, and missionaries.

The first Christian missionaries to work in Anioma were the agents of the Church Missionary Society (CMS), who, despite a very zealous start and a fairly warm welcome, made very slow progress. Their poor performance can be attributed to the series of conflicts that their missionary strategy sparked off. They were, for example, tight-fisted and generally reluctant to pay for their ministry or to finance the building of churches and schools. They also treated the people of Anioma with utter disrespect, which angered the local communities. More important, perhaps, is the fact that the Christians were brought face-to-face with a very strong traditionalist society that was prepared to defend its religion and independence with great courage and determination. The relationship between the Christians and the people of Anioma was a catalogue of misunderstanding and hostilities, yielding almost no immediate benefits. Asaba was the primary center of these inter-religious conflicts.

THE ASABA MISSION

European-trained Christian missionaries were sent to Africa as agents of imperial penetration and domination, but their sponsors must have been disappointed with the very slow spread of the faith in "the Dark Continent." At the Niger mission, for example, after an encouraging start at Onitsha in 1857 it took the CMS over twenty years to establish itself effectively anywhere else in Igboland. Even Asaba, an important commercial center only three miles from Onitsha, remained without a Christian mission post until 1875.

Christian missionary beginnings in Asaba can be dated to September 1873, when Rev. John Buck, from his base at Onitsha, visited Asaba to view the prospects but it was not until 1875 that Rev. M. Romayne bought a piece of land for the mission.[11] Romayne paid the agreed-upon price which was ten pieces of grey cotton baft valued at £5, to Obi Igweli, who Bishop Samuel Ajayi Crowther described as "a chief of the first rank of Asaba."[12] A few months later, the Niger Mission of the CMS instructed Rev. Edward K. Phillips to take over the new station.

The relationship between the CMS and the people of Asaba was particularly unsavory. Crowther and his colleagues were soon to learn that Asaba was an especially difficult field for missionary work. For, even though its people were generally peaceful and hospitable, or "sociable and tractable," as Bishop Crowther preferred to describe them,[13] they had no immediate desire to replace their gods and ancestors with some strange and unknown saints, virgin mothers, and winged angels. However, since they did not quickly comprehend the political motives of the Christian visitors, they allowed them to carry on with their activities unmolested even though the Asabans pitied them for gainlessly occupying themselves with preaching and fraternizing with outcasts and undesirables.

The missionaries, for their part, showed a determination to undermine and destroy the customs and belief systems of their hosts. Crowther, who saw his ministry as a battle between light and darkness, did not hesitate to call them all sorts of names.[14] In an attempt to incite the British government and traders against the people of Asaba, he described them in his copious correspondence to England as thieves who regarded "the property of a stranger . . . as a lawful prey, which, if not stolen, is extorted by cheats and rougery."[15] Crowther also tried to conceal the poor performance of his mission by warning that the country was "morally dark and full of cruel habitations" and charged that Asaba was "one of the places where the Satan's seat is."[16] Rev. Edward Phillips, a colleague and close associate of Crowther, denounced what he termed the "heathen" practices of the people. Barely one year after his arrival at Asaba he reported that its people were "still following the wicked customs of their forefathers."[17]

The people of Asaba, who were familiar with the Igbo proverb that warned against mixing with ill-intentioned guests, decided to stay away from the missionaries. Parents would not send their children to school or allow them to receive the water of baptism. Some youths who ran away to the mission center were quickly whisked back home by irate parents.[18] Crowther was soon to complain that some citizens of Asaba failed to make an open confession of Christ for fear of being laughed at, and that "even the few persons who were timidly coming forward to hear the word of God on the Lord's day were persecuted."[19]

Despite the misunderstanding, however, a small congregation worshipped at the mission center, some of them baptized. Each Sunday the missionaries were pleased to see a gathering of "some fifty or eighty humble worshippers, who, a few years ago had no knowledge of their maker."[20] Also, a few boys enrolled at the school, and as time went on, the congregation of converts grew, though extremely slowly.

It is not surprising therefore that by 1888—that is, after thirteen years of continuous missionary activity at Asaba—the CMS could not boast of more than a handful of converts drawn principally from two groups who had no status whatsoever in the traditional society of Asaba. The first group consisted of strangers, mainly the soldiers and laborers of the Royal Niger Company, who in 1888, were attending service regularly.[21] The second group consisted of slaves, and because they dominated the congregation of worshippers, the CMS earned the appellation "uka-n-nguali," that is, "church for slaves" or "the assemblies of slaves."[22]

Despite these problems, however, the CMS missionaries continued to strive to achieve success in Asaba. They arranged their work under "three principal heads," namely, "Sunday duties, School work, and Visiting and Itinerating."[23] Their industrial center attracted some youths who produced cotton, bricks, and furniture.[24]

One major source of continued conflict was the CMS's practice of meddling with local customs. By openly preaching the equality of all men and women before God, for example, they wittingly or unwittingly incited the slaves to rebel against their owners. This gave rise to much friction, culminating in the British conquest of Asaba in 1888.[25] Some converts went so far as to violate local customs in the name of Christianity. They also spied for the missionaries, reporting most of the things that went on in the villages. It was at this time that the people of Asaba nicknamed all Christians *ndi na ka anyi uka* or simply, *ndi uka*, that is, "those who backbite us."[26] The people of Asaba went further to regard Sunday as *ubosi uka*, "the day of gossip," because it was on that day that most Christians gathered together in one place. In fact, the depth of this feeling of betrayal is further illustrated by the fact that though the Christian missionaries introduced the English names for days of the week into Igboland, only Sunday was given an Igbo name. The expressions *ndi uka* and *ubosi uka* have been so completely absorbed into the Igbo language that the present-day generation of Igbo people do not seem to care to find out their origins.

Even the slaves of Asaba, who had benefited from the missionary presence and had embraced Christianity *en masse,* eventually protested against the reckless methods of the CMS by quietly withdrawing their association with it.[27] Disturbed by what he considered as an act of ingratitude, Rev. Julius Spencer charged that nearly the whole of the slaves who began to attend church in 1888 only paid lip service to their confession of Christ. He then went "from one slave village (*ugwule*) to another, exhorting and urging them to come out of their old customs and be separate and give themselves entirely to serve God," but all that he received were "fair promises" of their intention to follow the righteous way.[28] Until well into the twentieth century, the CMS remained a small and almost despised establishment in Asaba as the vast majority of the freeborn still refused to associate themselves with those they regarded as bad guests and the dregs of society.

PENETRATION INLAND

By the last quarter of the nineteenth century, Asaba had become a very important place for the Europeans, partly because it was "a starting point for journeys westwards to the Yoruba country,"[29] and partly because it was the administrative headquarters of the Royal Niger Company. In 1900, when the British government revoked the charter of the company and took over its territories, which extended as far north as Gwandu and Adamawa, Asaba was virtually the seat of the government of Nigeria.[30] Thus, even though the CMS did not make much progress in Asaba, the town had become an important center from which Christianity and British colonial rule—the Bible and the Flag—spread into many parts of southern and northern Nigeria.

One of the most colorful expeditions into the Asaba hinterlands was made by Rev. Julius Spencer to Ubulu-Ukwu in 1878. This journey had been planned for 1877 but the succession dispute that marked the death of the Obi of Ubulu-Ukwu and the accession of his son, Nwadishi, warranted a postponement.[31] Accompanied by two guides, Rev. Spencer left Asaba on February 27, 1878 and arrived at Okpanam an hour or so later, where he was warmly welcomed. After explaining why the CMS had come to Anioma, Rev. Spencer preached the words of God and tried to warn the people against "the folly of heathenism and its heinousness in the sight of God."[32] The people of Okpanam listened attentively and at the end of the sermon replied with what Spencer described as the stereotypical phrase, "It is the custom of our ancestors."[33]

Leaving Okpanam, Spencer and his companions went to Issele-Ukwu, where reports had gone around that an *oyibo,* a white man, was coming. Crowds gathered all along his route and it was with great difficulty that he and his companions were conducted to the house of the regent. The mob pressed so hard behind them that the regent locked the door and conducted them into the inner room where they remained until the throng dispersed. When eventually the missionaries left the Obi's palace, the crowds reassembled and followed them shouting, "Our fathers and grandfathers never saw an Oyibo."

It should be remarked that Spencer was not a white man but a black missionary trained in Sierra Leone. It should also be stated here that to most southern Nigerians, an *oyibo or onyibo* is a white person. But the word can also be used for a very light-skinned black person, or a very dark-skinned black person who behaves like a white person. To distinguish between a true white person and a black person who "resembles" a white person either in complexion or behavior, the Yoruba people may speak of *oyibo pupa* (literally, "white-white person") and *oyibo dudu* ("black-white person"). The Igbos, who later borrowed these expressions from the Yoruba, speak of them as *oyibo ocha* and *oyibo oji,* respectively. The early Christian missionaries, like Samuel Ajayi Crowther and Rev. John Buck, defined an *oyibo* differently; understandably they stated that an *oyibo* was a "civilized" person.

After his interview with the Obi of Issele-Ukwu, Spencer presented him with some tobacco, cloth, pipes, plates, and tumblers, and then asked for permission to proceed to Ubulu-Ukwu. The Obi of Issele-Ukwu had no intention of keeping his guests any longer than they wished to stay. He provided them with five guides and, early the next morning, Spencer expressed his gratitude and left.

He arrived at Ubulu-Okiti at noon and was met by the governor of the town, "a viceroy of the king." This man persuaded the Christian to spend at least an hour in Ubulu-Okiti to enable the townspeople, who had already crowded in, an opportunity to look into the face of an *oyibo*. Spencer reported that the pleasure the townspeople enjoyed by his presence was "manifested by loud shouts, clapping of hands, and screams on the part of the women and children, and furious, continued deafening blasts of the ivory horns from the men, which would make one at a distance think that the whole race of elephants were at war with themselves."

Spencer and his escort left Ubulu-Okiti at 1 P.M. and were followed for some time by a large crowd. They arrived at Ubulu-Ukwu at 5 P.M. and were warmly received by the prince, Modi. Because of the multitude that pushed forward to see the missionary, Modi requested Spencer to retire into the inner chamber and to prepare to see the Obi after dinner. From a conversation that lasted three hours, Spencer was able to learn from Modi that Ubulu-Ukwu was "tributary to the king of Benin," that Nwadishi, "the newly crowned king of Ubulu-Ukwu, was about to send messengers to Benin to announce his coronation and to present the Oba of Benin with some gifts and to have his accession confirmed." He also learned that all the settlements on the road to Benin were quiet and "peacefully disposed to each other." Spencer gathered from Modi the names of the towns situated between Ubulu-Ukwu and Benin and the distances between each pair of towns. In appreciation for this valuable intelligence, Spencer gave some presents to prince Modi.

When Spencer was summoned to the palace, he observed that the Obi of Ubulu-Ukwu was attended by twelve eunuchs, some of them carrying the scepter and other insignia of royalty. The Obi was also "flanked and followed by a large body of his nobility and gentry." After the usual exchange of kola nuts, gifts, and greetings, the Obi praised Spencer for the trouble he took to travel so far inland and added, "as long as ages and traditions last, it shall ever be remembered that in my reign an Oyibo penetrated thus far."

In the meantime, "thousands of people continued to pour into Ubulu-Ukwu from fifteen to twenty miles away to look at an Oyibo." The next day being Sunday, Spencer collected a small number of people together, including Modi and his brothers, and addressed them from John 3:16. These people listened with wonder and amazement to the story of Adam's fall and of God's inestimable love in sending his Son to bear and expiate our sins on the cross. Spencer ended his sermon by warning that "God desired no more burnt-offerings and sacrifices . . . we simply [must] believe and be saved." Spencer reported that when his sermon was over, the people of Ubulu-Ukwu burst out with the exclamation, "We never heard of such wonderful things before." The missionary and his escort ended their tour of parts of Anioma by returning to Asaba, passing through Ubulu-Okiti, Issele-Ukwu and Okpanam. They had been away from their headquarters at Asaba for seven days altogether.

What should be emphasized here is that up to 1888 the agents of the Church Missionary Society received a very warm and friendly reception wherever they went in the interior. When, for instance, Rev. John Buck, who, like Spencer, was an *oyibo oji* (black-white man), visited Igbuzo in 1874, he was overwhelmed with surprise to discover that thousands of people came to see him: "Some climbed up on top of houses, some on top of trees and some on men's shoulders, simply to see me and my curiosities." As he went from one house to another to pay his respects to the titled chiefs, he was glad that "a single step of mine throws many down through fear of my person." Buck visited only one of the quarters of the town—Ogboli-Igbuzo—and there he saw about twelve eze title-holders, from whom he received presents of cowries and cattle. Even his guide was lavishly praised for "having done or accomplished what his great-grandfather never did by bringing civilized persons to their country."[34]

It is, however, ironic that after these warm receptions of the early days, the same Anioma people began to burn down church houses, murdering Christians and terrorizing all those who showed sympathy for the *oyibo*. This change of attitude may well explain the failure of the CMS to establish itself in such large towns as Igbuzo, Ogwashi-Ukwu, Issele-Ukwu and Ubulu-Ukwu until after the effective imposition of colonial rule in the area. Instead, the Akwukwu station, opened in 1925, became the second station of the CMS in Anioma.

The Akwukwu station was run by Lazarus Odibosa, a native of Asaba. When Rev. T. J. Dennis, secretary of the Niger Mission of the CMS, visited Akwukwu in 1901, he was able to report good attendance at both the morning and evening Sunday services. He estimated that there were about fifty baptized adults and children. He felt that there had been a marvelous change there since he and Lazarus Odibosa first came there six years earlier. He wished that things had moved in the same way in other places.[35]

In the same year, a woman missionary visited Akwukwu and was able to report that during her call to the homes of some Christian women she was pleased to find entire families in which the husband, the wife and the children were all baptized.[36] She also told about a chief of Akwukwu who attended services in the company of all his household. This chief had many wives, she said, "on account of which he was refused baptism even though some of his wives had been baptized."[37] According to this missionary's account, yet another Akwukwu man, together with his two wives, had embraced the Christian faith. However, this man was denied baptism even though his wives had been baptized. To remove his disqualification and be baptized, this man sent away one of his wives, who, sadly enough, was nursing a baby, but the wife who was sent away "took kindly to her disgrace" and when her suckling baby was to be baptized, instead of feeling angry, she asked the first wife to stand as godmother to her baby.

By 1907, when the CMS celebrated its silver jubilee, it had stations in the following places: Onitsha-Olona, Onitsha-Ugbo, Idumuje-Uno, Issele-Azagba, Igbodo, Atuma, Ogwashi-Ukwu, Ubulu-Ukwu, Ubulu-Okiti, Umunede, Ugbolu, Obior, Ukwunzu, Ubulubu, Ani-Ofu, Akwukwu and Asaba. All these stations were established after 1895.

CONSTRAINTS ON GROWTH

The impact of the CMS on Anioma during its first fifty years (1857-1907) was minimal. Most of its stations were located within a twenty-mile radius of Asaba. The Agbor district had only one mission post, at Umunede. The Kwale district was not touched at all. Even in the Aniocha district, where the CMS succeeded in erecting churches and schools, only a small proportion of the inhabitants was baptized. Most of the elements of the traditional religion remained unchanged. In fact, some of the baptized Christians continued to observe their traditional religious rites, while others returned to traditional practices after a few months or years of adherence to the Christian faith. The whole unsatisfactory situation was summed up by Rev. Johnson when he moaned that one "should not have believed that after 30 years of . . . labour . . . the general mass of the people could yet be content to remain in a state of wilful ignorance and barbarism. Signs of idolatry and superstition meet the eye everywhere in the streets and in the houses of the people."[38]

Twenty years after this observation was made, the situation had not improved; instead it had deteriorated when the Ekumeku freedom fighters began to destroy mission establishments as well as harass converts. In 1904, Rev. Julius Spencer recalled grimly: "During the months of January and February all the out-stations, with two exceptions, presented a sorrowful spectacle. Mission-houses and churches were either razed to the ground or burnt down. The houses of converts were destroyed and the converts themselves had fled. During these months it seemed as if the labour of years had been brought to naught."[39]

From the missionaries' standpoint, one of the greatest obstacles to the spread of Christianity in Anioma was the difficulty in recruiting suitable agents. The health problem was real. Although quinine helped to reduce mortality among Europeans, Africa remained the white man's grave for a long time. It was largely because of the health problem that the authorities of the CMS decided that the Niger Mission should be manned largely by black agents.[40] Even so, qualified black agents were few and very difficult to find. In 1887, Crowther regretted that there were no less than twelve important centers from which he had received requests for mission establishments, "but which we could not answer for want of agents."[41] He said that if his mission had sufficient suitable agents, it would have occupied at least twenty-six centers. Bishop Crowther recalled that both "legitimate trade" and Christian missions were established in the same year (1857) on the Lower Niger, but while no less than forty-six trading stations had been opened by the traders, the CMS could boast of only eight mission stations.[42]

To further appreciate the magnitude of the problem posed by the manpower shortage one has to realize that the CMS Niger Mission was expected to cover a very large area. According to Crowther, "Considering the extent of the Niger Mission, taking it from the mouths of the Rivers at the Delta to Rabba and Shonga, 400 miles from the coast, and from Ilorin northward to Sokoto, Condu [Gwandu] and Hamaruwa on the Binue [Benue] Branch, about the same extent or more, we need a large army of missionaries to occupy the land and evangelise the ignorant inhabitants."[43]

If the mission could not import sufficient qualified agents from Europe, Sierra Leone, Lagos, and elsewhere, could it not have resorted to local training? In fact, this strategy was considered. Some baptized Igbo Christians were trained locally but these men were then considered unsuitable for the positions for which they had been trained. Crowther painfully recalled that since the commencement of his mission, he had sent no less than fourteen promising youths to Sierra Leone and Lagos grammar schools and training institutes, to be educated with the intention of employing them as teachers. Out of this number, continued Crowther, only five remained with the mission, the rest defecting to the trading firms. It is interesting to note that of the five who stayed with the mission, only one was an Igbo from Onitsha, a man named Isaac Mba, who helped the Church Missionary Society translate the Bible into Igbo. Nevertheless, he too was soon to leave the mission to join the Protectorate Government. "I am sorry to say that we are losing the service of Isaac Mba," reported H. H. Dobinson. "He has got an important offer of work under Major [Claude] MacDonald and has accepted the same. He applied for this months ago, before he came to work with me as a Translator: and now the offer has come."[44]

The problem posed by the drift of mission-trained personnel to the trading firms and civil service was exacerbated by the inability of the missions to pay their employees reasonable wages. The pay scale of the National African Company was considered the standard, and parents expected their children to earn this after training, whether they were employed by the missionaries or by the government.

Coupled with the difficulty of recruiting qualified personnel was the problem posed by "relapsing" or "backsliding" agents and converts. "The news here is far from cheering," reported Bishop Crowther, "Stephen Obori who ceased to be employed as our interpreter only in June last, and who often preached in the Church, and has great influence with the Onitsha Christians has become a Polygamist, with four wives."[45] Crowther went on to say that the re-conversion of Obori to the traditional way of life made a great impression on the "native" mind. The residents, Crowther said, decided that "Obori must know what is right as he has read the Bible . . . and preached in the Church." Like the slaves of Asaba who left the CMS en masse, many early Christian converts soon reconsidered their affiliation with the Church.

More disturbing to the Christian missionaries was the realization that the inhabitants of the Lower Niger had become generally hostile. As we have seen, the first visits were met with rousing welcome but subsequent visits were increasingly less friendly, and sometimes downright antagonistic. As early as 1878, Rev. John Buck had warned that "the state of things in the middle part of the Niger is becoming more and more alarming" as the lives of the Christians were in "jeopardy every hour." He complained of what he called "the difficulties, trials, and oppositions" the missionaries were encountering with the populations among whom they lived. He claimed that black missionary agents were often beaten and at times killed. According to Buck's report, the "late Mr. Joshua Smith was killed by Ogene's son of Onitsha . . . [and] the Rev. S. Perry was severely beaten when he went to rescue Mrs. John who was equally guiltless and [had] done nothing to provoke them." Buck warned that "this dreadful contagion is not only seizing large towns, but small villages also. Alenso now is far from being what it was years gone bye. . . ."[46]

It is normal to expect conflicts between the followers of different religions but a complication in the present was the additional fact that the local populations regarded all Europeans—traders, missionaries, and imperial agents—as one, and did not differentiate in their treatment of them; in the event of a disagreement with one party, the native inhabitants would not hesitate to antagonize the rest. For instance, in 1879 the chiefs of Asaba closed down trade, denying all Europeans the permission to purchase provisions for their sustenance based on a grievance against the traders. Crowther protested against this action, describing it as "the injustice of including the mission agents with the merchants." His protest was received with close attention by Obi Igweli who, according to Crowther, "acknowledged the wrong" but explained that "as one party of civilized people was forbidden, the other should be included also."[47]

Following a similar dispute at Obosi, on the other side of the river, Crowther took the trouble to explain to the residents that Christian missionaries, "being messengers of God, sent to teach all nations according to his book [and] being innocent persons . . . should not be made to suffer for the faults of others with whom they had no business." The chiefs of Obosi, who did not wish to contest this distinction, agreed with Crowther, but strongly protested against the tendency of the Christians to ignore the objects of worship of their forefathers, to kill and eat sacred snakes and fishes, and to pull down objects of worship and shrines. The chiefs warned that the new religion was undermining Igbo customs, and suggested that "converts should confess the wrongs done to the gods, make restitution by paying for all the damages they had already done, and promise not to repeat them in future." The chiefs also told the bishop that if he would copy something from the Bible, which they could bury in the ground "as an insurance to them of long life, multiplicity of children, and fruitful productions of their land, they would go to the worship of God. . . ."[48]

One can imagine that such encounters were not likely to produce any mutual understanding. Bishop Crowther charged that in this instance the chiefs of Obosi did not give a decided consent that the worship of the Christian religion should be continued unmolested, or that the converts should not be persecuted. "As no compromise was made to meet their superstitious wishes, they were not satisfied," he wrote.[49]

Such incidents suggest still another source of conflict between the Christians and the people of Anioma, namely, the wanton disregard by the former for the religious practices of the latter. These disputes led to sporadic, often violent outbursts. Generally, such misunderstandings, combined with the other difficulties the missionaries encountered, slowed the spread of Christianity considerably.

CMS/CATHOLIC RIVALRY

Neither was the evangelical strategy of the CMS sufficiently progressive to survive the rigor of establishing itself on often hostile ground. Unlike the Roman Catholic fathers, who first came to Anioma in 1888, the CMS did not entice converts with gifts and services intended to increase the well-being of the inhabitants. The CMS school at Onitsha was nearly undermined by the Roman Catholics because, as Archdeacon Henry Johnson put it, "children were enticed away by promises of clothing and free food." He also complained that the Catholics gave medical care "without insisting upon patients embracing their system," and were prepared to baptize people who they knew already belonged to the CMS. The Catholics, he further charged, accepted those who were known to be "lax in Church discipline," and offered higher salaries to CMS agents who were "led to join their ranks" and even indulged in the practice of "circulating Romanish literature" among CMS agents, "seeking to draw them aside."[50]

More galling to the feelings of the agents of the CMS was the fact that at one time or the other, not only single individuals, but also whole communities defected to the Catholic camp. A good illustration comes from Ossomari (Osamala), where most of the Christians, "under the leadership of their townsman, Mr. Jacob Akubueze, severed their connection with the CMS and united themselves to the Romanists." This particular event was blamed on the reluctance of the Church Missionary Society to pay its agent. Its executive committee had refused to appoint Akubueze to superintend the work at Osamala unless the people of that place undertook to provide one-third of his salary.[51]

It was only in 1905 that the executive committee of the CMS took a positive step toward solving some of the problems posed for them by the Catholics. The archdeacon attacked the policy of avoiding stations where Roman Catholics were at work when in fact the Catholics were not avoiding CMS stations, but were "settling down often in close proximity to us." At the same time the Archdeacon explained that certain towns, such as Issele-Ukwu, Igbuzo, and Illah, were within easy reach and in some cases on the main road between CMS stations; these towns had sent appeals to the society to establish missions in them but had been refused because the Catholics already were present. The CMS committee then resolved that the government should be informed that in view of the occupation of some of their own recognized stations, such as Asaba and Onitsha-Olona, by the Roman Catholics—apparently with the approval of the government--the CMS would no longer feel bound to limit their ministrations to towns not occupied by Roman Catholics.[52] These excuses notwithstanding, the greatest problem of the CMS stemmed from the fact that they operated with inadequate finances to train and pay their employees, to open up and maintain new stations, and to assist the communities in which they worked by providing them with medical care, orphanages, and other welfare services. This situation is clearly demonstrated in the case of Aboh, where the CMS spent sixty-six years preparing to establish themselves but never succeeded.

THE MISSION TO ABOH

Obsessed with their own feeling of moral and commercial superiority, some British adventurers sailed up the Niger River in a steel steamboat in 1841 on an expedition which, as already mentioned, was "conjointly commercial and missionary in its object."[53] On board the steamboat were British imperial agents, traders and missionaries. The British government representatives were instructed to conclude treaties of trade and friendship with African chiefs and people, the traders to explore the prospects of establishing direct trade with the interior, and the missionaries to introduce the Christian religion among the natives of Africa. Of special relevance to this study were the two missionaries who made the voyage. Samuel Ajayi Crowther and Simon Jonas. Crowther was a Yoruba man and a former slave who later became the first African to be ordained a bishop by the Anglican Church. Jonas was an Igbo man raised in Sierra Leone, apparently by ex-slave parents. Jonas was fluent in the Igbo language and was brought to the Niger as a preacher and interpreter.

When the steamboat arrived at Aboh, the representatives of the British government concluded a treaty of "protection" and trade with

Obi Ossai, the paramount chief. Crowther preached from the Bible and Jonas translated the sermon into the Igbo language. Obi Ossai was so touched by this visit that he requested the visitors to open a school and a church in his chiefdom, and was assured that his request would be granted. Obi Ossai was also so moved by Jonas's flare in both the Igbo and English languages that he requested him to extend his stay in Aboh. The leaders of the expedition could not turn down this appeal and, before the boat steered north, they instructed Jonas to remain behind in order to prepare for the establishment of Christian mission stations in Aboh and the neighboring Igbo settlements. Jonas complied with this order; during his stay he moved about freely and visited a number of towns and villages in the Aboh district. He made several visits up the river, to Ossamere [Osamala], Onitsha, and the Asaba markets, preaching the gospel. "He was respected by all, both chiefs and people" who saw and listened to him. When the expedition returned prematurely to Aboh, Jonas was found in good health.[54]

The boat's precipitous return was caused by tragedy, the second in a series that dogged the first European attempts to establish themselves on the Niger. In 1832, an expedition up the Niger sponsored by MacGregor Laird, had ended in disaster when thirty-eight of the forty-eight members died from tropical diseases.[55] The 1841 expedition had gone up the Niger to establish a trading post, a Christian mission station, and a model farm at Lokoja, but like the expedition of 1832–34, this one soon had to be abandoned. Of the 145 Europeans on the boat, 48 died from disease.[56] These mortalities, together with those that occurred in other parts of Africa, earned for the African interior the nickname, "the whiteman's grave."

The disaster of 1841 was a major setback. Apart from the lives lost and the reputation it earned for Africa, the expedition's closure also brought Simon Jonas's ministry to an untimely halt.[57] For over ten years, neither the British imperial government nor the private sponsors of expeditions into the interior of Africa showed any serious interest in sending British citizens to an almost certain death.

It was only after thirteen-year lapse that another group was sent up the Niger. The expedition of 1854 was commanded by MacGregor Laird, with Dr. William Balfour Baikie as the naval surgeon.[58] The party stopped again at Aboh only to learn that Obi Ossai had died a few months earlier. The town was in an interregnum, as the people of Aboh disputed over a suitable choice of a successor. The explorers conferred with the leading chiefs before sailing up the Niger and returned to Aboh a few months later; this time, none of the passengers or crew—fifty-four Africans and twelve Europeans—had died from fever, thanks to the use of quinine.[59] The British explorers spent a few days in Aboh and then returned to Sierra Leone and England.

In 1857, a more ambitious expedition sailed up the Niger, stopping at Aboh as others had before it. The traders who accompanied this group promptly established a trading station there, while the returning Samuel Ajayi Crowther, rather than build a school and a church as promised to Obi Ossai in 1841 and to Aje, Obi Ossai's son, in 1854, asked the people to clear a piece of land which the chiefs had reserved for his mission thirteen years earlier. Crowther told them to get building materials ready "so that when required there might be no delay in the erection of a temporary [mission] house."[60] Delighted that the long-awaited school and church would at last become reality, Obi Orise (Olise) accepted the responsibility of supervising the preliminary work.

Rather than establish itself at Aboh, however, the Church Missionary Society diverted its energy to Onitsha. A CMS report of 1858 stated that Onitsha was selected as the headquarters of the mission on the lower course of the Niger because it was important for its market and because of the large number of people "of various races" who assembled there for commercial purposes. The European traders established a trading post on the riverbank, while the Christian missionaries went to "the suburbs of the town, about a mile and a half inland and chose a site for the mission station." This station was headed by Rev. John Christopher Taylor, an Igbo man born in Sierra Leone.[61] Thus Onitsha—not Aboh—became a very important center of the CMS; it was from here that Christian missionary propaganda began to spread into the adjoining districts and across the Niger into Anioma.

Even after opening the Onitsha mission, the CMS did not consider it urgent to do likewise at Aboh. Instead, mission posts were erected at Asaba, Osamala, Alenso, and Obosi, even though some of these were subsequently abandoned or often remained vacant for lack of suitable agents. One CMS source attributed the late start at Aboh to the fact that the town was no longer an important trading center, having been ruined by the British imperial presence, gunboat diplomacy, and commercial rivalry.

The chiefs and people of Aboh were not discouraged, however. They continued to invite the CMS to come and build a church and a school in their town. In 1883, Bishop Crowther decided to visit Obi Ugboma, the new paramount chief of Aboh, "on the subject of his letter of invitation" to him. The letter had been written in 1881 and, according to Crowther, he "had not been able to answer till now." Obi

Ugboma was exceedingly pleased to see the bishop. The chief was also delighted to learn that his letter to the bishop had been received. He then re-affirmed his request for a church and a school. He told the bishop that he had already selected for the mission a "perfect piece of land" that would never flood, and hoped that he would not be disappointed as his grandfather and father had been.[62]

Bishop Crowther then explained in some detail the circumstances which had made the delay inevitable. He told Obi Ugboma that he had been on the Niger for over forty years and had witnessed the opening of mission centers in many towns. He said that lately, he had received numerous applications from various rulers to come and work among them. Some of those rulers, he went on, were prepared to meet half the cost of the establishments. He said that the king of Okirika had already volunteered to contribute thirty casks of palm oil toward the cost and the townspeople had promised to mold the necessary bricks. Obi Ugboma was greatly moved by this revelation. The bishop wrote: "King Bomai [Obi Ugboma] looked round on his courtiers . . . with an air of dignity, [and] said, 'I shall pay the expenses of both Church and mission house,' to which all of them gave their affirmative assent." After a discussion that lasted for many hours, the paramount chief took the bishop out to see the piece of land that he had chosen for the proposed mission, but the Obi was warned by his courtiers that portions of the same piece of land had already been reserved for some deities. The Obi did not support this reservation and, as Crowther put it, "the king overruled the information."

In spite of this very cordial and most encouraging visit, neither Crowther nor his co-religionists returned to build a church or school at Aboh. Some years later, the bishop wrote in his journal: "We visited Aboh and saw the ground the chiefs proposed to give us for our station," but rather than state when construction on the site would start, he added that "the chiefs here are a very greedy and avaricious set of men, but I still hope they will give us some assistance in building a house for our Agents."[63]

After this disrespectful remark, Aboh was scarcely ever mentioned in the Niger mission reports until the CMS jubilee celebrations of 1907. In other words, sixty-six years after Crowther and Jonas promised Obi Ossai a mission, Aboh still had none. During these six and one-half decades, several paramount chiefs had sat on the throne of Aboh and the CMS had made each of them the false promise of a church and a school.

This was a crucial event in the history of missionary beginnings in Anioma. The late start at Aboh meant that Christianity would spread late into the surrounding hinterland. This largely explains why the Christian religion made little or no progress in the entire Ukwuani district until well into the colonial period. The late start at Agbor also explains the late spread of Christianity in the Ika districts. As we have seen, Christian missionary activities in Anioma were concentrated in the Asaba district, and when the Ekumeku society began its anti-Christianity campaign, this district became the hub of violence and counter-violence.

Despite the apparent failure of the CMS missionaries in the region, we must not lose sight of the fact that they were pioneers and, like all pioneers, were bound to grapple with countless difficulties, especially among a people who had no inclination yet to abandon the customs of their ancestors. But it could also be perceived that the appearance of the Catholics on the scene, far from slowing down the progress of the CMS, helped to speed up the Christianization process of Anioma by, at least, creating among the people a familiarity with Christianity. During subsequent years, some converts oscillated between one brand of Christianity and another. After 1930, some became the leaders and flocks of the emerging African churches. At the same time many converts and baptized Christians, whether Anglican or Catholic, became nominal Christians who would not go to church. In the next chapter we shall show how the Catholic fathers came to Anioma and how their presence affected the cultural and political history of Anioma.

NOTES

1. *Church Missionary Intelligencer* (1879), 239.
2. CMS, CA3/04/1875, from the annual reports of Bishop Crowther, 1875.
3. Percy Amuray Talbot, *The Peoples of Southern Nigeria* (London: Frank Cass, 1969), 2: 28.
4. Francis A. Arinze, *Sacrifice in Ibo Religion,* (Ibadan: Ibadan Univ. Press, 1970), 22.
5. Talbot, *The Peoples of Southern Nigeria*, 2: 26-27
6. Ibid., 26-27.
7. Ibid., 46.
8. Elizabeth Isichei, "The Elizabeth Isichei Collection" in *Western Igbo*, ed. Don C. Ohadike and Rick N. Shain, *Jos Oral History and Literature Texts*, Vol. 6, (Jos: Univ. of Jos, 1988), 22.
9. Ibid., 9-10.
10. Talbot, *The Peoples of Southern Nigeria*, 2:27-28.
11. CMS, CA3/09 from the journal extracts of John Buck from September 1873 to September 1874.

12. CMS, CA/04/1875, from the annual reports of Bishop Crowther, 1875.

13. CMS G3/A3/1882/131, November 5, 1887, Crowther to Lang.

14. Peter R. McKenzie, *Inter-Religious Encounters in West Africa* (Leicester: U. K., Univ. of Leicester, 1976).

15. CMS, CA/04/1875, from the annual reports of Bishop Crowther, 1875.

16. Ibid.

17. CMS, CA3/031, from the annual letters of Rev. Edward Phillips, October, 1875.

18. CMS, CA3/04/744/761, from the reports of Bishop Crowther, 1876.

19. Ibid.

20. Ibid.

21. Ibid.

22. Clara Nkechi Onianwa, "The Coming of Christianity to Asaba," research project, Department of History, University of Jos, 1980, 45.

23. *Church Missionary Intelligencer* (1879), 230.

24. CMS CA3/09 journal extract of John Buck, 1873-74.

25. See Chapter 6.

26. Onianwa, "The Coming of Christianity to Asaba," 45.

27. CMS, G3/A3/1888/77, Johnson to Lang, July 5, 1888.

28. CMS, G3/A3/1892/52, Rev. Julius Spencer reporting from Asaba, December 1891.

29. *Church Missionary Intelligencer* (1879), 238.

30. CMS, G3/A3/1900/84, memorandum of interview, June 21, 1900, between Sir Ralph Moor and Dr. Harford Battersby, Rev. H. E. Fox, and Rev. F. Baylis.

31. *Church Missionary Intelligencer,* 1879, 239.

32. Ibid.

33. Ibid.

34. CMS, CA3/09 from the journal extracts of John Buck, from September 1873 to September 1874. See also CMS, CA3/031, from the annual letters of Rev. Edward Phillips, October 1875.

35. *Church Missionary Intelligencer* (1895), 292.

36. *Church Missionary Intelligencer* (1901), 388.

37. Ibid., 715.

38. CMS, G3/A3/1888/77 Rev. Johnson to Lang, July 5, 1888.

39. *Church Missionary Intelligencer* (1908), 767.

40. CMS, G3/A3/1889/166, observations of Bishop Crowther on new arrangements for the Niger Mission, 1889.

41. *Church Missionary Intelligencer* (1887), 222.

42. CMS, G3/A3/1889/66, observations of Bishop Crowther, 1889.

43. *Church Missionary Intelligencer* (1887), 223-224.

44. CMS, G3/A3/1892/69, H. H. Dobinson to Lang, January 2, 1892.

45. CMS, G3/A3/1887/131, November 5, 1887 Crowther to Lang.

46. CMS, G3/04, John Buck to Bishop Crowther, December 23, 1878.

47. CMS, CA3/04, Crowther's report on annual visits to the Niger Mission, February 14, 1879.

48. CMS, G3/A3/1886/39, Crowther to Lang.

49. Ibid.

50. *Church Missionary Intelligencer* (1897), 837.

51. CMS, G3/A3/1899/26, from the Annual Letter of Rev. T. J. Dennis, received February 10, 1899.

52. CMS, G3/A3/1905/133, minutes of the executive council, 1905.

53. *Church Missionary Intelligencer* (1857), 194.

54. *Church Missionary Intelligencer* (1855), 117–19.

55. MacGregor Laird and R. A. K. Oldfield, *Narrative of an Expedition into the Interior of Africa, by the River Niger in 1832, 1833 and 1834* vol. 1 (London: Richard Bently, 1837) passim.

56. William Allen and T. R. H. Thomson, *A Narrative of the Expedition to the River Niger in 1841* vol. 1. (London: Richard Bently, 1848).

57. *Church Missionary Intelligencer* (1857), 194.

58. Samuel Crowther, *Journal of an Expedition up the Niger and Tshadda Rivers in 1854* (2nd ed. with a new introduction by J. F. A. Ajayi), (London: Cass, 1970).

59. *Church Missionary Intelligencer* (1855), 117–19.

60. *Church Missionary Intelligencer* (1858), 28–29. The ensuing account is from this source.

61. Rev. Samuel Crowther and John Christopher Taylor, *The Gospel on the Banks of the Niger* (London: Dawsons, 1868).

62. CMS, G3/A3/1883/86, Crowther to Lang, April 5, 1883. The ensuing account is from this source.

63. CMS, G3/A3/1887/131, November 5, 1887, Crowther to Lang.

5

~~~

THE PEOPLE OF ANIOMA MEET THE ROMAN CATHOLIC FATHERS

IN THE BEGINNING

THE STORY of the establishment of a Catholic mission at Lokoja and its subsequent evacuation to Asaba forms an interesting link between the foundation of the Société des Missions Africaines (Society of African Missions, or SMA) and the spread of Roman Catholicism into Anioma. The SMA was founded in 1856 in France by Msgr. Marion de Bresillac. Like the Church Missionary Society, the SMA was one of those evangelical societies that were launched in Europe with a multitude of aims, one of which was to bring Christianity to Africa, partly as a means of driving out completely the slave trade and partly as an agency of colonial penetration.

On August 28, 1860 the entire territory extending from the mouth of the Volta River to the mouth of the Niger was committed by the Congregation of the Propagation of the Faith in Rome to the SMA.[1] In the beginning it was known as the vicariate of Benin, and Lagos was named as its headquarters.

Soon after the formation of this district, the SMA attracted to its work a number of young men, commissioned to man the vicariate. The Reverend Jules Poirier was its first superior, and from his headquarters at Lagos he started the famous farm at Topo, near Badagry, "where it was intended to found a Christian village living on the improved methods of farming begun and supervised by the Mission."[2]

Father Poirier also planned to use this method of evangelization in the area around Lokoja, where he dreamed of founding a nucleus of Christian villages.[3] In 1882 Father Poirier dispatched two priests to tour Bida, which at this time was the overlord of Lokoja. The tour was successfully undertaken and, because the Niger and the Benue rivers were an established trading area and a potential fruitful missionary field, the SMA lost no time in designating it a separate missionary jurisdiction.[4] Hoping that the gospel would spread rapidly in this "virgin" area, in 1884 Pope Leo XIII formally declared the new Prefecture Apostolic of the Upper Niger.

The new mission territory was to be run by the SMA fathers who had been working in the vicariate of Benin. Father Poirier was appointed its first prefect in 1884 and in the same year he was requested to proceed to Bida. Accompanied by Rev. Philip Fiorentini and Rev. Piollet, Poirier left Lagos by boat, hoping to get as far as Bida, but was forced to stop at Lokoja because the region above the Niger-Benue confluence was becoming politically unstable as the Muslim invaders advanced south.[5]

The priests had hoped that the French traders and officials who had already established a strong presence on the Upper Niger would assist them on arrival, but when they got to Brass (in the Niger Delta) en route to Lokoja, they learned that the French firms trading on the Niger were abandoning their factories to an English firm (the Niger Company), which was scheming to take possession of both banks of the Niger.[6] Though saddened by this information, the Catholic fathers sailed up the Niger and arrived safely at Lokoja, where they were received *avec cordialité* by Commandant Mattei, who confirmed that the French were about to leave the town but consented to postpone his departure for another month in order to help the missionaries settle in.[7] The priests were also warmly received by the agents of the Niger Company and the CMS.

Meanwhile, Mattei acted on behalf of Father Poirier and his colleagues, enabling them to secure a piece of land for their mission. Their "little resources" could only cover the cost of erecting a small hut which served as their entire establishment. Meanwhile Mattei promised Father Poirier that representatives of the French government would soon arrive and come to their assistance. After a whole month of patient waiting, during which the missionaries almost died from violent attacks of fever, no representative of the French government appeared, and finally Mattei left Lokoja "with tears in his eyes."[8]

Lokoja had been a prosperous city until the assaults by the Islamic jihads of the nineteenth century. Situated at the confluence of the two major rivers, the town was strategically located for trade. The CMS and some English and French trading companies had established themselves there before the jihadists menaced the area, but as war and insecurity advanced southward, the CMS and the European traders began to transfer their activities elsewhere. As the unrest increased, Captain (later Sir) George Taubman Goldie amalgamated the remaining British and French firms trading on the Niger into the National African Company; in 1886 the company was granted a Royal Charter and moved its administrative headquarters from Lokoja to Asaba. The CMS also abandoned Lokoja and concentrated its efforts at Onitsha and Asaba.

Rather than follow the Niger Company and the CMS to Asaba, and despite the obvious difficulties, the Catholic fathers stubbornly remained in Lokoja and suffered greatly. Father Fiorentini was attacked by fever, from which he never recovered; he died on October 25, 1885 and was buried at Lokoja. Father Dornan also died soon afterwards. Of the four newly ordained priests who had been sent to reinforce the original priests at Lokoja, two died on arrival. These men were soon followed to the grave by two nuns who had just been sent out to Lokoja. "It soon became clear to the Fathers," wrote J. J. Hilliard, "that as far as evangelization was concerned they were up against a stone wall."[9] The mission had no future whatsoever.

Perhaps more discouraging than these personal tragedies was the fact that they all appeared to be in vain, since during the four years (1884–88) that the fathers labored in Lokoja, they failed to win a single convert. All they could boast of were a dozen youths redeemed from slavery by Father Poirier with a few yards of Lyoneese silk in Bida; at that same market between three and four hundred slaves were being sold every day.[10]

In 1888, the surviving priests were more than glad to accept an invitation from Sir James Marshall, an official of the Royal Niger Company, to evacuate Lokoja and come over to Asaba. The process of withdrawal began in 1888 and lasted till 1892 when all the priests and nuns, together with their "small army of redeemed slaves," abandoned Lokoja and settled in Asaba, which became their new headquarters.[11]

THE CATHOLIC FATHERS COME TO ANIOMA

The Society of African Missions started off at Asaba with a number of advantages that the Church Missionary Society (CMS) did not initially enjoy, the most important being official patronage. When the CMS established itself at Asaba in 1875, Britain had no foothold in that town. Relations between British subjects and the people of Asaba were regulated only by goodwill. In 1884, a British colonial agent, Consul Hewett, managed to conclude a treaty with the chiefs of Asaba, article 6 of which read: "All ministers of the Christian religion shall be permitted to reside and exercise their calling within the territories of the aforesaid Kings, Queens, and Chiefs, who hereby guarantee to them full protection. All forms of religious worship and religious ordinances may be exercised within the territories of the aforesaid kings, queens and chiefs, and no hindrance shall be offered thereto."[12]

This treaty was concluded before the Berlin Conference of 1884–85, certainly at a time when Britain still did not have effective control of the Niger. There was therefore no means of guaranteeing that this clause of the treaty would be observed. However, after the conquest of Asaba in 1888 by the forces of the Royal Niger Company, the British began to exercise some political control over the town. It was at this time that, Sir James Marshall, who ordered the conquest of Asaba, "personally" invited the Catholic fathers to establish themselves in the town.

Marshall was a high court judge in addition to being an employee of the Royal Niger Company. He had already acquired great influence in other parts of West Africa before the company requested that he establish a regular judicial system at its headquarters at Asaba.[13] Sir James was also a good Catholic. By the time he arrived at the Lower Niger, the Holy Ghost Fathers, who belonged to another branch of the Catholic church, had established themselves at Onitsha, and Marshall demonstrated his adherence to the Catholic faith by crossing the Niger River every Sunday morning to take part in divine worship at Onitsha.[14] At the same time he urged that a Catholic mission be established at Asaba. In a letter to Father Poirier at Lokoja, he assured the priest that he would give the Catholic missionaries every possible assistance if they would come to Asaba.[15] Father Carlo Zappa was later to write that Marshall showed himself to be a good Roman Catholic by insisting that the Catholic mission benefited from the presence of the Royal Niger Company in Asaba.[16]

In May 1888 Fathers Poirier and Zappa responded to Marshall's invitation by coming down from Lokoja to examine the prospects. On May 17, they were welcomed by Marshall and his Roman Catholic colleague, V. N. Kaner.[17] The Company acted swiftly to enable the priests to secure a suitable site for a mission overlooking the Niger. Father Zappa remained behind to direct the work of the new mission while Father Poirier returned to Lokoja to begin closing down the mission there.

Though Marshall left Asaba in the same year, he was succeeded by Chief Judge V. N. Kaner, another staunch Catholic, who continued the policy of assisting and protecting the Catholics.[18] The political and economic situations at Asaba were infinitely different from and better than at Lokoja and before the end of the year the missionaries had succeeded in erecting a house for the fathers and a convent for the sisters.

Apart from official patronage, the Catholics benefited tremendously from the tireless ministry of Father Carlo Zappa who did for the SMA what Bishop Crowther did for the CMS on the Niger. The difference, however, was that while Crowther spent only two or three months of each year in his diocese,[19] Zappa, apart from an occasional leave of absence abroad, stayed permanently on the Niger. Many years after Zappa's death, people in the Asaba district still remembered him as Father *Ozo-kpo-kpo*. This was an expression coined by the local people to depict the tireless steps that he paced up and down the streets of the towns. In fact, as we shall see below, the history of the Catholic mission in the Asaba district from its foundation in 1888 to 1917 could be written around the life and work of this man.

However, despite official patronage and the role played by Father Zappa, the Catholics did not immediately make much headway at Asaba. Although the Catholic mission attracted a sizeable following, the membership did not comprise the indigenous people. On the contrary, some of the earliest members of the flock were employees of the Royal Niger Company, while others were slaves. The situation at Asaba remained unpromising for Father Zappa and his colleagues until 1892, when the mission post at Lokoja was completely abandoned and Father Voigt, accompanied by the sisters and some former slaves who had been converted to Christianity, came down to settle at Asaba.[20]

Some Asabans abhorred the sight of the white priests, who fraternized with slaves and outcasts, but the fathers and sisters were not dismayed by this disapproval.[21] Instead, they continued to show compassion for the needy, the destitute, and the sick, as a report by Sister Boniface of the Asaba mission indicates. "Last week," she wrote, "we received a poor old woman who used to sleep outside because her relatives didn't want her. When I brought her to the house of our protected ones she was dancing with joy." Sister Boniface further reported that they received children whose mothers died when giving birth to them. "Ordinarily," she wrote, "they leave them to die. We are happy to take them and care for them as long as God leaves them with us."[22] What Sister Boniface did not tell her readers was why the old woman was left to sleep outside, or why children whose mothers died when giving birth to them were abandoned. She ignored the ramifications of Igbo culture, and like other European-trained missionaries of that period, instead emphasized "African barbarity" in order to justify the mission to the "Dark Continent." In any case, to win converts, the Catholic priests adopted a number of strategies which the CMS did not consider. First, Father Zappa set up a center for the training of catechists. Second, he concentrated a great deal of the mission's effort on giving medical attention to the sick.

Despite these charitable acts, the bulk of the people of Asaba still shunned the new religion, with only a negligible number impressed by these acts. It appears that the first "native" convert of the Roman Catholic Mission at Asaba was one Thomas Okolo, who was converted in 1893.[23] Okolo may have been attracted to Christianity by the compassion the Catholic pioneers showed toward a dying man, an assumption supported by some of Zappa's letters. In a dispatch of 1894, he stated that the baptism of Okolo influenced others, while a year later, he attributed the conversion of some Asabans to works of charity.[24]

Despite his seemingly tireless effort, Zappa himself was faced with a problem; he could speak Italian, French, and English, but did not know how to communicate with the local people, nor did he believe that education was the best method of spreading the gospel. He never favored the strategy of mass preaching. He would rather visit people in their homes, to impress on them the "foolishness" of following the traditional religion. Zappa therefore had the need to learn the Igbo, Edo, Urhobo, Itsekiri, Ishan, Afenmai, and Igbira languages since his ministry brought him in contact with the speakers of these languages.[25]

However, to Father Zappa, Igbo was the most important of these, and he therefore took a number of Igbo catechists with him to France, where they studied the French language. When they returned, they helped him to compile a French-Igbo and Igbo-French dictionary.[26] With the aid of this dictionary and his catechists, Zappa was able to quickly master the Igbo language. He subsequently promoted the study of local languages as a strategy for Catholic expansion.

By the early 1890s the Society of African Missions had become firmly established at Asaba and from then onward missionary activity into the hinterland became frequent. As more and more priests arrived from Europe, and as more and more catechists were trained locally, the Catholics made some progress in the neighboring districts. However, by December 1899 only four stations had been effectively occupied in Anioma. These were Asaba, Illah, Issele-Ukwu, and Igbuzo. Others, such as Okpanam, Ezi and Onicha-Olona, were out-stations.

The Illah Station

From Asaba Father Zappa began to visit the neighboring settlements with a view to opening up stations in them. For a time, however, the SMA could not carry on its work effectively in any other town outside Asaba. For one thing, the people of the Asaba district remained generally hostile to Europeans, and for another, Zappa could not find enough co-workers.

In 1893 a priest was sent to him, bringing the number of the fathers in the prefecture to five. The newcomer was Father John Baptist Frigerio, whom Alexander Nzemeka, a later-day Catholic priest, described as "an inexperienced young man of twenty-five, just ordained only a few months earlier." Nzemeka further stated that "by the time of Father Frigerio's appearance on the scene of the nascent mission enterprise acquaintance with the people around Asaba had developed to the extent that Fr. Zappa . . . felt confident enough to approach the native chiefs for a formal grant of land on which churches could be built."[27]

At Illah, the SMA dealt with the chiefs through the agents of the Royal Niger Company, which at that time had a palm oil factory and a fairly large trading post in the town. On January 22, 1895, the SMA acquired a piece of land for the purpose of erecting a church. Following the usual mission policy, Father Frigerio and his assistant, André Gex, built a convent there for the nuns who joined the priests later in the year.[28]

For nearly thirty years (1893–1920) Father Frigerio labored at Illah. From there he made several attempts to evangelize the neighboring towns, but his efforts were almost negligible because of Anioma's mistrust for Europeans. For example, he was attacked by the people of Ebu during one of his visits to their town. It was only after the consolidation of British rule in the area that Frigerio succeeded in establishing new stations in Ezi, Onicha-Olona and Ebu.

What Father Frigerio was able to accomplish was bringing the Catholics of Illah into a closely knit group. This small community of converts gave him a large piece of land on which they also cultivated yams and rubber for him.[29] Father Frigerio visited the sick in their homes and was able to baptize many children. Some orphans were cared for at the orphanage, which was run by the Sisters of Our Lady of the Apostles. The missionaries built a school in 1899 and Frigerio insisted on school attendance for children. As the people of this district recognized the importance of western education in the new colonial situation, they flocked to the mission centers to enroll for classes. The Catholic fathers capitalized on this rush by insisting that baptism was a prerequisite for enrollment.[30]

In 1920, Father Frigerio was transferred to Igbuzo by order of the new bishop of the prefecture, Bishop Broderick. "It was with much reluctance that he consented to go," wrote Nzemeka. "His work at Illah had been so fruitful and Illah had become such an important station that it was a place of constant resort by Fathers all around."[31] Father Frigerio labored at Igbuzo for several years and eventually returned to his hometown in Italy, where he died in 1928.

The Issele-Ukwu Mission

Since coming to Anioma, Father Zappa had contemplated opening up a mission post at Issele-Ukwu, and in time he sent word to the Obi of Issele-Ukwu requesting his permission to visit his chiefdom. The necessary permission finally came, and Zappa, accompanied by guides and carriers, left Asaba on May 15, 1893. They made brief stops at Okpanam, Issele-Asaba, Anifekide, and Ubulu-Okiti and arrived Issele-Ukwu the following morning.

The king's messengers received the party and took them to "an influential personality, Moque [Mokwenye] an intimate friend of the King." Zappa also visited the king's mother, Sidi (Chidi). From Mokwenye and Chidi Zappa learned that "the king was favorably disposed" toward the Catholics.

Father Zappa's interview with Obi Egbuna of Issele-Ukwu was cordial even though it was packed with emotion. The priest seized the opportunity to preach against certain aspects of the Anioma culture.[32] Though enraged at the unwarranted attack on the customs of his fathers, the Obi calmly dismissed the priest, telling him that he needed time to consider his request.

Fifteen days after this visit, Father Zappa again travelled to Issele-Ukwu. The Obi received him with great cordiality. "His answers were clear and to the point," noted Father Zappa, and in the end, he gave the Catholics a "vast area" of land. In a report that Zappa sent to Europe, he attributed his success in acquiring this piece of land to Chidi, the queen mother.

A portion of the land allocated to Father Zappa was immediately cleared and a hut was built on it with wood supplied from the nearby forest. One year later, the Catholics added more structures to the establishment. Soon, instead of just a single hut, the compound included a collection of several mud houses, some of which the Catholics used as a church and a place for instruction in catechism. Father Rousselet was placed in charge. Like the Illah mission, the one at Issele-Ukwu made progress and in 1898 a large house for the priests was completed. In 1899, the Issele-Ukwu mission had in its register the names of twenty baptized adults and twenty-seven baptized infants, figures that represented a slow but encouraging progress.[33]

The Igbuzo Mission

From the outset the people of Igbuzo had opposed the establishment of European trade and missions, so that despite its large population and proximity to Asaba, the town had no Christian mission establishment or European trading post until after its destruction in 1898 by the forces of the Royal Niger Company (See chapter 6). As early as 1890, "long before a Father took up residence in the town,"[34] the Catholic mission at Asaba had sent catechists to Igbuzo to carry out private evangelization, resulting in many private baptisms. In 1899, after the temporary subjugation of the warrior chiefs, Father Ignatius Hummel was appointed the first pastor of Igbuzo. Work on the church building commenced at once and was completed the following year.

It would appear that despite the late start, the Igbuzo mission made more rapid progress than the other Catholic missions in Anioma. The report of the prefecture which Father Zappa sent to the Society for the Propagation of the Faith for the year 1899–1900, showed that Igbuzo had the largest number of both infant and adult baptisms:[35]

Town	Adult Baptisms	Infant Baptisms	Total
Asaba	17	81	98
Illah	7	64	71
Ezi	2	22	24
Issele-Ukwu	20	27	47
Onicha-Olona	—	4	4
Igbuzo	1	80	81
Okpanam	—	30	30
Total	47	308	355

Although the total for Asaba appears to be higher than that of Igbuzo, the fact is that by 1900 Asaba had been evangelized by the Catholics for twelve years as compared to only one year at Igbuzo. The total for Igbuzo includes all the private baptisms administered by the catechists who came from Asaba prior to the official opening of the Igbuzo mission. Also interesting is the number of adult baptisms compared with infant baptisms.

THE SMA 1900-20

The Society of African Missions entered a new period of challenge and difficulty after 1900 when Britain, having revoked the charter of the Royal Niger Company, assumed direct responsibility for administering the Niger territories. Although the Catholics succeeded in opening up many stations in the two decades beginning in 1900, their work was very much disturbed by two major factors, namely, opposition from ritual specialists and chiefs, and the First World War.

Opposition from Ritual Specialists and Chiefs

The people of Anioma were particularly hostile to the Roman Catholic fathers, but we must remember that the Catholics inherited the legacy of prejudice which the local populations had developed against the first European visitors. The conquest of Asaba and the activities of British gunboats were still fresh in the mind of the people, and as the years passed, rather than tensions easing, the people instead conceived the grand aspiration of driving the white men back into the sea.

An atmosphere that was already charged with suspicion and distrust was worsened when the Catholic fathers, like the Anglican preachers before them, denounced in clear terms all aspects of the traditional customs and religion. On a number of occasions, the priests took it upon themselves personally to destroy the objects of worship of the local people. For instance, Rev. Father Voigt, while en route to Illah, set fire to a shrine. The local inhabitants, who were baffled by this unprovoked behavior of the white priest, "decided to revenge this desecration of their shrine,"[36] which they soon carried out under the banner of the Ekumeku movement (see chapter 4)

For much of this time the traditional healers, seers, and chiefs protested against Catholic interference with their cherished religion, but were ignored. The Anioma grievances were not just religion-based, but were also based on economic and political considerations because in the traditional context, ritual and political powers issued from the same source; one could not be separated from the other, as one implied the other.[37] The chiefs and ritual specialists rightly judged that their power and influence over their people would diminish in the same proportion as the influence of the Catholic fathers increased. Like Madam Tinubu, a prominent Lagos merchant and community leader, the chiefs and ritual specialists of Anioma were quick to realize that missionaries were "pathfinders" of European imperialism.[38] Elizabeth Isichei has noted that if the indigenous rulers initially welcomed missions and trade, experience often taught them to "distrust the Greeks bearing gifts." This, Isichei noted, explains why the initial welcome was often succeeded by a period of persecution, for it did not take the traditional rulers much time to realize that missionary teaching tended to undermine the customs of the society and even challenge their own authority. These, Isichei continued, were the fundamental circumstances surrounding the martyrdom of Joshua Hart in Bonny, where the local chiefs on many occasions persecuted their Christian slaves in the fear that the latter, who were becoming numerically superior, might declare their freedom.[39]

While the Anioma communities were already worried about slaves who began to take advantage of the European presence to assert their freedom, many were alarmed about a growing tendency at the other end of the social spectrum—chiefs who began to convert to Christianity and receive the water of baptism. Some of these very chiefs had helped to organize the Ekumeku movement and had led the people into a protracted war against the Europeans, yet at the turn of the century some of them began to embrace Christianity. Among the first Anioma chiefs to accept the Roman Catholic faith was Obi Ajufo of Igbuzo, a wealthy and prominent man with twelve wives and many children, who decided in 1901 to give up the traditional religion of his fathers and follow Christ. Fearing that his conversion would have serious consequences for the community, the townspeople rose against him. The chiefs of Igbuzo shunned him, his wives threatened him, and his children warned that they would kill him if he failed to return to the religion of his fathers. Obi Ajufo fled to the Catholic mission compound where he confronted the holy fathers with his woes:

> Petitions, insults, curses, the most biting gibes—my ears heard all these. My children declared they would no longer cultivate my farms, the eldest threatened me, axe in hand. My wives swore they would all sleep on the public way, outside my gate, so that I might be put to shame. The chiefs of the town have excluded me from the great council because my mouth no longer speaks the language of our fathers.[40]

Even well into the colonial period, the people of Anioma continued to protest against the Catholics. "It was not rare," wrote Father Hilliard, "for the chiefs to falsely accuse prominent members of the church in order to discredit the work of the Missionaries in Government eyes."[41] The government itself was opposed to Catholic interference with local politics. In 1899 the agent general of the Royal Niger Company attributed the Ekumeku rising to "fathers mixing in politics," in the same year Sir Ralph Moor insisted on abstention from politics as a necessary condition for allowing Christian missionaries to establish themselves in these territories, and the Government asked the Catholics to leave Issele-Ukwu and Illah entirely.[42]

These conflicting forces explain the dilemma of the Catholic priests. In their attempt to assist the colonial government they incurred the wrath of the local people. During the numerous encounters that ensued, their work was greatly disturbed as missions were destroyed and missionaries chased off. Recalling the effects of one such encounter, Father Strub wrote that the conflict had "done us considerable harm. Our progress has been retarded. . . . Sums which would have been used for the establishment of new missions are used for the restoration of old. Our converts are so frightened that they have gone into hiding, not to be identified as those who supported the white men. . . . The question of new missions is not envisaged for the moment."[43] In addition, the colonial administration turned the Catholics into scapegoats for their own bad administration. As already stated, for example, some colonial administrators strongly believed that the Ekumeku society was opposed, not necessarily to British imperial presence, but to the Roman Catholics in particular.[44]

Certainly, this indictment was exaggerated. The truth is simply that, in the event of any misunderstanding between the government and its colonial subjects, the latter regarded all foreigners and their property as legitimate objects of prey. Even before the people of Ogwashi-Ukwu attacked the Catholic mission in 1909, for example, they had already destroyed the CMS buildings at Azungwu (September 11, 1909), and the Government Rest House (some time in August 1909).[45] Also, during the Agbor rising of 1906 several Benin paramount chiefs were killed by the resisters.[46] In 1911 the people in the Kwale district attacked Yoruba traders as well as government officials.[47] These incidents confirm that the people of Anioma did not direct their opposition specifically against the Catholics, but against all foreigners whose activities were suspected of tearing the social fabric.

Before 1900 the Catholic fathers were virtually the only Europeans living among the Anioma people. Only at Asaba and at Illah could other Europeans be found. These other Europeans were traders and soldiers of the Royal Niger Company, whose pretensions to imperial authority were already provoking much discontent in the area. But in the event of any outbreak of hostilities between these Europeans and the local people, the priests were singled out for special harassment. Referring to the Ogwashi-Ukwu expedition, after which the Catholics were asked by the colonial administration to remove themselves from that town, Father Hilliard defended the fathers, saying they were "in no way responsible for any violation of law or order, but on the contrary they were most helpful to the officers of the expedition."[48] Father Strub concluded, on the other hand, that the local populations opposed the fathers because the native residents were "incapable of distinguishing between the traders who dictated disagreeable laws to them and the Fathers who tried to make them accept the laws of Jesus Christ."[49]

But the people of Anioma knew fully well the difference between European traders and the holy fathers; they knew that one oppressed them in the name of profit, and the other in the name of Jesus. They knew that in those hostile times, the line that ran between "the disagreeable laws" of the traders and "the laws of Jesus Christ" was as thin as air. They were certain that Father Zappa, who spied on them and disclosed their war plans to their enemies, could not have been their friend. If, therefore, they directed their hostility toward both traders and missionaries, it was because they knew that both were dangerous. In any case, what Father Hilliard and Father Strub did not seem to perceive was that if two parties were in conflict, any assistance given to one party was assistance denied the other or, as is commonly said, "One who is not with us is against us."

Apart from the political problems posed by the Christian missionary presence, the people of Anioma were disturbed by some nonpolitical issues. As Rev. M. Toner rightly pointed out, "Breaking with paganism and joining the Church often required great courage because sickness in the home, failure of crops and many other disappointments were conveniently blamed on the defection of individuals from pagan sacrifices."[50] The Sunday rest, said Toner, was looked upon as laziness or escapism. Since the Christian way of life was inconsistent with the traditional way of life, the Christians were blamed for introducing disobedience into the society. He argued that these charges were not always untrue, since some young catechumens, finding themselves freed from traditional fears that had formally restrained them, took some time to gain their poise in a Christian way.[51] Such misunderstandings were sometimes serious enough to provoke head-on collisions.

It was also true that Father Zappa, like all his conferees, acted as an informal, unpaid spy for the colonial administration. This role of the Catholic fathers greatly annoyed the people of Anioma, contributing in large measure to their ill feelings toward the Catholics. In fact, throughout the period of the Ekumeku wars, the Catholic fathers never gave up the habit of creating divisions within the ranks of the resisters, as by taking the confessions of condemned Ekumeku veterans awaiting execution or by persuading the Obi of Issele-Ukwu to dissociate himself from the movement.[52]

The Impact of the First World War on the Performance of the SMA

The first World War was another factor that affected the performance of the Catholic mission in Anioma. Prior to 1914, only one SMA priest, Father Dornan, an Irishman who died only a few months after his arrival at Lokoja in 1885, was recruited from an English-speaking country. The rest were either French, Italian, or Alsatian, the latter being regarded as German at the time. The British government and private citizens treated these priests, not only as Papists, but also as foreigners. Since the days of the Royal Niger Company, the British had developed great jealousy for the French and Germans because of the competition for trade, and had generally regarded the Catholic fathers as agents of their respective countries.[53] For the time being, however, as long as these "foreigners" remained neutral in politics, no open hostility was shown them based on their faith or nationality, but the First World War changed that unwritten policy.

In July 1914, the colonial government of Nigeria announced to the people of the region that Serbia and Austria were at war with each other, and that Germany had declared war on France and Russia. On hearing this news some Catholic priests quickly fled. Fathers Anezo, Bourget and Lelierre left Asaba for Porto Novo while Father Ollier followed them from Forcados.[54] Three Alsatian fathers at Onitsha never had the chance to escape, even if they had so wished, for they were at once arrested and sent to Lagos as prisoners of war.[55] Although the French priests were not arrested, they were asked to enlist in the army.[56]

All the fathers—French, Italian, and Alsatian—were subjected to one form of harassment or another. At one time the French Consulate at Lagos demanded a list of all French reservist priests. At another time certain French fathers were told to appear before the consulate in Lagos where they were placed at the disposal of the French Military Authority. They were subsequently dispatched to Porto Novo to have their cases reviewed by French military officials and consulate there. In June 1915 the colonial government of Nigeria wanted to know if there was any German mission in the Niger region, and if any German priests had left the territory since the commencement of war.[57]

More disturbing was the order of the colonial government of Nigeria that all Alsatians should leave the country. A government dispatch of October 1914 directed that all German and Austrian firms in the Warri, Sapele, and Benin districts should cease trading, and that all subjects of these nations be sent to Lagos.[58] Fathers Frederich, Burr, Krauth, and Hebting were summoned to Asaba by the district commissioner. When they appeared, they were ordered not to leave their districts without official permission. This order was soon changed and these Alsatians were asked to prepare to leave the country entirely. "An order from home says that all German subjects are considered as prisoners and will be sent home," they were told.[59]

If this order had been followed to the letter, it would have seriously drained the manpower available to the Catholic mission. Already many mission stations were not fully operational because of a shortage of priests. Moreover, the activities of the mission continued to expand to distant places, particularly after 1915, when the Igbo converts began to follow railway construction up to the north, and the priests had to follow too, increasing the shortage of priests to a critical level.

All the Catholics at Asaba protested the decree which required all German and Alsatian priests to leave Nigeria. Father Zappa fought vehemently against it. In a letter to the authorities, he pointed out the danger the colony faced if missionaries who had devoted themselves to educating British subjects "without human reward" were compelled to leave the country.[60] Zappa's protest, notwithstanding, the Alsatians temporarily left their districts. The acting district officer of Onitsha later informed the Catholics that the Alsatian fathers could return to their stations and that it would be acceptable for them merely to report to the authorities once a week.[61]

From this sudden change of attitude toward the Alsatian fathers, Zappa and his colleagues concluded that Alsace had declared for France. Further in August 1914 Fathers Anezo, Bourget and Lelierre, who had been detained at Dahomey, returned to Asaba by the steamboat SS *Dilimi*. These men, including the rest of those on parole were, however, restrained by order of the assistant district officer "not to speak to the natives about anything concerning the war."[62]

Equally affected by the war was the financing of the Catholic mission, which prior to the outbreak of hostilities had been supported mostly from France. Over the years, funds had been dwindling and by 1905 the Fathers were forced to decree that parents must pay school fees for their children.[63] Even so, only very little cash was derived from this measure, and the war made matters worse as all assistance coming from France virtually stopped. Father Zappa was compelled to order the stations to cancel all expensive projects in view of a prolonged war, and he decreed that all expenses involved in building and expansion should be reduced to the barest minimum. The supreme council also decided to deduct ten shillings per month from each priest's allowance, as war indemnity.[64]

Priests could not go home on leave, as they had to wait for the cessation of hostilities. This was very painful because all Europeans serving in the tropics eagerly looked forward to occasional leave abroad, as it afforded them the opportunity to get away from the climate and the concomitant tropical diseases. However, because of the war, some fathers served for more than nine years without going home on leave.[65]

Apart from these staffing and financial problems, the war sparked off panic within the European communities in Nigeria over real and imagined dangers. All Europeans were alarmed at the reports of sporadic violent outbursts by Nigerians. These outbursts were connected with the war, for there were rumors that Germany had defeated Britain in Europe, and many colonial subjects felt that the time had come to finally drive the British out from Nigeria. In the Awka area, the people attacked the police and opened the prison gates, and in northern Nigeria, the Tiv refused to pay their taxes and attacked the officials who came to collect them.[66] In the Muslim emirates, some religious activists, together with members of the ruling oligarchy who were not profiting from the colonial arrangements, seized the opportunity created by the war to call for a resumption of the jihad. Two policemen were imprisoned by the chief of Nsukwa[67] and, as we shall see in due course, the Kwale district became the scene of a widespread revolt against British rule. Some protests were passive and others somewhat sympathetic to the chaos in Europe. In southeastern Nigeria, where the priests of the Holy Ghost sect were laboring, several chiefs of Aguleri, Anam, and other places assembled themselves together and "solemnly decided" that Father Bubendrof should be sent home to Europe "to settle the palaver between the big chiefs in Germany and England."[68]

THE DEATH OF FATHER ZAPPA

From the second half of 1915 onward, the political climate began to look brighter for both African and European residents of Anioma. This change resulted from an effective British propaganda campaign which discredited the Germans and promised their colonial subjects a better life after the war. The native inhabitants believed this propaganda and began to cooperate with the British, first by maintaining "law and order," and then by making both cash and human contributions to the war effort.

For the SMA, the year 1915 was a turning point in another significant way. Father Zappa was allowed to re-open the Catholic mission stations at Obwashi-Ukwu and the neighboring districts; they had been closed in 1910 by order of the high commissioner. During the next two years the number of converts grew and there were few cases of molestation of Christians. However, in the midst of the improving situation, the Catholics were thrown into mourning by the death of Father Zappa. Describing the loss, a fellow priest stated that in 1917 Father Zappa, prefect apostolic of Western Nigeria, was feeling the increasing pinch of his fourth wartime Christmas at the Catholic Mission at Asaba. He was then in his fifty-sixth year and had spent thirty-one of them in the mission. Father Zappa had complained that he was very tired, the priest reported, a fact which "caused the fathers to stroke their beards in wonder." For, in all of Zappa's journeying up and down the Niger, his endless trekking from station to station, he was never known to make such an admission.[69]

The wonder caused by Zappa's admission of fatigue, notwithstanding, the fact remained that the man had been strained by the hardships and anxieties of the First World War. Although he carried on as usual after Christmas, it was clear that he was far from being well.[70] On January 15, 1917 he was hospitalized at Onitsha, where he was treated for a liver problem. After a few days in bed he seemed to be responding to treatment and was able to take short strolls in the evenings, but on January 25, his condition deteriorated. "Seeing that his end was near," wrote Father J. J. Hilliard, "he asked to be brought back across the Niger to Asaba to die."[71]

Father Zappa was granted his final request and was brought back to Asaba on a government river craft. He could speak only very faintly and, as Father Piotini observed, "He no longer had any hope of recovery." On the following day he received his last rites. He called in his fellow priests and received their blessing, after which he gave his to them. "The sick man," wrote Father Piotini, "was perfectly resigned and offered the sacrifice of his life for the conversion of the people." But it was with much difficulty that he muttered his last words. "Do not weep for me and do not pray for my recovery: pray rather that the good Lord will have mercy on me," Father Zappa told the fathers and sisters who pressed forward to see him. He died on January 30, 1917.[72]

To the Catholics the years 1900–17 had been difficult, but they had been able to brave many hardships under the leadership of Father Zappa. Now that the prefect had suddenly departed, the question was, "What next?" For two years the missionaries searched for a replacement, eventually finding him in Bishop Broderick, who in 1919 took over at Asaba. After the death of Father Zappa the SMA also made positive moves to address two of its most pressing problems, namely, the difficulties created by the ethnic origins of the fathers and the role of the Catholic mission in the educational progress of Nigeria. Until the war most priests had been French, Alsatian, Italian or German, but this ethnic mix had presented the missions with both political and language problems. The Niger mission of the SMA now had to decide whether or not it would continue to use these non-English-speaking ministers in an English colony.[73] They finally came to the decision to replace them with Irish priests. No consideration was given to western-educated Africans, and in 1920 the Nigerian mission field was handed over to the fathers of the Irish province of the society.[74]

The missionaries addressed the question of education by redefining the educational objectives of the Catholic mission, which had hitherto been unclear and sometimes nebulous. In fact, the most important contribution of the Catholics to Anioma was western education and its real inception can be dated to 1920 when this new approach was officially adopted. We shall look more closely into this in the concluding chapter of this book which summarizes the impact of the European presence and colonialism on Anioma, but for the time being, suffice it to say that ensuing generations of Nigerians would be increasingly exposed to the culture and belief systems of Europe and the west as the missions continued and expanded their educational outreach efforts.

NOTES

1. SMA, Rev. M. J. Walsh, "Catholic Contribution to Education in West Africa, 1861–1926." thesis, SMA Archives, Rome, 301.
2. Fr. J. J. Hilliard, "Father Zappa and his Mission," *EXIIT*, no. 3(May 1963): 14.
3. Ibid., 14.
4. SMA, Ref. SMA 3 B 45, 4.
5. Aaron Ekwu, "The Establishment of the Catholic Mission in Western Nigeria by the Society of African Missions, 1868–1920," Ph.D. dissertation, University of Vienna, 1967, 212.

6. SMA, Les Missions Catholiques, no. 1130, January 30, 1891, from the letters of R. P. Poirier, Vice-Prefect Apostolic of the Niger, 49.

7. Ibid., 49.

8. Ibid., 49–50.

9. Hilliard, "Father Zappa and his Mission," 15.

10. Ibid.

11. Ibid., 11.

12. For the treaties with chiefs of the Lower Niger, see for instance, PRO, FO2/167.

13. Ekwu, "The Establishment of the Catholic Mission," 214.

14. CMS, G3/43/1888/77 Johnson to Lang, July 5, 888.

15. Ekwu, "The Establishment of the Catholic Mission," 214.

16. SMA, 14/80302, Asaba, Zappa to superior, October 4, 1888.

17. Ibid.

18. CMS G3/1888/77, Johnson to Lang, July 5, 1888.

19. CMS, CA3/04/2893, copy of Consul T. L. McLeod's letter to the Bishop of Oxford asking him to appoint a white bishop for Lokoja. Dated February 24, 1868, part of the letter read: "The Native Mission here [Lokoja] is in complete failure. The worthy old Bishop Crowther is on the Niger excepting for two months of the year, and in consequence, everything gets worse and worse. . . ."

20. Hilliard, "Father Zappa and his Mission," 15.

21. Strub, L'Echo des Missions Africaines de Lyon, 1937, 106.

22. SMA, Les Missions Catholiques, no. 1282, December 29, 1893 from the letters of Sister Boniface of the SMA, Lyon, 615.

23. Clara Oniawa, "The Coming of Christianity to Asaba," research project, Department of History, University of Jos, 1980, 51.

24. SMA, 14/80302/15897, Zappa to Superior, July 21, 1893; SMA. Annals of the Propagation of the Faith, 1895, 197–98, from the letters of Father Zappa.

25. Ekwu, "The Establishment of the Catholic Mission," 218.

26. Ibid.

27. Alexander Nzemeka, One Hundred Years of the Roman Catholic Church at Illah (Benin City: Bendel Newspaper Corp., 1980), 10, 11.

28. SMA, Ref. SMA 3 B. 45, 10.

29. Nzemeka, One Hundred Years, 16.

30. Ibid., 17–19.

31. Ibid., 28.

32. SMA, Les Missions Catholiques, no. 1279, December 8, 1893, 586. The ensuing account is from this source, p. 587.

33. SMA, Ref. SMA 3 B. 45, 14.

34. Ibid., 13.

35. Ibid., 14.

36. SMA, 14/80404/15794, Strub, "Le Vicariat Apostolique de la Nigerie Occidentale depuis sa fondation jusqu'à nos jours," Folio 14.

37. Michael A. Onwuejeogwu, "An Outline Account of the Dawn of Igbo Civilization," Odinani: The Journal of Odinani Museum, Nri, 1, no. 1(1972): 48.

38. Emmanuel A. Ayandele, "The Missionary Factor in Northern Nigeria, 1870–1914," *Journal of the Historical Society of Nigeria* 3, no. 3(December 1966): 505. See also Ogbu Kalu, ed., *Christianity in West Africa: The Nigerian Story* (Ibadan: Ibadan Univ. Press, 1978), 21.

39. Elizabeth Isichei, *The Ibo People and the Europeans* (London: Faber and Faber, 1973), 102, 103.

40. SMA, *Annals of the Propagation of Faith,* 1902, letters from Father Zappa, 70.

41. SMA, Ref. SMA 3 B 45, 60.

42. SMA, 14/80302, 16005, Zappa to superior, September 14, 1899.

43. Strub, folio 15.

44. PRO, CO 520/36, telegraphic dispatch of June 12, 1906. (Signed) C.S. to Mr. Oliver.

45. SMA, Ref. SMA 3 B. 45, 38.

46. PRO, CO 520/36/30466, August 18, 1906. "Native Rising, Agbor District."

47. PRO, CO 583/21/02579, December 1, 1914, confidential report by Frederick Lugard to Lewis Harcourt.

48. SMA, Ref. SMA 3 B. 45, 24.

49. Strub, entry no. 15794 14/80404, 1928.

50. SMA, Fr. M. Toner, "A Co-operative in Nigeria," *EXIIT,* no. 3(May 1963): 18.

51. Ibid.

52. PRO, CO 520/3/270/36867, November 26, 1900, draft comment on report on result of inquiry made as to the actual losses sustained by the Catholic Mission at Illah. (Signed) C.S. to Antrobus, Colonial Office.

53. Felix K. Ekechi, *Missionary Enterprise and Rivalry in Igboland, 1857–1914* (London: Frank Cass, 1971), 71.

54. SMA, from the journal entries of Father Lelierre, in *Journals of Some Early Fathers* (July, 1914): 147–49.

55. From Father Zappa's diary, in ibid., 82.

56. Ibid., 82.

57. Ibid., 83.

58. PRO, CO 583/20/48783, December 8, 1914. Lugard to Colonial Office, November 18, 1914.

59. SMA, from Father Krauth's diary in *Journals of Some Early Fathers,* 149.

60. SMA, Ref. SMA 3 B. 45, 30.

61. SMA, from Father Zappa's diary, in *Journals of Some Early Fathers,* 73.

62. Ibid., 74.

63. SMA, from Father Hummel's diary, in ibid. February 1905.

64. SMA, from Father Lelierre's diary, in ibid. 71.

65. SMA, Ref. SMA 3 B. 45, 73.

66. SMA, from Father Zappa's entries, in *Journals of Some Early Fathers,* 75.

67. Ibid., 44.

68. Ekwu, "The Establishment of the Catholic Mission," 227.

69. SMA, Father Hilliard, "Father Zappa and His Mission," 13.

70. SMA, from Father Krauth's Diary in *Journals of Some Early Fathers* 153; SMA, Hilliard, "Father Zappa and his Mission," 13.

71. SMA, from Father Piotini's diary in *Journals of Some Early Fathers* 88–89. For the full account of Zappa's death.

72. SMA, from Father Krauth's diary, in *Journals of Some Early Fathers,* 154.

73. SMA, Ekwu, "The Establishment of the Catholic Mission," 15.

74. SMA, Walsh, "The Catholic Contribution to Education," 301

≈

6

~~~

POLITICAL HISTORY, 1860–1960

THE BRITISH CONQUEST OF ANIOMA

THE DISINTEGRATION of the Igbo society, which the Europeans initiated in 1857 with the establishment of commercial and cultural presence at Onitsha, was accelerated by the British imperial government when it embarked on a mission of conquest of Igboland in 1879. I have provided a detailed account of the British invasion of Western Igboland, otherwise known as Anioma elsewhere.[1] In order to establish the proper historical context, however, I will summarize here the major events in that invasion.

Because Anioma was the gateway into the Niger territories, the British saw it as a strategic location in their bid to expand their hegemony into that part of Africa. By the last quarter of the nineteenth century, British traders and government officials, because of the expeditions of the 1840s and 1850s, had gained access to but not effective control of the areas in the upper stretches of the Niger River. They established trading posts on both sides of the river and tried to monopolize both the import and export trades and, as time went on, began to defy the constituted authorities of the African chiefs in whose territories they did business. This defiance was made possible by the sudden appearance of gunboats in global politics; the disparity in technological levels between Europe and Africa had begun to manifest itself very decisively in favor of Europe.

Some African rulers in southeastern Nigeria who had welcomed the Europeans as trading partners were disturbed by this sudden change of attitude. Many, like the chiefs of Brass, Opobo, Calabar, Aboh,

Onitsha, and Asaba, protested the British intrusion. Some sent letters to the British Foreign Office in London, complaining that British traders were depriving them of their means of livelihood.[2] The Efik chiefs complained that the missionaries, who had been invited to provide basic education to the people were instead loading the school curriculum with religious instruction of which the Efiks already had enough.[3] Many communities warned that the Christians were inciting the wrath of the ancestors by desecrating the objects of worship, but rather than listen to their petitions, the British government in London sent gunboats to bombard them. In October 1879, Captain Burr of the warship *Pioneer,* acting under orders from the British War Office, sailed up the Niger River and opened fire on Onitsha. He also landed troops who destroyed "every object" they could find, killing many of the residents of the town in the process.[4] Four years later (1883), following a misunderstanding between a British trader and some Aboh merchants, three British ships stood in the middle of the Niger River and shelled Aboh, after which troops were sent ashore, drawing the people of the town into a war of resistance that caused the loss of many lives.[5] Again in the same year, some British gunboats shelled the town of Idah, razing it. Then in 1888, the forces of the British Royal Niger Company attacked and destroyed half of Asaba (See map 3).[6]

That was not the end of the atrocities perpetrated against the Niger communities by the British. Throughout the period 1886 to 1898, the forces of the Royal Niger Company remained busy with the wars of territorial annexation, which overwhelmed fifty-two towns in such scattered places as Patani and Akassa in the Niger Delta, Keffi and Wase on the Jos Plateau, Ilorin and Bida in the northwest, and Gloria Ibo and Oguta in the southeast.[7]

After the destruction of Asaba, the practice of protecting British citizens and of attacking African communities became an accepted British foreign policy. There also emerged a new pattern of conquest and penetration of parts of southeastern Nigeria. British agents used the slightest excuse as an opportunity to demonstrate their strength, to make the Africans fully understand that the British were their overlords and were determined to control them.[8] This policy resulted in incredible amounts of unnecessary violence; disputes that would have been settled amicably were approached with head-on confrontations. Ultimatum became a substitute for dialogue.

Anioma communities were still fragmented; the powers of the elders, chiefs and religious cults were still small and restricted to the villages and clans. There was a high level of discontent; what was lacking was mobilization. They could not organize their resistance

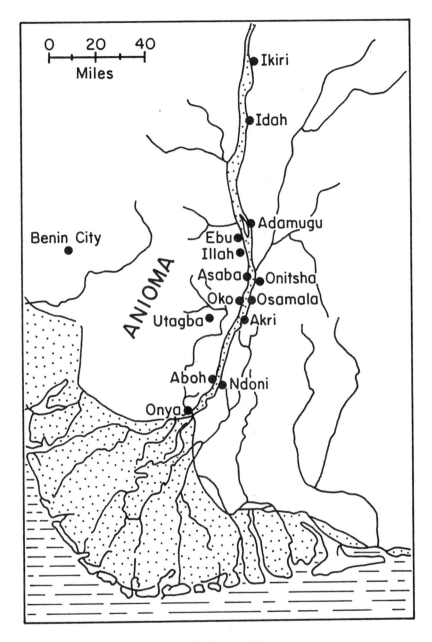

Map 3: The major towns of the Lower Niger

around charismatic figures, nor around centralized, shared religious beliefs, but when pushed to their limits the native inhabitants rallied around some groups of local power-holders. These were the local chiefs who had become increasingly militant in their dealings with the Europeans. These chiefs were the patriots who finally mobilized the peasants of Anioma against British military penetration.

However, partly because of its proximity to Asaba, the center of most British imperial activities at this time, and partly because of the militant nature of the people of Igbuzo, it was here that resistance initially flared. The warrior chiefs of Igbuzo formed companies of young warriors, *otu aya,* each company numbering between twenty and fifty men and named after its patron. In 1895 almost fifty of such companies had been formed in Igbuzo, the most popular being Otu Elikwu, Otu Ofogu, Otu Chidi, Otu Umejei, and Otu Uwechua. The patrons of these companies went further to form a coalition of warrior chiefs, called the *Otu Ochichi,* which met periodically to discuss matters relating to the British military invasion and the undermining of ancient customs and traditional belief systems. Patrons enabled their followers to secure firearms, charms, and military training. They managed to engage the forces of the Royal Niger Company in small-scale skirmishes until fighting of a different nature broke out in Issele-Ukwu when the warrior chiefs expanded their theater of operations.

In 1898, the people of Issele-Ukwu, alarmed by the excessive religious zeal of the Roman Catholic fathers who had recently established themselves in the town, rebelled against their paramount chief, contending also that the chief had exhibited a grave disrespect for the customs and democratic institutions of his people. A civil war broke out and the warrior chiefs of the neighboring towns who had joined the *Otu Ochichi* society, rather than act as mediators, flung themselves into the battle, siding with the Issele-Ukwu rebels. They dispatched the military arm of the society, soon to be known as the Ekumeku warriors, to fight side-by-side with the Issele-Ukwu rebels. Father Zappa, whose interests were identical to those of the paramount chief of Issele Ukwu, appealed to the Royal Niger Company for help.

Early in January 1898, the company's soldiers left Lokoja and entered Anioma to assist the paramount chief of Issele-Ukwu and his supporters. But rather than attack the rebels and their Ekumeku supporters in Issele-Ukwu, the soldiers attacked Igbuzo, forcing the Ekumeku warriors to abandoned their locations in and about Issele-Ukwu and to rush to the rescue of their headquarters. The forces of the Royal Niger Company, under the command of Lieutenant Festing, maintained the attacks against Igbuzo for six weeks, eventually razing the town. They also killed or captured many of the Ekumeku warriors. The Issele-Ukwu rebels and their Ekumeku supporters, seeing their cause hopeless and their capital in ruins, dispersed, and William Wallace, the head of the company, and Lieutenant Festing imposed a forced peace on Igbuzo. Thus, what had appeared to be a minor misunderstanding between the people of Issele-Ukwu and their paramount chief became the first battle in a series of military engagements that later became popularly known as the Ekumeku Wars.

Although the Ekumeku warriors were disappointed with the fall of Igbuzo, they were not defeated. Rather, they quickly reorganized their ranks and moved their center of resistance to the northern district, specifically, to Ezi and Onicha-Olona. Two months after the fall of Igbuzo, the Ekumeku entered Illah, which was well garrisoned by the forces of the Royal Niger Company, and destroyed the Roman Catholic mission church which had been causing much annoyance to the people. However, during a counter-offensive, the soldiers of the company successfully dislodged the insurgents from the town, but not before the news of the Ekumeku's bold moves had spread like a bush fire, encouraging the chiefs of the various communities, including some Ishan towns, to send their own warriors to aid in the struggle. Within a short time the Ekumeku warriors ransacked and burned down the Christian mission stations at Ezi, Ebu, and Ubulu-Ukwu and drove away their personnel. The Royal Niger Company responded by intensifying its military offensive. It bombarded all the settlements that were within reach of gunfire, compelling the Ekumeku warriors to give up fighting in December 1898.[9]

The Royal Niger Company did score a local success, but it was soon apparent that a curtailment of its privileges was necessary if the British government were to be saved from further embarrassments.[10] Officials within certain imperial circles also suggested that if additional territories were to be gained, diplomatic action was needed.[11] The Britisn, who were anxious to expand their influence in the Nigerian region, were certain that the power of the company's authority did not extend much beyond a few miles inland from the Niger River, and that it could not maintain law and order in the hinterland. The Company was also proving itself incapable of extending British influence in the territories north of the Niger-Benue confluence, nor could it keep the French out of Sokoto and the Germans out of Adamawa. As a result, on December 31, 1899, the charter of the company was officially withdrawn; by this act, the company was forced to surrender the administration of the Niger territories to British imperial agents.[12]

If the defeat of the Ekumeku in December 1898 did not bring the

Anioma resistance to a sudden close, neither did the withdrawal of the charter of the Royal Niger Company bring about any improvement in the violent political situation. After abolishing the charter, the British imperial government went on to dissolve the company's military forces, replacing them with a new administrative machinery and a new military force. Asaba, the company's former administrative headquarters, was turned into a new seat of imperial government, complete with a Native Court Council, judicial personnel, warrant chiefs, and soldiers of the Southern Nigeria Regiment, a branch of the recently formed West African Frontier Force. At the same time, British military officers continued with the conquest of Nigeria, a task that the Royal Niger Company could not complete. Frederick Lugard resumed the campaign in Northern Nigeria, and Ralph Moor dispatched his troops to fight the people of the Lower Niger.

Since most southeastern Nigerians organized themselves like the Igbos and had no centralized institutions, the British had to conquer each town and village separately, thereby finding themselves embroiled in annual military engagements. East of the Niger, the Aros were a major target, and west of the river it was the Ekumeku, which British officials described as an anti-foreign association. The Aro used a great many mercenary soldiers and forged military alliances against the British, but the Aniocha communities of Anioma, rather than confront the British in the open, adopted silence and guerrilla tactics as their primary war strategy. As the British were determined to impose themselves, so were the people of Anioma determined to resist the imposition. The communities that had engaged the forces of the Royal Niger Company in intermittent wars since 1888 and had gone underground after what had appeared to be a decisive defeat in December 1898, suddenly reemerged.

Meanwhile, in 1900, Ralph Moor, the high commissioner of Southern Nigeria, warned the Colonial Office in London that the entire territory between Benin City and the Niger was "still in an unsatisfactory state." He reminded the British government that the whole district beyond Aboh and Asaba had been hostile, and had given a great deal of trouble to the Royal Niger Company. He therefore suggested that it was "essential that some demonstration of an established government should be made in this direction." With such a demonstration, he continued, "practically all the territories in the protectorate to the right or west of the Niger will be brought fairly under Government control."[13]

The soldiers of the Southern Nigeria Regiment, which the new colonial government stationed in Asaba and Agbor, were better drilled and better armed than the soldiers of the dissolved Royal Niger Company. Some of them were recruited in the Gold Coast (modern Ghana), some from northern Nigeria, and others from Yorubaland; none was Igbo. The Yoruba recruits were mostly "Ibadan Warboys," who hated "an agricultural life after being so long engaged in warlike operations against Ilorin."[14] Many of the recruits from northern Nigeria were former slaves who had deserted their masters following the British invasion of the Sokoto Caliphate.[15] Other soldiers were drawn from thousands of fleeing slaves who had been seen trooping in 1897 behind the victorious soldiers of the Royal Niger Company as they withdrew from Ilorin. Frederick Lugard, the head of the new Northern Nigerian administration, insisted that those he considered as Hausa-speaking pagans should be given special treatment during recruitment into the Nigerian armed forces.[16] Despite Lugard's fear of what he described as "Muslim fanaticism," he instructed his subordinate European officers to give special treatment to Hausa Muslims over Yoruba Muslims.[17] The reason for these preferences is not clear, but as early as the 1880s, the British had given up the feeling, then current within certain British imperial circles, that the Hausas, many of whom were Muslims, would be unwilling to fight against Muslims from the other parts of Nigeria. That feeling had given birth to the policy which required that men should be recruited in the Gold Coast for service in Nigeria, and vice versa.[18] Major Claude MacDonald, who favored the lifting of the restriction, testified that Muslims had been tested on more than one occasion in Royal Niger Company expeditions against Muslims on the Benue and had raised no objection, and "considering that Mohammedans [Muslims] of India have frequently fought in India and in Egypt against their co-religionists, there seems to be no reason why the Mohammedans [Muslims] of one part of Africa should not fight against those of another part."[19]

Whether or not Lugard shared this reasoning, the fact is that he specifically instructed his deputies to give preference to the Hausas over other Nigerian groups when recruiting men into the colonial armed forces. Till this day, despite independence, this policy has not changed and explains why the Nigerian military is dominated by Hausa-speaking men. In any case, whether Muslim or not, most of the soldiers whom the British deployed to Anioma were already familiar with military operations and a rough life in a tropical environment and therefore proved a very useful instrument for colonial conquest and consolidation.

The Ekumeku warriors were totally unfamiliar with the military capability of these new forces. They were aware, however, that the society had been infiltrated by a large number of collaborators and European sympathizers, especially Christian converts and warrant chiefs, and therefore insisted on secrecy and silence as a war strategy. They held their meetings at night and in secret places. Only those who had taken the oath of secrecy were admitted. No one, except Ekumeku members, knew how the society organized its activities or where its headquarters were. Now that war had broken out, the society was thrown open to all-able bodied young men who wished to demonstrate their prowess and local patriotism. But the movement was still organized around such prominent chiefs as Dunkwu, Elumelu, Obiora, Idegwu, and Chiejina of Onicha-Olona; Elikwu, Ofogu, Umejei, and Uwechua of Igbuzo; Nzekwe and Nwabuzo Iyogolo of Ogwashi-Ukwu; Awuno Ugbo, the Obi of Akumazi; the Obi of Ubulu-Ukwu; Nkwo and Modi, also of Ubulu-Ukwu; and Onwuadiaju of Issele-Azagba.[20]

Contacts among these prominent men were usually achieved through the use of emissaries. Neither the leaders nor their followers were seen in action during the day. The mode of summoning meetings, which was kept secret, involved the shaking of bullet containers around private homes in a carefree manner to announce the time of the gathering without actually saying a word. Other covert calls to meetings involved the use of trumpet notes intelligible only to initiated members, or secret hand signals.[21] The Ekumeku truly was a secret war cult, and because it carried out its activities silently, it earned the nickname "the League of the Silent Ones" or simply, "the Silent Ones."

The Ekumeku clashed with the British in 1902-3, 1904-5 and 1909-10. The battles of the first year began when the British rushed to the rescue of a group of besieged Christian missionaries who had continually disturbed traditional customs and religions. The initial objective of the Ekumeku was to halt the spread of Christianity, which they believed was corrupting society. The clashes of 1904-5 were largely instigated by the colonial government's attempt to introduce the native court and warrant chief systems into various districts. The uprising of 1909-10, on the other hand, started as a succession dispute in Ogwashi-Ukwu and rapidly spilled into the adjacent settlements, triggering missionary and colonial government interventions.

As already mentioned, the Ekumeku rising took place in the immediate hinterland of Asaba, but other groups in Anioma were also independently opposing British political intrusion. The Ukwuani resisted the British in 1905 and 1914, the Ika in 1906. The latter rising was a protest against the practice of imposing Benin chiefs on the Ika communities and the excessive demand on them for free labor. The Ukwuani outbreak of 1905 began as a protest against a British attempt to introduce the native court system, while the 1914 outbreak was triggered by the attempt of some Ukwuani communities to take advantage of the upheaval of the First World War to violently expel the British from the district.[22] These issues will be considered at more length later in this and the following chapter.

On the whole, however, these conflicts created a deep feeling of distrust for the colonial government. They slowed the pace of political development, the consolidation of colonial rule, the spread of Christianity and the westernization of Anioma. The clashes also slowed economic development and ushered in food scarcity and rural poverty.

INDIRECT RULE: THE WARRANT CHIEF SYSTEM

Several leading Nigerian historians have already examined the warrant chief system and aspects of native administration in parts of Southern Nigeria. Adiele E. Afigbo is well known for his *Warrant Chiefs*, Philip I. Igbafe for his *Benin under British Administration*, and Obaro Ikime for his "Native Administration in the Warri Province."[23] However, despite the large number of materials that have appeared since the publication of these pioneering works, indirect rule in Southern Nigeria cannot be regarded as over-studied. Its existence in certain parts of southern Nigeria has not been studied at all. A good example is the Aniocha district of Anioma which, somewhat paradoxically, had the largest concentration of native courts and warrant chiefs in southern Nigeria. In this section, we shall trace the history and functioning of the system, focusing our attention on Anioma responses to the activities of the warrant chiefs and native courts, the most visible features of the system during the first half of the colonial period (1900–30). We will also see how the warrant chief system and the Native Administration system that replaced it in the 1930s overturned the indigenous judicial system.

Officials of the British colonial government decided to introduce the warrant chief system in Anioma, not because they had searched without success for traditional rulers but because they failed to comprehend the working of the Igbo political systems.[24] The Igbo political systems were inconsistent with British notions of governance, and anything that did not meet European standards had to be destroyed, not developed. The first "problem" in governance the British encountered was the fact that each clan was ruled by elders in alliance with a large number of titled chiefs and age-grades. Under these circumstances, it was difficult for an uninitiated mind to identify the real center of authority. Second, the political organization of Anioma was fragmented and small in scale; its people did not develop centralized institutions beyond the town or clan level. Third, even though the political systems remained kin-based and small in scale, they were not uniformly organized. For instance, while such towns as Aboh, Ogwashi-Ukwu, Ubulu-Ukwu, Issele-Ukwu, Ukwunzu, Owa, and Agbor had paramount or head-chiefs (obis), others like Asaba, Okpanam, Igbuzo, Onicha-Olona, Kwale (Utagba-Ogbe), Abbi, Amai, and Obiarukwu had bought titles. Even in the towns where paramount chiefs were found, the authority they exercised was very minimal indeed. In the first place, they had no police force or a standing army to enforce their authority. In the second place, their positions were fundamentally elective in the sense that every adult freeborn member of the community had some say in the selection of a new paramount chief. Finally, government was rooted in the concept of personal freedom and social equality. A paramount chief was simply *primus inter pares* when he sat among other men in the council of chiefs and elders.

With the establishment of colonial rule, therefore, British officials were faced with the problem of "introducing a system that would nullify these ancient tribal customs and usages," and forge an administrative machinery that would bring together what Afigbo has described as a "large number of tiny, politically equivalent and autonomous units."[25] In particular, there was the need to curb the political powers of the mosaic of obis, titled chiefs, age-grades, and elders who shared power in these communities. Since no traditional rulers exercised the type of authority that the British could rely on, and since by their nature the people of Anioma recognized no single authority, the British were faced with a real political problem. This frustration was compounded by their failure to comprehend the working of the Igbo social and political organization. J. Macrae Simpson, like many of his colleagues in the colonial service, regretted that the Igbo social organization was "the most difficult of explanation . . . [and] the most confusing to the European mind." He observed that "it is sometimes but a few minutes walk from a village whose social structure is founded solely on ancestorality to one where a system of bought titles has almost completely overwhelmed the basic organization."[26] To cope with their confusion, the British colonial administrators decided to destroy the indigenous systems and replace them with a system of "indirect rule" that would be based on native courts and warrant chiefs.

Native courts were the product of colonial proclamations. In 1900 the Native Courts Proclamation No. 9 was issued, authorizing colonial officials to set up native courts and to appoint native chiefs to them. Though European officials were allowed to supervise these courts, in practice they and native chiefs were "appointed by the High

Commissioner, or by his representative, by authority given under his hand and seal."[27]

The first major implication of the Native Courts Proclamation was that all traditional judicial institutions were thenceforth ignored even though the new courts were ingeniously called native courts. It also implied that all men who served in the new courts did so at the pleasure of the high commissioner. Under a proclamation issued in 1901, resident commissioners were vested with arbitrary powers which enabled them to overrule the decisions of warrant chiefs.[28] In other words, a vast amount of power was concentrated in the hands of colonial officials; not only could they alter the decisions of local chiefs, but they were also authorized to remove those chiefs who did not represent British interests. In fact, native courts were not meant to protect the rights of Africans nor to preserve their institutions but to advance British interests. According to Igbafe, "the native courts were part of the process of the consolidation of British rule whose principal ingredients were patrols, escorts and military expeditions. The courts were not only the props of the British judicial system in Benin but also the basis of the administrative and executive aspects of British administration."[29]

WARRANT CHIEFS: UPSTARTS OR ACCREDITED REPRESENTATIVES OF THEIR COMMUNITIES?

Afigbo described warrant chiefs as "certain natives whom the British thought were traditional chiefs and [who] were given certificates of recognition and authority called warrants." The warrant, Afigbo wrote, "enabled each of these men to sit in the Native Court from time to time to judge cases. It also empowered him to assume within the community he represented executive and judicial powers which were novel both in degree and territorial scope."[30]

The warrant chiefs of Anioma, like their counterparts in the other parts of southeastern Nigeria, were the tools with which the colonial government centralized the fragmented political institutions of the people. These courts became the major local government body, and, as Igbafe has pointed out, the warrant chiefs "accepted measures from the administrative officers and enforced these through the courts."[31] Because they were in alliance with district officers and the police, the chiefs wielded great powers both locally and regionally. They made by-laws and regulated local affairs. They controlled the local police and summoned those who broke colonial regulations to appear before them. They decided cases coming to their courts and sent offenders, including other chiefs, to prison. They could call offenders and witnesses from distant towns to appear before them. The members of one native court could be asked by a colonial official to try cases in towns other than theirs. In 1902, for instance, three chiefs of Issele-Azagba were tried in their own town by native court chiefs drawn from Asaba.[32] In 1909 the chiefs of Ogwashi-Ukwu, including Nzekwe, were asked to appear before the native court of Igbuzo to answer to charges concerning a murder that had been committed at Ogwashi-Ukwu.[33]

These were great changes which baffled the various Anioma communities. To allow themselves to be tried by strangers or by men of doubtful origins, and under strange laws, was galling to the pride of men who had been accustomed to trying their own cases. At first some communities tended to ignore these courts, but as district officers and warrant chiefs continued to assert their political powers, the local people resorted to armed resistance against the strange system.

Opposition to the native court system continued in Anioma until 1928, but scholars seem to be divided in their view about the immediate source of the discontent. Was opposition directed specifically against the native courts or against the warrant chiefs? If the latter, could it have been because warrant chiefs were not the accredited representatives of their communities? Afigbo has described warrant chiefs as upstarts, that is, people who had no real following in their respective communities but "whom the British thought were traditional chiefs."[34] Obaro Ikime, on the other hand, considered it "an over-generalization to argue that all warrant chiefs were upstarts who possessed no influence within their respective communities before the advent of the British."[35] Ikime explained that when the native court system was introduced British officials consulted the local communities before appointments were made, although over time such consultations declined and the warrant chiefs were essentially drawn from their own class. In other words, Ikime wrote, the first warrant chiefs "were in a real sense the accredited representatives of their communities" even though that became less and less the case as the years rolled by.

There is enough evidence to show that in the beginning there were indeed consultations before appointments were made. What has not been explained is whether the right sort of men were actually presented. Evidence from Anioma shows that, whereas in the beginning colonial agents specifically requested some communities to bring forward their "nominees," the fact remains that the true leaders did not always come forward. Under the circumstances, British officials were constrained, even after some consultations, to appoint upstarts. A good illustration of this point comes from Onicha-Olona, where a native court was opened in 1903 and the first warrant chiefs appointed in the same year.

WARRANT CHIEFS AS UPSTARTS: THE EXAMPLE OF ONICHA-OLONA

Four of the most notable chiefs of Onicha-Olona in 1902 were Dunkwu, Elumelu, Ebora, and Ikemefuna. Dunkwu was the Ekumeku general who had led a successful expedition to Illah in 1898 against the Royal Niger Company. Ikemefuna was the *iyase* (a prominent war lord) of the town while the other two occupied comparable positions. The Ekumeku War of 1902–03 was launched from Onicha-Olona and the British colonial troops immediately attacked and captured the town. They then proceeded to destroy the houses in those sections of the town which they considered hostile. The so-called hostile quarters, with the assistance of hundreds of Ekumeku warriors who had promptly arrived from Ezi, Akwukwu, and the other neighboring towns, adopted guerrilla tactics in their effort to flush the British out of Onicha-Olona. The engagements lasted many months, and while Dunkwu, Elumelu and Ebora were fighting the colonial troops in the bush, Widenham Fosbery, commissioner for the central division, decided to initiate a native council in Onicha-Olona. He singled out Ikemefuna, as the spokesman of the "friendly quarters" of the town and specifically asked him to "get nominations" to the proposed native council.[36] In other words, Ikemefuna was expected to send nominees from half the town since out of the six quarters of Onicha-Olona only three (Ishiekpe, Idumuoji, and Ogbekenu) were regarded as friendly while the other three (Ogbeobi, Umuolo, and Agba) had declared their opposition and were prosecuting the war from their bush camps. Ikemefuna, rather than comply with this order, tried to sabotage it.

First, he sent a message to the commissioner explaining that all the chiefs had declined to be nominated, and that instead, they proposed that representatives be sent from each quarter. The divisional commissioner raised no objection to this suggestion but was disturbed when no representatives came forward. He then sent word to Ikemefuna, asking him to call a meeting of the chiefs of the friendly quarters with a view to dispelling the confusion but Ikemefuna sent word saying that the chiefs would not attend; and when he was himself sent for, he and a number of the leading chiefs of Ogbekenu fled.

Surprised at the flight of Ikemefuna and several leading chiefs, the divisional commissioner decided to set up a body to inquire into these events. As would be expected, the rest of the "friendly chiefs" denied ever hearing of the proposed native council or of nominations, nor had they ever been informed by Ikemefuna about a meeting. The district commissioner was also told that Ikemefuna had taken the leading part in reactivating the Ekumeku in Onicha-Olona and had personally participated in organizing the war against the British, but at the last moment had "left the others in the lurch as he saw that the soldiers were many." The chiefs further alleged to Fosbery that Ogbekenu was a hostile lineage as was Ikemefuna, but his timely defection to the side of the British saved his quarter, Ogbekenu, from being destroyed.

Adu Boahen, a later day African historian, described some African leaders as what one may call "benevolent collaborators."[37] These were Africans who collaborated with the European invaders, not for personal, selfish gains, but to save their communities from destruction. The validity of this thesis has not been sufficiently tested, but if it is accepted, then we have here a good example of such a "benevolent" collaborator. For, by his prompt defection, Ikemefuna temporarily saved his maximal lineage, Ogbekenu.

However, now convinced that Ikemefuna and Ogbekenu were hostile, Fosbery sent a message to the chiefs to warn that if they failed to bring in Ikemefuna within two days, he would order the soldiers to blow up their homes. The next morning, Ikemefuna and another chief, who did not wish to see the people killed and their property vandalized, gave themselves up. They were arrested, and tried for bearing arms against His Majesty, the King of England. Fosbery, who presided over an assembly that he himself appointed, declared that the presence of Ikemefuna and his accomplices was "an obstacle to the establishment of peace and good order in the town." They were at once removed to Asaba as prisoners. Before Fosbery left Onicha-Olona, he received the names of some men who "at once agreed to form a native council and to do their utmost to end the palaver by finding Dunko [Dunkwu]."[38]

What we have seen is that although the divisional commissioner actually consulted some sections of Onicha-Olona before making some appointments, his appointees were not necessarily the appropriately accredited members of the community. Instead, many of these "upstarts" earned their warrants by virtue of the fact that the divisional commissioner regarded them as "friendly," while chiefs like Dunkwu, Elumelu, Ebora, and Ikemefuna were rejected because they were implicated in the Ekumeku movement.

As soon as these "upstarts" had received their warrants in 1903, however, they began to exercise undue authority over the people. Early in 1904 the majority of the chiefs of Onicha-Olona, whom British officials described as "Ekumeku chiefs," decided to get rid of the native council and the warrant chiefs. First, they established another court in the town, which some British officials described as an "Ekumeku court." Second, they tried to mock the colonial system by electing one of their members to the rank of "district commissioner" and provided him with a number of "court messengers" who greeted him as the white man was greeted.[39] Finally, they arrested the warrant chiefs and others suspected of "nursing European sympathies." These "traitors" were tried before the "Ekumeku court" and were all found guilty of showing disloyalty to the community by providing water and provisions for the white men. As enemies of the people, they were to be executed by a firing squad. A leading "Ekumeku chief" is said to have warned: "As the white man has come suddenly upon us, as if it were from the skies, so we have equally suddenly, and now people will have to carry water for us instead, for the white man and those people friendly to him are to be driven into the sea, the white man being unable to exist inland from the water." Preparations were underway to shoot these warrant chiefs when colonial troops arrived from Asaba and attacked the Ekumeku warriors, thereby starting the Ekumeku War of 1904–5.

THE NATIVE COURT AT UBULU-UKWU

Also in Ubulu-Ukwu, opposition was directed against the native court and corrupt warrant chiefs. Before the advent of the British in Nigeria, the obi was the paramount chief of Ubulu-Ukwu and the nominal overlord of the Ubulu-Uno, Ubulu-Okiti, and Ashama clans. But the obi's dominance was threatened when the colonial administrators passed the antislavery laws of 1901–3, established a native court in Ubulu-Ukwu in 1903, and appointed warrant chiefs to sit in this court to try cases coming before them. The obi and his subjects were alarmed by these innovations. The native court threatened to strip the obi of the position he had inherited from his father and father's father as the ultimate court of appeals in the clan. Also, the antislavery laws threatened to strip him of his slaves, his major source of labor. Should he decide to contest these colonial enactments, he would have to stand side-by-side with his slaves and argue the matter before colonial ad-

ministrators and warrant chiefs. Worse still, barely one year after the
native court of Ubulu-Ukwu was established, its officials became very
corrupt in the discharge of their duties.

The people of Ubulu-Ukwu protested the unjust practices of the
court and, as government officials took no action to remedy the situation, the local inhabitants decided to boycott its proceedings. Thenceforth, the public refused to answer its summonses; court messengers
and policemen who carried summonses were beaten up by angry crowds.
W. E. B. Coupland-Crawford, the divisional commissioner, later testified that sufficient supervision was not given to this and similar
courts in the district and that "abuses as were inevitable to some extent crept into their conduct." He admitted that the courts in some
cases inflicted heavy fines for minor offenses, frequently accepted
bribes, and showed favoritism in the decisions given.[40]

In January 1904, Coupland-Crawford ordered an aide to proceed to
Ubulu-Ukwu "to enquire into the matter," but the party was turned
back by messengers from the chiefs who insisted "they would not allow Government representatives to enter their town." Coupland-
Crawford later reported that he made several more attempts "to settle
the matter by peaceable means and to enquire into the grievance," but
the chiefs and people of Ubulu-Ukwu would not rescind their decision. Coupland-Crawford viewed this refusal as an act of rebellion
and contemplated a punitive expedition, which was hastened by the
arrest and trial of the warrant chiefs of Onicha-Olona by the "Ekumeku
chiefs."[41]

A CONFLICT AT EZIONUM

The available evidence points to the fact that virtually all Anioma
communities opposed the establishment of native courts in their towns.
There is also considerable evidence that many men shunned the prospect of becoming warrant chiefs. These feelings were clearly manifested in a small town in the Kwale district, where a district officer
attempted to set up a native court.

On September 2, 1905, according to a British Colonial Office
source, James Davidson, the assistant district commissioner of Kwale,
sent summonses to the town of Ezionum, about three miles from
Amai, via a court messenger accompanied by an interpreter and two
policemen.[42] The duty of the interpreter was to explain to the people
of Ezionum the aim of the government, which was to install a native
court. When these men arrived, the townspeople gathered to hear the

message from the white man, but halfway through the discussion that followed, the crowd seized the court messenger and flogged him severely, then threw him and his companions out of the town. The next morning, the people of Ezionum, who were still determined to make their feelings clearly known, armed themselves and invaded Amai, the seat of the assistant district commissioner. The official had no choice but to flee to Warri.

Infuriated by this incident, colonial troops invaded Ezionum but were defeated by the Ukwuani warriors. It was several months later that the colonial government sent a more extensive expedition against the Ukwuani, who put up stout resistance but were finally subdued. James Davidson, the assistant district commissioner whom the warriors of Ezionum had chased off from Amai in the previous year, was reinstated. Thenceforth, the Ukwuani people were subjected to closer imperial supervision and saddled with native courts and warrant chiefs, and could not rise again until 1914, when the First World War situation encouraged them once more to try to expel the British from their midst.

The three situations just described show that many Igbo harbored a strong revulsion for the native courts. Even when the British consulted the people and supposedly appointed the "right sort of men," society at large was nonetheless appalled by certain inherent contradictions of the native court system. The fact was, this judicial system was inconsistent with the Africans' ideas of justice.

The overbearing attitude of British colonial officials who presided over these courts certainly was another factor in native people's revulsion. In the Agbor district, certain accredited men were in fact vested with warrants, but these same chiefs soon found their position most pathetic, as they were made to fetch water and firewood for colonial officials. On a number of occasions some of the warrant chiefs of Agbor were stripped in their court house, placed on the ground, and then flogged on the orders of British officials. In 1905, Chief Meri of Agbor-Alaesima, who was a warrant chief and next in rank to the Obi of Agbor, was publicly flogged because he was not found present when S. O. Crewe-Read, the district commissioner, arrived at the native court. In the chief's own words, "I was flogged in the Agbor Court in the presence of all the chiefs. . . . The District Commissioner called me up and asked me why I was not present to attend the meeting. . . . My statement was not believed and I was put on the ground and flogged. I also had to pay a fine of £1:26d." Chief Meri had actually turned up for the meeting of the Agbor native council on the appointed day and in good time. He and the other members of the council had awaited the arrival of the district commissioner but when it appeared that he was not coming, Chief Meri and a few others returned to their homes. However, soon after their departure, Crewe-Read arrived for the meeting, and as Chief Meri's town was not far from Agbor, he was sent for.[43]

Chief Bingi of Ogan (near Agbor) was also publicly flogged when he did not complete the work assigned to him. This chief had been told by the district commissioner "to get the Ogan people to help him with the road work." The chief attended to the work but the district commissioner soon returned and demanded an explanation as why the work was not finished. The chief tried to explain but his plea was rejected. He was put on the floor and flogged twelve strokes.[44]

Chief Niago of Umunede and a few of his subordinate chiefs were also publicly flogged; they 'were given 12 strokes apiece," for failing to roof properly the government rest house, and for failing to provide the district commissioner with enough free yams, livestock, and clean water. The district commissioner had arrived at Umunede during a heavy downpour of rain only to find the roof of the rest house "leaking badly." And while he fumed over what he saw as a gross dereliction of responsibility, Chief Niago presented him with an utterly inadequate free supply of "200 yams, 7 fowls, some eggs and water."[45]

Enraged by this endless official highhandedness, these oppressed people of Anioma rose in arms in 1906, killing the district commissioner, together with other men who had oppressed them, thus compelling the government of Southern Nigeria to give up, temporarily, the more obvious abuses such as flogging and forced labor.

Apart from the personal misconduct of district commissioners, the manner by which business was discharged in these courts was burdened with abuses and corruption. The courts were controlled by district officers who presided over the sessions, and in the absence of a district officer, one of the principal chiefs substituted. But even so, the district officer had the overriding decision in any matter that came before his court. In other words, if cases were decided during his absence, he had the right to reverse the decisions already reached. Sometimes he did so without consulting the warrant chiefs, and without consideration for their views. When the district commissioner presided over a proceeding, the warrant chiefs were relegated to the role of ordinary observers. Thus, it could be said that whereas in principle the court was held responsible for its decisions, in practice, these decisions were those of the European district officers.

One other problem with the native courts emanated from the fact that some district officers who presided over them were completely ignorant of native laws and customs, so that most of their decisions contradicted what the Africans would consider as justice. Some of these officers were very young army officers or administrators—Crewe-Read was only twenty-six, for example—who, as Igbafe has noted, "found themselves invested with wide judicial powers which made them the arbiters of the fate of many indigenous people whose own judicial system had been disorganized and driven underground." As Igbafe further pointed out, the native courts were controlled by the supreme court, meaning that the ideas of English law and procedure were used to decide issues that had local origins. Also, appeals reaching the supreme court were reviewed by judges who might have been trained in English law but had little or no knowledge of native law and custom.[46]

More disturbing than these irregularities was the behavior of corrupt warrant chiefs and other court officials like clerks, interpreters, and messengers. These men soon became so powerful, corrupt and overbearing that in some parts of Southern Nigeria they were dreaded even more than the white men. "The issue," wrote Ikime, "was not so much whether the right men were appointed warrant chiefs but the nature of the authority which they exercised." This authority was strange in that it transformed "mere delegates into effective rulers" concentrating vast amounts of power "in individual hands to an extent unknown in traditional usage." These irregularities provoked so much discontent, Ikime observed, that during the anti-tax riots of 1927–28, warrant chiefs were the primary target of hostility while, somewhat paradoxically, government property, including court houses, prisons, and rest houses were not destroyed in the areas of outbreak.[47]

Opposition to this new class of "upstarts" was widespread in Nigeria. Even in Yorubaland, where the concept of centralized institutions was very familiar, the colonial people's "hostility was everywhere directed at illegitimate chiefs or illegitimate powers given them, and at the native court clerks' and messengers' abuses of power."[48] At Iseyin, the agitation of 1916 was not directed against taxation, because at that time none had been introduced, but against the abusive power exercised by illegitimate colonial appointees, and the unfamiliar "centralizing influence which the British administration was bringing into the Oyo area generally."[49]

THE NATIVE COURTS OF ANIOMA TO 1930

Nevertheless, whether the people of Anioma gave the native courts and the warrant chiefs a try before rejecting them (as in Ubulu-Ukwu), or whether they fought against the idea from the start (as in

Ezionum), the fact was that the courts had come to be an integral part of the colonial administrative system in the period 1900 to 1930. Each rejection called forth a punitive expedition and each punitive expedition was concluded with the establishment or reestablishment of a native court. For the colonial subjects, there was no way out of the dilemma.

The most notable native court to be established in Anioma was at Asaba. It was opened in 1900 and had eight members selected from the several hundred chiefs of the town. Out of these eight, one was a stranger who represented the Hausa community resident in Asaba, while another man from Oko represented the people of Oko. Over the years, the jurisdiction of this court extended in stages until it reached as far as Aboh.[50] Cases from many parts of Anioma were referred to it for decision while by-laws made there had legal force in distant districts.

Another powerful native court established in Agbor had members drawn entirely from titled men from the Agbor clan while chiefs from the adjoining districts were rejected. The result, noted J. Macrea Simpson, was that "the Agbors were given a preponderant voice in the administration of the District." Over the years, Simpson further reported, a bureaucracy of warrant Chiefs developed in Agbor whereby some people "obtained appointment by virtue of their fathers having been assessors in the original court." In 1908 fifteen of the Agbor title-holders were elected to attend the native council at Benin, and in 1918 the Agbor and Asaba divisions were joined under the name of Asaba Division. The district officer was stationed at Ogwashi-Ukwu while an assistant district officer was left at Agbor in charge of the Agbor district.[51]

The Asaba district had more native courts than any other district of southern Nigeria. This, as Igbafe has suggested, was because Asaba was one of the most "unquiet and troublesome" districts where "there were perpetual disturbances and opposition to British rule."[52] Thus, whereas by 1910 there was only one native court in the Benin district, there were eight in the Asaba district, located in the following places: Asaba (1900), Issele-Uku (1902), Igbuzo (1902), Illah (1902), Onicha-Olona (1903), Ogwashi-Ukwu (1903), Ubulu-Ukwu (1903), and Ukwunzu (1904).[53] These towns were the hottest spots of the Ekumeku movement. Widenham Fosbery, the colonial officer who was largely responsible for starting these native courts, wrote that he had hoped "a change for the better will soon be apparent when the Native Courts which have now been inaugurated are in proper working order and I do not think there will be any further trouble in this part of the Division. . . . The power of the Government [has been] fully demonstrated. The country must however be regularly visited and the Native Council constantly supervised by the officers of the District in future."[54]

By the 1920s all the districts of Anioma had been effectively brought under the jurisdiction of one native court or the other. Also by 1930 the process of bringing the former autonomous Anioma polities under one administration had been completed. That process had been accelerated in 1927 with the introduction of direct taxation into Ogwashi-Ukwu for the whole of Asaba Division.[55]

Anioma was saddled with an unduly large number of native courts and warrant chiefs, not because the area was the most troublesome in Nigeria, as Igbafe has suggested,[56] but because the introduction there of indirect rule was accompanied with much haste and reckless violence. In other words, the British attempt to introduce the indirect rule system sparked much violence. In order to keep the freedom fighters in check, the British multiplied the native courts and then expanded their military presence.

Opposition to the native court system was also part of a reaction to official insensitivity to the welfare of local communities. In their desire to introduce what they called a "more just and civilized method of government," British agents overthrew indigenous institutions. Although colonial officials tried to work through and with the assistance of the chiefs, in some cases they appointed the wrong persons to sensitive positions, completely disregarding the social and class structures within which the native Africans operated. Determined to exploit their new stations, these upstarts demanded bribes and imposed heavy fines on those who disobeyed their authority. For example, under the pretense of implementing the provisions of the Roads and Creeks Proclamation of 1903, which required all ablebodied men and women between the ages of fifteen and fifty to work without pay in accordance with the wishes of the chiefs, warrant chiefs compelled youths to render forced and unpaid labor on their private farms, and flogged or imprisoned all those who refused to work for them.

The people of Anioma were particularly disturbed by the manner in which the business of the native courts was conducted. During the precolonial days, they had used a variety of judicial techniques to settle their disputes. The nature of the dispute, Simon Ottenberg observed, determined which judicial agent would be sought; sometimes the disputants and their relatives decided where to present their case— before patrilineal elders, village elders, clan elders, famous oracles, or simply by swearing innocence to a spirit which they believed would kill those who lied to it.[57] The Igbo had no prisons or jails, and no matter the offense, the accused remained a free man, carrying out his daily activities, until his guilt was established. The idea of locking people up, depriving them of their freedom and livelihood even before their guilt was established, was most disgusting to the traditional Igbo mind.

ADMINISTRATIVE REFORMS: THE INTRODUCTION OF NATIVE ADMINISTRATION

Opposition to the native courts and warrant chiefs continued throughout southern Nigeria during the first two decades of this century. Meanwhile, in the late 1920s, the British began to consider extending the principle of direct taxation into the "untaxed provinces" of Nigeria. When implemented, however, this policy sparked much unrest, culminating in the anti-tax riots of 1927–28 in parts of Anioma and the Western Delta. It also was instrumental to the outbreak of the famous Aba women's riots of 1929, which compelled the colonial administration to reorganize the native authority government in the 1930s and 1940s.[58]

Colonial officials had justified their decision to tax these provinces on the grounds that they needed to raise revenue to support the administration; they ignored the fact that no satisfactory system of local government had yet been established. It was only during the anti-tax riots that officials recognized that the warrant chiefs could not be relied upon to collect taxes and discharge a host of administrative and judicial functions. When the riots were finally quelled, officials decided to tackle the problem by initiating large-scale investigations into the causes of grievances and, if possible, to suggest means of building centers of political power around the ancient indigenous political systems. The exercise resulted in the introduction of a system of native administration which was an improvement on both the native court and the warrant chief systems. In other words, the political agitations of the late 1920s resulted in the introduction of administrative reforms which, in the following decade, paved the way for constitutional reforms and prepared Nigerians for political independence. Indeed, as Terence Ranger and A. B. Davidson have observed, not all African resistances were in vain; many of them not only forced concessions and preserved pride, but they also left their mark on the most important internal process of African political development.[59]

Although the decision to introduce the system of native administration could be regarded as a progressive one, its operation was still rife with contradictions. For example, in the Warri Province, some colonial administrators wanted to structure the native administration along ethnic lines such that "each tribe would be endowed with its own native administration, the homogeneity of culture and sameness of culture and sameness of social and political institutions being the decisive criteria."[60] Obaro Ikime explained that under this scheme, the Igbo-speaking areas of the Warri province were to be placed under a single native administration. Superficially, he noted, this idea was progressive, but to group all Igbo-speaking people of the province under one head would be difficult to implement. As we have seen in chapter 3, the people of Anioma, like most Igbo groups, were organized in independent towns and clans and would not recognize any other authority. Further, some clans in the Kwale and Aboh areas, such as Abraka and Orogun, had emulated so many non-Igbo customs that, as was shown in chapter three, they would prefer not to be administered as part of the Igbo-speaking clans. When, therefore, the colonial administration tried to designate the Obi of Aboh as sole native authority for the Kwale and Aboh districts, the move was stoutly opposed since not all the clans in the area acknowledged his suzerainty.[61] Similar opposition arose in the other districts of Anioma. Eventually, however, the colonial administration decided to use paramount chiefs as the centers of authority whenever possible, as in Agbor and Aboh, or to allow the elders of the towns and villages to collect taxes, using customary executive agents like the titled chiefs and age-grade associations.

By 1932, a number of native authorities had been established in Anioma. They became the new centers of local administration. They were, to a large extent, councils of elders presided over by either a paramount chief, a titled chief, or the most senior elder. Their principal functions were to collect taxes, which they were required to deposit with the treasury. They were also empowered to try cases in the native courts and refer appeals to the district officers. The members of the native councils were appointed by the district officers; the notion of election to office was still out of the question. Until the 1940s, most councilors were male elders. Women, younger male adults, and those educated in the west were not considered fit to serve in these councils.

As Obaro Ikime has pointed out, the native administration system "was not an administrative revolution but a modification and, in some respects, an intensification of the old ways of running local government."[62] He described them as a school for councilors, that is, chiefs and elders, for "learning the finer points of local government." On the other hand, Ikime wrote, the period 1945–50 witnessed some rapid reforms "amounting at times to revolution." During this period committees were set up to consider grievances against the agents of the native administrations and cases involving disciplinary measures against ineffective or high-handed councilors, the imposition of closer supervision of expenditures, the appointment of tax assessment committees, the introduction of wider representation, and the election of educated young men into the finance committees and the clan and central native authority councils. Perhaps the most important change of this period was this introduction of the elective principle into the selection of members of the native administrative councils.[63]

The Aboh native authority experienced other important changes in the 1940s. When the Ase clan wanted to break away from the Aboh native administration, colonial authorities conducted an investigation, after which the Obi of Aboh ceased to be the sole native authority. His advisory council was dissolved and replaced by an executive council made up of representatives from every clan in the district. The Obi was thenceforth to be treated simply as the president of the council.[64]

Another change involved election to the councils. While the other native councils in the Asaba, Agbor, and Ukwuani districts were opening their doors to western-educated young men, hardly any educated person served in the Aboh native council, except the Obi himself. This reluctance is understandable, however. As was shown in chapter four, western education and Christianity were late in coming to Aboh. Obi Oputa, who might have received a western education, remained the only effective link between the native administration and the provincial government at Warri. When he became too old to discharge his duties, the dissatisfied clans in Ashaka, Ushie, and Ase asked that they be transferred to the Ukwuani native administration. Fearing a disintegration of the entire native administration, the colonial government introduced the elective principle for all subordinate native authority councils and the central executive council.[65]

Similar changes were also taking place in the Agbor district. The Obi, who was president of the native court, was also the statutory native authority and was authorized to issue orders through the native court and its members. By the 1930s the Obi's salary was £200 per annum, a very large sum in those days.[66] He and the native council were expected to collect taxes on behalf of the government and were allowed to keep 10 percent of the total. The warrant chiefs of Agbor had been treated as village heads but after the introduction of the administrative reforms in 1931, they were thenceforth considered simply as representatives of the villages to which they belonged, unless they were legitimately chief functionaries. This change in policy suggests that previously, some "upstarts" may have presented themselves as village heads, for, as Simpson testified, by 1931 "of the eighteen members only three or four were village heads in actual fact."[67]

POLITICAL CHANGES IN ASABA, 1886–1960

While it is not practicable to examine every local native administration in Anioma, we nonetheless cannot consider the treatment of this aspect of Anioma history complete without a discussion of the political changes that took place in Asaba in this period. Some of the changes were based on the increasing heterogeneity of the populace, as diverse groups settle in the region. For example, in 1886, the Royal Niger Company was granted a charter by the British government, in the same year the company established its administrative headquarters in Asaba, introduced a judicial system for its employees, and built a large military barracks for its soldiers. These barracks were literally iron houses mounted on iron columns, with iron roofs. The rooms were very small, each containing two narrow beds, and the passage that ran down the center of each structure was only broad enough for a man to pass, sometimes with great difficulty. During the hot season—and Asaba was always hot—these iron houses were extremely uncomfortable, so that most of the soldiers lived outside the barracks, in a section of Asaba which was nicknamed "Soja Town" ("Soldier Town"). "Soja Town" was a collection of more than 300 huts which the soldiers built for themselves, some distance away from the barracks. It was a place where the soldiers could live a life of relative ease, away from the constant and harsh supervision of their superior officers. It was here that they kept their wives and female friends.[68]

This settlement helped diversify the population in significant ways. The soldiers of the Royal Niger Company were foreigners to the Lower Niger; none was from southeastern Nigeria, and none was Igbo. They were recruited mostly from the Gold Coast (modern Ghana), northern Nigeria, and Yorubaland. According to a report from Major Claude MacDonald, out of every eight soldiers, five were Fanti from modern Ghana, two were Hausa from northern Nigeria, and one was Yoruba from western Nigeria.[69] A section of "Soja Town" was occupied entirely by Muslims and was called the Mohammedan section. The other half was called Elmina (a name derived from a coastal town in the Gold Coast), suggesting that a large number of the soldiers recruited in the Gold Coast lived there. In 1888, the missionaries reported that some of these soldiers were attending mass regularly and that some had been baptized.[70] The soldiers themselves made sure that each group in Soja Town kept rigidly apart from the others. While it is not clear where the Yoruba soldiers lived, whether in the Mohammedan section or in Elmina, we can infer that most of them would have lived in Elmina, since the first Yoruba recruits of the colonial armed forces were mostly Ibadan war boys (*omo okun*) who had engaged the Hausa-Fulani jihadists in a prolonged war of resistance.

Apart from the soldiers, the company kept in Asaba a small force of policemen and employed hundreds of Africans, most of them from coastal West Africa. These employees worked as servants, porters, crews of the river crafts and trading agents.

In addition, partly because of the presence of the company and its soldiers and partly because of its historical role in the trade of the Niger River, Asaba attracted a large population of Hausa traders, craftsmen and craftswomen, and former slaves many of whose original homelands were located in areas beyond the Niger-Benue confluence. These people lived mostly in the "Hausa" quarters (*ogbe Hausa*) of the town, where the Hausa language became the lingua franca.

The presence of these military and nonmilitary employees of the company, together with the presence of the Hausa immigrants, helped to transform Asaba into a truly cosmopolitan center. In addition to thriving native quarters, the city boasted officers' quarters, as well as homes for the Commandant, the judges and the doctors. These houses were very comfortable, with wide verandas, and were situated one hundred feet above the river. The town also had military and civil hospitals and a prison. Initially, the prison had only 33 cells, but was later expanded as the population and resistance to British rule increased. Until 1910, the prison at Asaba was the only such structure in Anioma and many people who violated oppressive colonial laws and could not be imprisoned there were transported to Calabar or Benin.[71]

In 1900, the Royal Niger Company lost its charter and the territories it had administered from Asaba. Its hegemony had stretched from the Niger Delta to Lokoja, then to Ilorin, Adamawa, and in fact, to some undefined territories in the interior. When the company surrendered its administrative headquarters to the British government, many more administrators, soldiers, missionaries, traders, and prostitutes flocked into town for, as H. Vaux later testified, Asaba had become "the virtual capital of Nigeria."[72] And despite the withdrawal of the Niger Company's charter, Asaba still harbored the homes of the chief justice and puisne judge, the military barracks, the military and civil hospitals, the headquarters of the medical department, the prison, and even an experimental botanical garden.[73]

Asaba's ascendancy continued well into the new century. Barely three decades after the revocation of the Niger Company's charter, Vaux was able to remark that the town had become "the cradle of Nigerian Education" which, for many years, "was the only source from which a local supply of suitable men could be counted upon to oust native foreigners from higher secretarial posts in government and commerce." In his reference to "native foreigners," Vaux was referring to many Africans from the Gold Coast, Sierra Leone, and Liberia, as well as blacks from Brazil, who dominated the wage labor market of southern Nigeria at this time. He also noted that a group of "highly educated and experienced" Asaba natives, who a quarter of a century earlier had migrated to other parts of Nigeria to occupy secretarial positions, were beginning to return home in middle age in the enjoyment of pensions, to join a quasi-political and quasi-social club known as the Asaba Union. Vaux described this union as "the most vocal and the least representative organ of the town," and suggested that its members would be capable of playing a dynamic role in the reorganization of the native administration system.[74]

Asaba remained a provincial headquarters until 1904, when the seat of the provincial commissioner was moved to Onitsha, leaving Asaba as the district headquarters of the Asaba district. Then in 1910, the district headquarters were moved to Ogwashi-Ukwu.[75] In 1926 the Asagba of Asaba was recognized by the government as the sole native authority, his position similar to that of the Obi of Aboh, who was native authority for the Aboh district. A year later, the native administration of Asaba was reorganized in preparation for the introduction of direct taxation. The Asagba remained the native authority until his death in January 1934.[76]

Until 1952, when the regional government system was introduced—or more specifically, when the Action Group Government of Western Nigeria passed the Local Government Law, which provided for the establishment of different classes of courts, the election of members of local, rural, urban, and divisional councils—Asaba remained important even though it had forfeited much of its administrative significance. Between 1952 and 1960, the dominant issues in Nigerian politics were constitutional development and the achievement of independence, so that the political history of Anioma became intricately bound with the wider Nigerian political situation. Also at this time, the political development of Asaba became somewhat synonymous with the political history of Anioma in the sense that both were influenced by the conflicts between the Igbo-dominated National Council of Nigerian Citizens (NCNC) and the Yoruba-dominated Action Group (AG) on the one hand, and on the other, between southern and northern Nigeria. The conflicts between the NCNC and the AG were particularly adverse for the people of Anioma because, while the Igbos of eastern Nigeria had their own government at Enugu, the Anioma Igbos were governed from Ibadan by the Yorubas, and were exposed to all the intrigues and repressions that characterized (and still characterize) Nigerian politics. Despite the intrigues, however, the people of Anioma, under the leadership of Dennis Osadebe, a native of Asaba and the deputy leader of the NCNC, continued to play a vital role in the politics that shaped the structures under which Nigerian independence was based.

In the next chapter, we shall examine some of the circumstances that led to the decline of the economic preeminence of Asaba, but it may be briefly mentioned here that the advent of the railway lines and motor roads diminished the importance of the Niger River as a commercial route and, concomitantly, the administrative and commercial importance of Asaba. Secondly, with the amalgamation of southern and northern Nigeria in 1914, the attention of the colonial government became centered on Lagos and Kaduna, to the almost complete neglect of Asaba and other previously important cities like Onitsha, Aboh, Old Calabar, Opobo, Bonny, Ogoja, Akassa and Lokoja. It was only in the 1940s that Asaba began to regain its former precedence, partly because of the rise of militant political agitation for Nigerian independence—a movement in which the Igbo-speaking people played a very active role—and partly because Asaba remained an important staging post for east-west commuters, that is, those who travelled to and from Calabar, Enugu, Ogoja, Port Harcourt, Benin City, Ijebu-Ode, Ibadan, and Lagos.

So far, we have presented an outline account of the political history of Anioma in the period 1883 to 1960. As we have seen, the period was marked by the British colonial conquest and the introduction of an indirect rule system based on native courts, warrant chiefs, and native administration. The warrant chief system was replaced by the native administration system in 1928. The latter remained operative until 1952 when it gave way to the regional government system, which remained the basis of local administration but was not changed at independence in 1960. In 1963 the midwest region was carved out of the former western region for the non-Yoruba speaking peoples of western Nigeria. Benin City was declared its administrative capital, and Dennis Osadebe its prime minister. In 1967 the Nigerian civil war broke out over many issues that had their origins in the colonial period, but which could conveniently be put together under one head, namely, disputes over the distribution of scarce resources. Our discussion will now turn to a consideration of Anioma's resources and their effects on the region's economy.

NOTES

1. Don C. Ohadike, *The Ekumeku Movement: Western Igbo Resistance to the British Conquest of Nigeria, 1883-1914.* (Athens: Ohio Univ. Press, 1991).

2. See for instance, PRO, FO 403/217, Confidential File no. 6668, Sir J. Kirk to Marquess of Salisbury, received August 30, 1895.

3. Monday E. Noah, *Old Calabar: The City States and the Europeans, 1800-1885.* Uyo: Scholars Press, 1980).

4. Felix Ekechi, "Traders, Missionaries and the Bombardment of Onitsha, 1879-1880," *The Conch*, 5, nos. 1 and 2(1973): 61-81.

5. Local Government Archives, Benin City, File no. 26769, E. A. Miller, "Intelligence Report on Abo."

6. Ohadike, *The Ekumeku Movement*, 68-76.

7. A. H. M. Kirk-Greene, "A Preliminary Note on New Sources for Nigerian Military History," *Journal of the Historical Society of Nigeria* 3, no. 1(1964): 135-38.

8. Joseph C. Anene, *Southern Nigeria in Transition, 1885-1906* (Cambridge: Cambridge Univ. Press, 1966), 220; on p. 221 Anene also quotes PRO, C0 520/2, Moor to Colonial Office, May 28, 1901.

9. Ohadike, *The Ekumeku Movement*, 86-93.

10. *Church Missionary Intelligencer* (1896), 433.

11. Godfrey N. Uzoigwe, *Britain and the Conquest of Africa:* The Age of Salisbury (Ann Arbor: Univ. of Michigan Press, 1974), 101.

12. John E. Flint, *Sir George Goldie and the Making of Nigeria* (London: Oxford Univ. Press, 1960), 267.

13. PRO, CO 520/3/320/2519, Ralph Moor to Colonial Office, December 29, 1900.

14. Kirk-Greene, "A Preliminary Note." 405.

15. Sir Charles Orr, *The Making of Northern Nigeria.* (London: Frank Cass, 1965), 203.

16. R. A. Adeleye, *Power and Diplomacy in Northern Nigeria, 1804-1906* (New York: Humanities Press, 1971), 220.

17. Ibid., 219-20.

18. PRO, FO 84/2019, military notes on the countries of West Africa visited by Major Claude MacDonald, July to November, 1889.

19. Ibid.

20. Philip Igbafe, "Western Ibo Society and Its Resistance to British Rule: The Ekumeku Movement, 1898-1911," *Journal of African History* 12 no. 3(1971): 444.

21. Ibid.

22. Ohadike, *The Ekumeku Movement*, 147-65.

23. Adiele E. Afigbo, *The Warrant Chiefs: Indirect Rule in Southern*

Nigeria, 1891–1929, (New York: Humanities Press, 1972); Philip I. Igbafe, *Benin Under British Administration: The Impact of Colonial Rule on an African Kingdom, 1897–1938* (London: 1979); Obaro Ikime, "Native Administration in Kwale-Aboh, 1928–1950: A Case Study," *Journal of the Historical Society of Nigeria* 3, no. 4(June 1967): 663–82.

24. For the British failure to seek traditional rulers see Margery F. Perham, *Native Administration in Nigeria* (London: Oxford University Press, 1937) 206–54.

25. Afigbo, *The Warrant Chiefs,* 7.

26. NAI, CSO 26/4, File no. 3038X, J. Macrea Simpson, "Intelligence Report on the Agbor, Oligie and Emuhu Clans, Agbor District, Asaba Division," 1935.

27. PRO, CO 583/1 Native Courts Proclamation No. 9 of 1900. See also Afigbo, *The Warrant Chiefs,* 39 and Igbafe, *Benin Under British Administration,* 81–82.

28. PRO, CO 588/1 Native Courts Proclamation No. 25 of 1901.

29. Igbafe, *Benin Under British Administration,* 182–83.

30. Afigbo, *The Warrant Chiefs,* 6.

31. Igbafe, *Benin Under British Administration,* 223.

32. PRO, CO 520/18/7937 of February 29, 1903, Widenham Fosbery, divisional commissioner, central divisions, to the high commissioner, Southern Nigeria, January 2, 1903.

33. PRO, CO 520/93/17110 of June 6, 1910. Lt. Col. H. C. Moorhouse to the governor of Southern Nigeria, April 24, 1910.

34. Afigbo, *The Warrant Chiefs,* 6.

35. Obaro Ikime, "The Anti-Tax Riots in Warri Province, 1927–1928," *Journal of the Historical Society of Nigeria* 3, no. 3(December 1966): 560.

36. PRO, CO 520/18/7937 of February 29, 1903, Widenham Fosbery to High Commissioner, January 2, 1903.

37. Adu Boahen, *African Perspectives on Colonialism* (Baltimore: The Johns Hopkins Univ. Press, 1987).

38. PRO, CO 520/18/7937 of February 29, 1903, Widenham Fosbery to High Commissioner, January 2, 1903.

39. PRO, CO 520/24/20839 of June 13, 1904. W. E. B. Coupland-Crawford to the high commissioner. The ensuing account is from this source.

40. Ibid.

41. Ibid.

42. PRO, CO 520/32/28260 of October 27, 1905. Enclosure no. 3, James Davidson, assistant district commissioner, Kwale District to divisional commissioner, Western Division, August 8, 1905

43. PRO, CO 520/38, Confidential enclosure of December 29, 1906, sworn statement by Chief Meri of Agbor-Alesima, taken at Abavo on November 23, 1906 by S. W. Sproston.

44. Confidential enclosure in ibid, sworn statement by Afidi, native court messenger, taken at Abavo on November 23, 1906 by S. W. Sproston.

45. Confidential enclosures in ibid, sworn statement by Chief Niago of Umunede, taken on 26 November, 1906 by S. W. Sproston.

46. Igbafe, *Benin Under British Administration,* 190, 192.

47. Ikime, "The Anti-Tax Riots," 560, 565.

48. Akinjide Osuntokun, *Nigeria in the First World War,* (Atlantic Highlands: Humanities Press, 1979), 133.

49. J. A. Atanda, "The Iseyin-Okeiho Rising of 1916: An Example of Socio-political Conflict in Colonial Nigeria," *Journal of the Historical Society of Nigeria* 4, no. 4(1969): 497.

50. NAI, CSO/26, File no. 30927, F. M. White, introduction to H. Vaux, "Intelligence Report on the Asaba Clan," 1936 and Vaux in ibid.

51. NAI, CSO 26/4, File no. 3038X, Simpson, "Intelligence Report on the Agbor, Oligie and Emuhu Clans."

52. Igbafe, *Benin Under British Administration,* 192.

53. PRO, CO 520/18/7937 of February 29, 1903, Widenham Fosbery to the high commissioner, January 2, 1903.

54. Ibid.

55. NAI, CSO/26, File no. 30927, Vaux, "Intelligence Report on the Asaba Clan."

56. Igbafe, *Benin Under British Administration,* 182–83.

57. Simon Ottenberg, "Ibo Receptivity to Change," in *Continuity and Change in African Cultures,* ed. William Bascom and Melville J. Herskovits (Chicago: Chicago Univ. Press, 1959), 138.

58. For an account of the women's riots of 1929 see, for instance, Nina Emma Mbah, *Nigerian Women Mobilized: Women's Political Activity in Southern Nigeria, 1900–1965* (Berkeley: Univ. of California, 1982); Judith Van Allen, " 'Aba Riots' or 'Igbo Women's War'? Ideology, Stratification, and the Invisibility of Women," in *Women in Africa: Studies in Social and Economic Change,* ed. by Nancy J. Hafkin and Edna G. Bay (Stanford: Stanford Univ. Press, 1976): 59–86.

59. Terence O. Ranger, "Connections Between Primary Resistance Movements and Modern Mass Nationalism in East and Central Africa," *Journal of African History* 9 (1968): 441; A. B. Davidson, "African Resistance and Rebellion Against the Imposition of Colonial Rule," in *Emerging Themes of African History,* ed. Terence O. Ranger (Nairobi: East African Publishing House, 1968), 177–88.

60. Quoted in Ikime, "Native Administration in Kwale-Aboh," 664.

61. Ibid., 665.

62. Ibid., 663–64.

63. Ibid., 672, 674–75.

64. Ibid., 677.

65. Ibid., 678.

66. NAI, CSO 2614, file no. 3038X, Simpson, "Intelligence Report on the Agbor, Oligie and Emuhu Clans."

67. Ibid.

68. PRO, FO 84/2019, military notes on the countries of West Africa visited by Major Claude MacDonald, July to November 1889.

69. Ibid.

70. See chapter 4.

71. PRO, FO 84/2019, military notes on the countries of West Africa visited by Major Claude MacDonald, July to November 1889. Major MacDonald noted that these soldiers were clothed in khaki jackets, blue shorts, white jersey, red kammerband, red fez (cap), but had no covering for their

feet. Crime, he said, was severely punished; it included 84 days in prison and up to 30 lashes of the cane. In addition to crime, another less welcome sign of the town's growth was the increase in the number of prostitutes who settled there. Some Christian missionaries complained about the influx which, they said, had been stimulated by the presence of the soldiers and other employees of the company.

72. NAI, CSO/26, No. 30927, Vaux, "Intelligence Report on the Asaba Clan."

73. Ibid.

74. Ibid.

75. PRO, CO 520/94/375 of January 13, 1911, confidential dispatch of June 16,1910, acting governor, Southern Nigeria to secretary of state for the colonies.

76. NAI, CSO/26, No. 30927, Vaux, "Intelligence Report on the Asaba Clan."

7

~~~

ECONOMIC HISTORY

THE SUBSISTENCE ECONOMY

LIFE IN ANIOMA did not center only on migrations, wars, politics, and cultural evolution alone; the populace also pursued a wide range of economic activities. The main occupations were cultivating yams and vegetables, processing vegetable oils, and weaving and dying cloth, with fishing and trading as auxiliary activities. While most families grew their own food crops and processed their own palm and coconut oils, others combined food production with craft manufacture, producing baskets, sleeping mats, and iron and wooden items. A few men and women worked as spiritual specialists.

Even though many people took part in many different types of economic activities, men generally cultivated the yams while women grew vegetables. Maize (corn) was introduced into Anioma in the seventeenth century, after the Portuguese arrived in the coastal towns on the Bight of Biafra, and its cultivation was adopted by both sexes. As we shall presently see, men allowed maize to be grown in combination with yams, but would not give a similar concession to cassava when it was introduced at the end of the nineteenth century.

The most important food was, by far, yams, but the people of Anioma cannot now remember when they first ate or cultivated them. Some elders would say that yams came from *Chukwu,* the Great Creator. A few Igbo clans in the Anambra valley might add that *Chukwu* created the first Igbo king, Eze Nri, and gave him yams to share among the Igbo people. They would also say that it was Eze Nri who introduced the yam festival (*iwa ji*) and the yam cult (*ifejioku*). Some

Igbo groups in the Anambra valley acknowledged Eze Nri as the provider of yams and each year, at the beginning of the planting season, they would journey to Nri for a special yam medicine which they believed would guarantee soil fertility and a bountiful harvest. According to Richard Henderson, "Since the cultigens upon which the Ibo-speaking peoples came to depend for their food staples were the 'son' and 'daughter' of Nri, Nri and his descendants gained the right to produce the sacred 'yam medicine' (*ogwu-ji*) for which surrounding peoples traditionally came to Nri and for which they paid him an annual tribute to insure the edibility of yams."[1] While most Anioma people are unfamiliar with this folklore many of their elders are certain that the children of Nri occupied a unique position in Igbo cultural history, largely because of the ritual activities of the itinerant Nri men and women whom they referred to as *okpala Nshi* and *ada Nshi*, respectively.

Regardless of its origins, to the people of Anioma, the yam was everything. It was the king of crops and the basis of their calendar. It was also the measuring rod of status, power, and authority; without it, their monetary system could not function. Their most important festivals and their dominant ideologies were linked to the yam. If the yam crop failed, everything failed. Anioma men derived much of their status in society from their ability to produce yams and manipulate the rituals that regulated their cultivation and distribution.

The farming system in Anioma can best be described as shifting or a kind of rough rotational cultivation. Under this system of production, the land was cultivated with yams (and sometimes maize) for a season and then abandoned. The land would soon revert to bush, and might stay so for five or more years until it was cleared again. This system of agriculture was labor intensive, but it enabled an already used piece of land sufficient time to naturally regain its fertility without the use of artificial fertilizers. Labor was sometimes communal during certain periods of the growing season. The common practice was to pool together the effort of a whole kindred or patrilineage to clear a given area at the onset of the planting season, after which each household was allotted a parcel of land according to its size or ability to cultivate it. In the following year, the process was repeated elsewhere. Although no one was forced to abandon an old farmland and move on to a new one at the beginning of a new planting season, most people did so because yams did best in virgin forests.

Down through the centuries, both sexes adhered strictly to the ancient gender relations of production, which was subsistence-oriented. With the introduction of the Atlantic slave trade into this region in the 1650s, changes in the gender relations of production occurred. Some men entered the Atlantic slave trade as slave dealers, to the almost total exclusion of women, at the same time maintaining control of the production of yams, the main food item of the provisioning trade. Furthermore, when overseas trade in palm oil was introduced into the lower Niger in the mid-nineteenth century, men entered it and became the main trading partners of European merchants. By the time of the onset of colonial conquest and rule, Anioma men had gained an indisputable dominance over women based on the influential roles they played in the slave, the provisioning, and palm oil trades. Thus, the gender inequality of wealth and power that became more pronounced in the colonial and post-colonial periods had its origins in the distant past.

Trading was a vocation in which the vast majority of the people of Anioma participated, though mostly on a part-time basis. Only a few individuals made their living on trade, and of that number only a few engaged in long-distance trading; the majority confined themselves to local trading. This characteristic of commercial enterprise lasted well into the colonial period. In the 1930s, a British colonial agent, J. Macrea Simpson, noted in regard to Agbor that "there are no large native traders in the clan. The bulk of the people are peasant farmers who sell their produce locally, but several enterprising aspirants are now exporting yams to Kwale and the creeks."[2] Simpson reported also that the main trade was still internal, and that yams and edible oil were the most important items. What Simpson described, however, was an ancient trading pattern that had simply been carried over into the colonial period.

A common feature of African commercial enterprise in general and Anioma in particular was the gender of the traders, based on the type of trade in which they engaged. Anthony G. Hopkins has noted that "traders involved in local exchange tended to be predominantly female, part-time, small scale, mobile and numerous. They were mainly female because local trade was a convenient adjunct to household and, in some societies, farming activities." Most women, he continued, engaged in local trading because they regarded it as "a supplement to primary [i.e., domestic] occupations."[3] Local trading operations remained small, partly because "they lacked the capital to be anything else," and partly because what a farmer was capable of selling was being equally cheaply produced and traded by her neighbors. In any case, Hopkins suggested, while local trading developed in response to the complementary needs of communities living in close proximity to one another, long-distance trade owed its origin to the demand for scarce and less bulky items which were constantly being moved around, sometimes over great distances. For example, dried fish from the Lake Chad region was transported a distance of one thousand miles by overland routes to Lagos. So also were cowries imported from the Indian Ocean islands, and copper, cattle, grains, and other food items from distant lands.

In Igboland itself, the Niger river was a particularly important highway for trade in foodstuffs. The commercial opportunities the river provided helped the precolonial West Africans as a whole to cope with hunger. The river also stimulated trade and occupational specialization, with some communities focusing on food production, some on craft manufacture, some on ritual practices, and others on trade and transportation of merchandise. For example, among the Igbo, the Anam specialized as farmers; the Awka as blacksmiths; the Umunri as itinerant ritual specialists; and the Aboh as long-distance traders and commercial intermediaries.

Two thousand or more years before the Portuguese felt their way down the West African coast, the entire valley of the Niger River had become a single economic region. Since there were no rigid political boundaries, traders, craftspersons, and farmers met in the Niger settlements in periodic, rotating markets. On an island in the river between Asaba and Onitsha was a famous market where traders from Aboh and the Niger Delta met once each week to exchange yams, livestock, salt, cloth, metal wares, and other goods with traders from Idah and Lokoja upstream.[4] Similar fairs were held further upstream at Ikiri, Idah, Lokoja, Jebba, and beyond. These fairs were intricately connected to the local markets which were located on the banks of the Niger and in the interior settlements. They were also linked to North Africa by the caravan routes and the major entrepots of Jenne, Gao, Timbuktu, Kuka, and Kano. (See maps 4 and 5.)

✳ The marketplace was important to the social, political, and economic structures of the Igbo and it was a ritual, political and commercial center as well.[5] A collection of settlements shared a central market but in the less thickly populated districts, several settlements shared a number of periodic, rotating marketplaces. The scheduling of these markets was embedded in Igbo culture and derived from Igbo concepts of time.[6] Periodic markets were thus held on each day of the four-day Igbo week (*Izu*), namely, *Eke, Orie Afo,* and *Nkwo.* Markets were sometimes located between settlements rather than within them "so that they might be seen by all to be common property."[7] While women handled the local trade, most long-distance Igbo traders were men. They relied on covenants at the personal level, *igbandu,* as the principal means of guaranteeing freedom of movement across the country and safety among strangers.[8] In some parts of Africa, this covenant was sealed by marriage ties, while in others, by the settlement of slaves and other dependents along the caravan routes. A caravan of traders was in most cases accompanied by a large number of such specialists as smiths, carvers, priests, diviners and doctors, whose presence and services added to the caravan's prestige and diplomatic immunity. Some traders and ritual specialists also acted as the agents of important oracles.

Scholars seem to be uncertain as to which came first, local or long-distance trade. The argument centers around whether local trading arose "naturally" in response to the "complementary needs of communities which were in close proximity to each other" or whether local trading was stimulated primarily by long-distance trade.[9] It would appear that throughout West Africa local trade arose naturally as a result of the complementary needs of the communities, but in some parts of eastern and central Africa, as Hodder and others have argued, there might have been some "marketless zones" in which local trading activity did not even exist until long-distance trade was introduced.[10]

Whatever its origins, local trading derived much of its sustenance from long-distance trading inasmuch as the latter could not have flourished without the former. In most parts of Africa, long-distance trade stimulated local trading when the commodities, especially luxury items like gold and kola nuts, that passing caravans brought provided local communities with the incentive to produce complementary goods.[11] Long-distance trade relied primarily on the non-bulky or luxury items like beads, salt, ivory, dyes, cloth, and ritual objects, while local trading involved, in most cases, the collection and distribution of bulky food items, some of which, depending on the strength of the demand, were invariably channelled into long-distance trade. For example, yams were a bulky commodity but were ferried down the Niger River, over a distance of two hundred miles, because of the strong demand created by the provisioning trade. Though small in scale and numerous, it was upon the local and periodic markets that most long-distance trade routes, such as the Niger and trans-Saharan trades, drew their sustenance.

THE ATLANTIC SLAVE AND PROVISIONING TRADES

By A. D. 1500 the Niger trading system had been well advanced. A sixteenth-century Portuguese explorer, Duarte Pacheco Pereira, described the canoes he encountered at the mouth of the Rio Real, a dis-

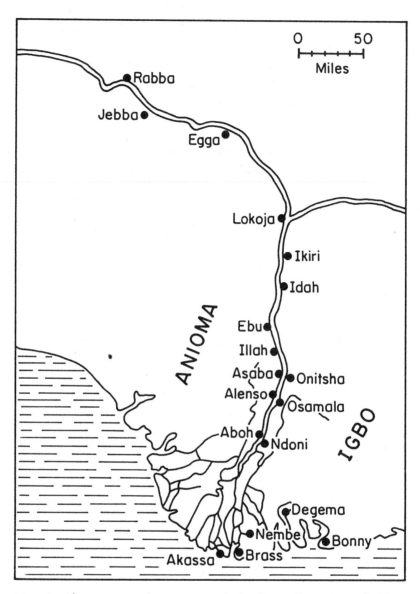

Map 4: The major trading centers of the Niger River from Rabba down to the Niger Delta

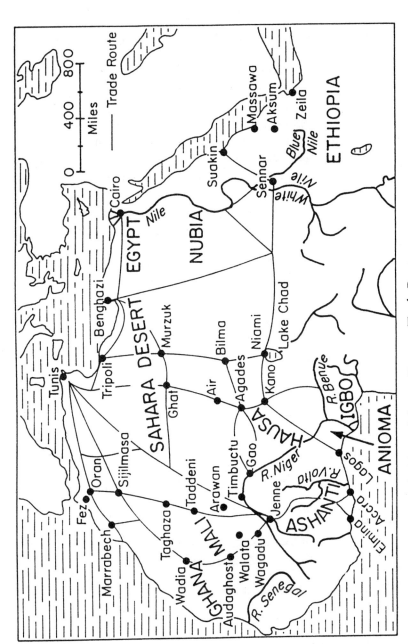

Map 5: River Niger and the Trans-Saharan Caravan Trade Routes

tributary of the Niger, as large enough to hold 80 men and travel down the river several hundred miles, conveying yams, cows, sheep and other commodities.[12] This report suggests that food trading on the Niger was well established even before the rise of the Atlantic slave trade in the sixteenth century. In fact, E. J. Alagoa has noted, "By the beginning of the sixteenth century this north-south trade was already far advanced, and carried on with huge canoes on a large scale over long distances." Alagoa emphasized that the overseas trade built on this ancient Niger trade.[13] David Northrup concurred, writing that "by the arrival of the Portuguese, the region was already a veteran of long-distance trade both up the Niger and westward to the Gold Coast, and in the case of the inter-coastal trade it was the Europeans who had to make the adaptation to existing African patterns."[14]

When the Atlantic slave trade became the dominant industry in the seventeenth century, some Africans in the region participated by producing large quantities of foodstuffs, including yams, palm oil, maize, and other food items normally purchased by European ship captains.[15] Slaves and crew had to be fed during the long periods that the ships spent at the coastal ports collecting their slave cargos, and also for sustenance during the middle passage. Thus, many communities made a good living of the slave trade by producing food for provisioning.[16] As the slave trade grew, so did the demand for provisions. David Northrup has estimated that at least 400,000 yams annually entered this trade from the Bight of Biafra at the beginning of the eighteenth century, a figure that increased to 1.2 million by the end of the century. Yams from the Lower Niger were also intended for sale to the coastal communities, which had experienced a population explosion and could not grow all of their food. These communities eventually neglected fishing, farming, and salt-making because of their preference for trading.[17]

These developments were observed and adequately documented by a number of nineteenth-century European explorers. During their Niger expedition of 1830, Richard and John Lander remarked that most of the yams which the Brass imported from Aboh were sold to European slave ships. The canoe in which the brothers were transported from Aboh to Brass contained over two thousand yams intended for sale to a Spanish slave ship on the Brass River.[18] Laird and Oldfield also commented on the trade of the Lower Niger, remarking that yams and foodstuffs from the hinterlands were exchanged for salt and European manufactured goods from the delta.[19] On the basis of these and other reports, noted Northrup, "one finds confirmation in the middle of the nineteenth century of trade in the same items that Pereira noted at the beginning of the sixteenth: food crops (especially yams) and livestock in exchange for salt."[20]

The people of Anioma participated in the slave and provisioning trades because their homelands had long been integrated into the trade of a region which itself had strong linkages with an interregional, multi-commodity commerce. Aboh chiefs and merchants maintained large fleets of war and trading canoes that plied the Niger, bringing foods and other commodities downstream to be exchanged for goods manufactured overseas. The Aboh were the most notable middlemen on the Lower Niger, acting as intermediaries between the Igala and the Niger Delta communities. Unlike slave raiding and slave trading, yam production required neither large capital investments nor elaborate regulatory structures to maintain. Throughout the period 1500 to 1900, the demand for labor to produce yams and other crops, to paddle the trading canoes, and to act as domestic servants was constant.

PALM OIL AND LABOR TRANSFORMATIONS IN THE NINETEENTH CENTURY

The people of Anioma were one of the most famous producers of yams and palm oil in precolonial Africa. In fact, they had produced and traded palm oil centuries before the Industrial Revolution in Europe generated a new demand in the early nineteenth century; until that time, Europeans had preferred cargoes of salves to cargoes of vegetable oils. When Europeans eventually decided to give up trading in human beings, Obi Ossai of Aboh assured them that if they stopped buying, he would stop selling.[21]

Thus the people of Anioma restructured their production to accommodate the expanded demand for palm oil. Statistical evidence shows that as the external slave trade declined, the palm oil trade increased, so that by the mid-nineteenth century, the overseas demand for palm oil and palm kernels had become too high for the available labor to meet. Not just a few hundred, but tens of thousands of tons of palm oil were being shipped to Europe annually. The rapid growth in the use of vegetable oils in Europe resulted from the demand for fats and oils of all sorts, together with the increased demand for soap for washing and candles for lighting. In addition, the new machinery of the factories and the railroads that proliferated during the Industrial

Revolution required lubricants. European traders, who hitherto had stayed on the coast, began to sail up the Niger to buy directly from inland producers, thanks to the age of the steamship. Between 1857 and 1879 European traders established over forty trading posts between Aboh and Lokoja, each spaced at approximately twenty-mile intervals.[22]

The rise in the palm oil trade also affected yam production. While demand for yams to sustain slaves and ships' crews declined with the external slave trade, internal demand continued to expand throughout the century because the growing Niger Delta communities often neglected farming in favor of more lucrative occupations.[23] In addition, the population of Onitsha, which grew rapidly in response to the European presence and the palm oil trade, had to be fed. Thus, apart from the labor required to produce palm oil and palm kernels for export, there was an increasing demand for labor to produce yams and other food crops for the internal market.

Since the amount of labor at the disposal of each household was limited in the short run, some enterprising local producers turned to the use of slave labor, secured through the normal process of trade, since Igbo homelands were situated on one of the most important trade routes in Africa. After 1840 the price of slaves on the Lower Niger dropped dramatically, which coincided with the expansion in the demand for palm oil. While the export of slaves to international markets was diminishing, thanks to British naval patrols on the coast of southern Nigeria, internal slave raiding in the regions north of the Niger-Benue confluence did not respond in kind. The humanitarians who had hoped that the "legitimate trade" would drive out the slave trade were disappointed. The supply mechanism which had delivered slaves to the coastal ports continued to function with greater efficiency; the Islamic reform movements launched from Sokoto in 1804 had spread to virtually every part of the grassland belt of Nigeria, generating wars on an unprecedented scale and yielding thousands of captives.[24] Slaves were ferried down the Niger, where they were sold for a pittance. The more enterprising male and female yam and palm oil producers in Anioma took advantage of the situation to amass cheap labor which, in turn, enabled them to climb rapidly onto higher rungs of the social ladder. For example, one Aboh woman in 1841 owned over two hundred slaves whom she kept to produce palm oil and yams.[25] In Asaba, Onitsha, and the other places, men became slave-owning chiefs almost overnight.

Some historians have wondered how the communities in the hinterland of the Bight of Biafra could have supplied millions of slaves to the Atlantic slave trade and yet after abolition, maintained dense populations. Where then did the slaves come from?[26] Baffled by this phenomenon, some scholars have argue that either the African slave trade was not as disruptive as was commonly represented in textbooks, or that the slaves sold at the coastal ports of southeastern Nigeria could not have been Igbo but instead were captives who had been marched through Igboland. It would appear that the latter argument is the more persuasive, but whatever the source, the available evidence confirms that during the peak period of the Atlantic slave trade (1650 to 1850) the people of Anioma, like many Igbo groups on the other side of the Niger River, shunned the prospect of slave raiding, even though they engaged in kidnapping. It would also appear that the Aros were the only Igbo group that accepted slave raiding as a vital part of their economic system, which they effectively combined with slave trading. But the Aro did not operate on the western side of the Niger and could not have influenced the Anioma communities.

All in all, the people of Anioma developed a complex, hierarchical social organization, a stable political system, and a lucrative trade during the one and half centuries following the repulsion of Benin military forces in 1750 and the conquest of Anioma by the British at the end of the nineteenth century. The society of Anioma was not particularly changed by the Atlantic slave trade; instead that trade encouraged the production of yams and palm oil for provisioning. Until the mid-nineteenth century, the bulk of these commodities was produced by family labor. It was only after the ending of Atlantic slaving from the Bight of Biafra and the arrival of the British in the interior that the society of Anioma entered a period of crisis that spanned the century between 1860 and 1960.

Meanwhile, from 1830 to 1920 southeastern Nigeria as a whole remained the world's premier palm oil and kernel producer. But this success could not have been achieved without female labor. Palm oil was processed by women because, traditionally, African men did not process foodstuffs. Large amounts of labor were required to meet the overseas demand for palm oil in addition to the palm kernels, foodstuffs, and other commodities that had to be produced at the same time. In the absence of mechanized devices, an efficient system of division of labor had to be worked out. Since the practice in most of Africa was to allocate roles on the basis of gender, families in southeastern Nigeria simply assigned to each sex a definite role in the new economy. As Susan Martin has shown, men cut down the ripe fruit bunches from the top of the trees, and women processed them into oil and kernels.[27]

Towards Colonial Economic Development: A Faulty Start

Meanwhile, palm oil remained profitable until the 1880s, when it went into a rapid decline, fluctuating rapidly in price, and bottoming out during the First World War. As early as 1905 many primary producers, mostly women, had lost interest in the palm oil trade because of what some colonial government officials described as the activities of middlemen. The primary producers, they said, were "somewhat unsophisticated" and could not or would not "see the reason for fluctuation of prices."[28] However, because southeastern Nigeria as a whole did not develop other cash crops, palm oil and kernel, remained for them the major source of foreign earnings. Experiments with cotton, rubber, and cocoa proved unsuccessful. Thus, while groundnuts (peanuts), cotton, cocoa, and rubber earned additional cash for the farmers of the other provinces of Nigeria, those farmers in the southeast continued to feel the pinch of a declining foreign trade till the 1920s.

The history of British enterprise in Anioma is further testimony that they had no vision of developing their colonial territories beyond converting them into sources of cheap labor, cheap raw materials, and markets for manufactured goods. Cotton was grown in some parts of Nigeria, not because the British colonial government and British industrialists wished to promote textile production in the country, but because, as Alan McPhee has boldly declared, they wanted "to divert the supply of cotton from the Nigerian hand-looms to the power-looms of Lancashire."[29]

The reason for developing Nigerian cotton for the benefit of British industries is not hard to find. In the nineteenth century Britian had begun to lose her traditional sources of cotton, notably the United States and India. If the British textile industry, the cornerstone of her industrialization, were to survive, other sources of cotton had to be found in the tropics. Nigeria, where cotton was already being widely cultivated, was a convenient starting point.[30]

While pursuing their policy of self-preservation, colonial administrators were required to discourage the development of any product that would not reinforce the necessary linkages between colonial raw materials supply and metropolitan industries. The fact that such products might be beneficial to the colonies was irrelevant. In addition, the construction of railway lines, harbors, and motor roads was not necessarily undertaken to provide the colonial subjects with a much-needed infrastructure, but to enhance the movement of troops and the rapid export of selected commodities to Europe. Thus, until after the Second World War, any discussion about the industrial development of the colonies for the colonies was either avoided or quashed.

Coupled with this unprogressive colonial economic policy was the concept of trusteeship. Trusteeship was rooted in the philosophy of minimum interference with native institutions.[31] Since trusteeship, as Lord W. M. Hailey has rightly pointed out, prescribed things to avoid rather than what should be done, British imperial agents were required to act as mere custodians or caretakers of their colonial estates.[32] The economic development of Anioma was delayed because the guiding principle of British colonialism in tropical Africa was based on this sentiment, and, in small measure, was also a result of the age-long Mercantile Policy which, in its classical form, discouraged the development of industries in the colonies for fear they would compete with "home" industries. It is regrettable that most scholars have neglected the economic aspects of the principle of trusteeship and have focused only on the cultural and political aspects when in fact the economic implications are more central to an understanding of the economic underdevelopment of Africa in the colonial period. In the pages that follow, we shall show how the trusteeship principle stifled the mining of the lignite deposits of Anioma and, at the same time, delayed the development of secondary industries and transportation infrastructure.

THE UNWORKED LIGNITE DEPOSITS OF ANIOMA

The reluctance of the British colonial government to promote industrial growth in the colonies for the benefit of their colonial subjects is illustrated by the failure to work the lignite deposits of Anioma and to construct a railway line that would have linked Asaba with Benin City, as proposed by some developers. The Nigerian colonial administration not only refused to extract, but also prevented others with proven interest and ability, to develop these lignite—a type of brown coal—deposits. This refusal, which hampered the development of a number of secondary industries in the area, emanated from the conviction that Anioma lignite would not in any way benefit British home industries. In fact, the colonial government feared that Anioma lignite would compete with coal imported from Britain which at that time was the only source of fuel for the Nigerian Railway and Nigerian river boats.

These new economic possibilities for Anioma had presented themselves when large deposits of lignite were discovered in Igbuzo (1904),

Obamkpa (1907), Okpanam (1908), and Nnewi (1909).[33] When these discoveries were announced, both the colonial administration and a number of private companies expressed interest in their development. In 1905 the Niger Company tested and reported favorably on the Igbuzo lignite. Samples of Obamkpa lignite were tested by the British Imperial Institute in London, and were considered a valuable source of fuel for the Nigerian railways, seagoing steamers, and steamboats plying the Niger River.[34] Developers hoped that, if produced in adequate quantities, the coal would save the administration large sums of money.[35] They were certain that the deposits extended over a very wide area, that the seams were of unusual thickness, that the deposits could be commercially exploited, and that the lignite was of high quality.[36] An analysis of the Okpanam lignite showed that it did not contain elements that might react with copper and brass engine fittings, and the researches concluded that the briquettes made from Okpanam lignite was a satisfactory and economic form of fuel.[37] Consequently, developers suggested that suitable machinery for the manufacture of briquettes be erected at or near Asaba.[38]

Sir Walter Egerton, the high commissioner of southern Nigeria, advised that since the director of the Imperial Institute, who was "the highest scientific authority," had satisfied himself that the Okpanam deposits were superior in quality to the lignite commonly used in Germany, he could not see the use for further tests. He went on to urge that all that was needed was to ascertain "the cost per ton of mining, transport to Asaba and briquetting this lignite."[39] The cost, he said, depended largely on output since the price per ton would fall if economies of scale could be established. Egerton also pointed out that he had little doubt that Okpanam lignite could be delivered briquetted for one-third the price of Welsh coal and could be used on the Niger, on the Baro-Kano Railway, and on the upper portion of the Lagos Railway.[40]

Egerton also requested approval for the construction of a railway line from Asaba to Okpanam. He reported that its extension west would render it a valuable line for the transport of forest and agricultural produce as well as the lignite. He estimated that the cost of the line and of the briquetting works would be very small compared with the benefits to be obtained and he had confidence that, even if the lignite works proved a failure, the rail line, if lengthened to twenty or more miles, would produce payable traffic.[41]

In short, colonial officials suggested that an economically viable mining industry should be opened up and that a rail line be constructed starting from Asaba, running westward to Agbor, Benin, and possibly Ijebu Ode and Lagos. Doing so would have opened the area, not by conquest, but by the introduction and expansion of trade and industry.

Rather than accept these recommendations, however, officials of the British government engaged themselves in a prolonged quarrel with a number of European companies and the people of southern Nigeria over these deposits. The major question was who should benefit from their exploitation.

The first to take up the matter was the Niger Company, which had seen the value of the mineral for fuel on its steamers. On August 21, 1907 the company applied for an exclusive license to prospect for minerals in certain parts of the Asaba district. The company's application was for an area of sixteen square miles, situated about eighteen miles due west of the Niger River.[42]

In his reply, the acting colonial secretary, P. F. Burrows, regretted that there had been a delay in issuing the license because the administration objected to the working of the minerals by persons other than the government. He expressed the wish that prospecting should continue and hoped that the difficulties in the matter would be surmounted. The issue of granting the company permission to exploit the mineral deposits dragged on for years and finally in 1911, the colonial secretary refused to entertain any applications for a license.[43]

Enraged by these delays, the Earl of Scarborough, who was chairman of the Niger Company, denounced the reluctance of the administration to permit the company to exploit "a mineral which might prove of incalculable advantage not merely to Nigeria but to the British Empire." His Lordship wished to ascertain, among other things, whether the colonial administration intended to keep some of the deposits in its own hands. He argued that if the administration "did not intend to prosecute these investigations energetically and systematically," then "the company which has been ready and anxious to do so for the past three years should be given encouragement and be allowed to go ahead." The Earl of Scarborough finally pleaded that the company's application for a prospecting license be given "due and early consideration" not only because of its large stake in the country, but also because it provided most of the river transport.

From the letters that passed to and from the Colonial Office and the various prospecting companies, it soon became evident that the Nigerian colonial administration was neither willing to allow other bodies to prospect for lignite nor to undertake the venture itself. At one time the administration proffered the excuse that it desired to reserve some portions of the deposit for its own use, in other words, that it had "from the first been the policy of government that it should itself undertake the development of the carboniferous area of Nigeria." At another time the Nigerian administration gave the excuse that the final decision in the matter rested, not with the Nigerian government, but with the secretary of state for the colonies.[44]

While one cannot immediately understand the reluctance of the Nigerian administration to exploit these deposits, one can fairly easily explain its reluctance to allow others to do so. As early as November 1910, Wyndham R. Dunstan, the director of the Nigerian Department of Mineral Surveys, had warned the Nigerian administration against the temptation to give concessions to private companies to work the lignite of Asaba, the coal of Udi, and the tin and timber of Uwet. He explained that as a result of the work of the mineral survey, the approximate nature and extent of the lignite deposits in the neighborhood of Asaba was now clear. Careful investigation of the Okpanam lignite, he went on, had shown that it was a valuable fuel and that its value would increase for certain purposes if the crude lignite was briquetted. He said that since lignite briquettes would be used largely as fuel on government railways and riverlaunches, the government itself should undertake the mining and briquetting of the material. If at a later period, he added, owing to increased demand or to other causes, the government should desire to transfer its responsibility to private concerns, there would be little doubt that the transfer could be arranged on profitable terms.[45]

A. G. Boyle, the acting governor of southern Nigeria, was of a different opinion. He warned that since the results of the tests were favorable, the question of the development of the lignite and coal areas could be definitely settled, and that persons of financial standing who were anxious to embark on the enterprise should be permitted to do so. He suggested, however, that the question of the reservation of certain areas for government purposes was of minor importance compared to the development of those areas, since "government interests can well be safeguarded by the insertion of a clause guaranteeing on behalf of the leases that such supplies as Government may require shall be supplied at a price to be agreed upon before the lease is signed." Finally, he warned that he personally was "averse to the Government embarking on a commercial enterprise of the nature of coal and lignite mining."[46]

Despite this and similar suggestions, the Colonial Office and the government of Southern Nigeria chose to play the "dog in the manger." They would not develop the lignite deposits, nor would they allow private enterprise to do so. This is particularly surprising because those

European companies wishing to prospect for minerals clearly stated that they were prepared to bear the entire costs of the operation. For instance, the South Nigerian Exploration Syndicate spent considerable sums in examining the fields and professed its willingness to set up a powerful company for the working of the deposits and to develop an export trade with the British and foreign colonial possessions on the West coast of Africa.[47]

THE SENTIMENT OF TRUSTEESHIP INVOKED

While the government sought to keep European companies from mining the lignite deposits of Anioma, it tried at the same time to deny the people of Anioma of any gains likely to be derived from the venture. In a confidential dispatch of July 28, 1910, Sir Walter Egerton, the governor of southern Nigeria, suggested that "arrangements should be made by agreement with the native communities for the transfer to the Government of their rights over various lignite fields, as in the case of mineral oil."[48] While the governor spoke of agreements between officials and chiefs, other administrators talked of outright seizure of the deposits. In a dramatic turnaround, Egerton, who had spoken of arrangements between chiefs and officials, now urged the government to seize "all lignite areas in the Niger valley, of which the chief are Okpanam, Ibusa [Igbuzo] and Obompa [Obamkpa] on the right bank and Nnewi on the left bank." He claimed that these areas fell well within the lands over which the Niger Company had obtained control by means of treaties with the chiefs and that therefore the government already had the necessary control.[49]

In making such declarations, officials of the colonial administration were already reversing Ralph Moor's proclamation of 1902, the first legislation that dealt with mining in southern Nigeria.[50] The proclamation was based on the theory that all lands in the Protectorate were vested either in the chiefs of native communities in trust for such communities, or in the government.[51] Thus, even though the government exercised the sole right to grant prospecting licenses, it could not issue a license without first obtaining the consent of the chiefs of a community in which the deposits were found. However, if the chiefs refused to give their approval, the Supreme Court was empowered to enforce the grant provided that the chiefs' refusal was held to be "detrimental to the interests of such community."

The proclamation further stated that all fees and taxes on profits were to be deposited with the treasury; where the lands subject to license or lease were the property of a native community, one fifth of the fees and one third of the taxes on profits were to be given to the chiefs of such community, to be distributed among its members or applied for their benefit according to native laws and custom, or as the high commissioner might direct.[52]

The colonial government was soon to brush these regulations aside. Under the Minerals Bill enacted in 1912 and amended in 1913, the native communities were deprived of any share of fees, rents, or profits to which they were entitled under the previous law. They could not even object to the government's decision to grant prospecting licenses or mining leases.[53]

As would be expected, a colonial government administrator defended the new law by stating that it was necessary to abolish the provisions for sharing fees, rents, and royalties with the natives while it could be done without hardship. He wondered how the government, which spent large sums in exploring the country for minerals, should take rents and royalties from Europeans and share it among natives who had done nothing for which they were entitled to be paid. He added that "the idea of mineral rights has probably never entered the native mind, and if the proposal is carried out he will only lose something which he didn't know that he had."[54]

These troubling illustrations corroborate the colonial government's unwillingness to deal fairly with its colonial subjects. They also exemplify trusteeship in action. Rather than acknowledge the injustices of the new ordinance, Lord Frederick Lugard stated that he shared the same view with Sir Walter Egerton, i. e., that mineral rights in the Eastern and Central Provinces "may properly be regarded as vested in the [British] Crown by right of Conquest."[55] Thus, while Egerton rested his claim to the wealth of Anioma on the forged "X" treaties of the Royal Niger Company, Lugard based his judgment on the right of conquest. Whatever the basis, the end result was the same: the rights of indigenous people to their own land and resources were summarily denied.

For reasons that yet have to be discerned—possibly the opposition which the Minerals Ordinance of 1913 aroused both in Nigeria and in Britain, or possibly the discovery of coal deposits in Udi, near Enugu— the British government soon decided to discontinue all mineral surveys in southern Nigeria, at least for the time being.[56] It also decided not to listen to any more requests for permission to prospect for lignite in Nigeria or to make any further attempts to exploit even the deposits that were already known to exist.[57] What is more, the idea of constructing a rail line from Asaba westward was put aside.

Thus British chose to exploit rather than develop its colonies. Under British colonialism, mineral deposits, agricultural products, roads, railway lines, and harbors were developed only if they would benefit the metropolitan country. Only the production of colonial resources necessary for the growth of British industries was to be encouraged; the welfare of the colonial subjects was secondary.

THE END OF DOMESTIC SLAVERY

By the end of 1914, the more serious British attacks and Igbo risings had come to an end, although as late as 1928, when direct taxation was introduced, the British continued to send troops to suppress sporadic violent outbursts. Despite the forced intrusion, however, the British imperial government did not immediately achieve its prime purpose of invading Anioma. This was due to certain problems associated with labor. First, the chiefs and elders of Anioma still controlled the local labor supply and, under the prevailing hostile conditions, there was no assurance that they would be willing to release their dependents to build roads and bridges, to produce and deliver commodities to the European buying stations, and to construct government houses and military barracks. Second, although the population of Anioma was dense relative to other regions of Nigeria, labor was not given enough incentives to freely offer itself for hire, nor could the colonial government, which had committed itself to the abolition of internal slavery, directly make use of slave labor. Rather than give the necessary incentives to labor by paying appropriate wages, officials resorted to covert strategies intended to recruit cheap labor.

Disguised as part of an antislavery campaign, officials passed several laws which in effect transferred the control of labor from the hands of chiefs and elders into those of officials. For example, under the Master and Servant Proclamation No. 12 of 1903, slaves were now to be called "apprentices," and both they and their masters were to be bound by contracts laying down terms of service.[58] The law made it illegal for any slave to leave his master's house and prescribed a term of imprisonment for any person wandering around or having no apparent means of subsistence. Another law authorized officials to call on chiefs or heads of houses to provide forced labor. It stipulated that "every chief may require all able-bodied men between the ages of 15 and 50, and all able-bodied women between the ages of 15 and 40 residing within his jurisdiction . . . to work in accordance with his direction on any river, creek, or road."[59] Anyone who refused to carry out the orders of his chief or house head was to be punished by fine, imprisonment, or flogging. Of course, the chiefs who would be giving orders to these workers were themselves also under the control of the colonial government. Officials explained that these enactments were necessary to accelerate the suppression of slavery and the establishment of a free labor market.[60]

These laws were to be enforced by the native courts. In the event of a dispute arising between a slave and his or her owner, the final decision in the matter rested with the courts; a detachment of the Southern Nigeria Regiment stationed in Asaba had policing powers. Since the warrant chiefs were government appointees, they were obliged to advance British interests rather than those of the Anioma communities they were supposed to represent.

The Christian missionaries and their new converts, together with the warrant chiefs and other government functionaries, drew the attention of slaves to the declining power of their owners. Although officials tried to discourage mass desertion and social unrest, thousands of slaves responded to the antislavery proclamations by simply walking away; no one stopped them and many were never heard of again. Several thousands more remained behind, not to work for the communities that previously owned them, but for themselves. Some went further to demand equal treatment, a fair share of the communal land, and full membership in the communities in which they lived. At Abala, for example, more than half the population of the town simply moved away in a body and established another settlement a few miles away.[61] Elsewhere, former slaves converted their slave villages, *ugwule*, into autonomous settlements, which they organized like the host lineages and with which in due course, they claimed fictitious relationships.

Many bitter conflicts took place between owners and former slaves who remained behind. The colonial government officials who had formulated the emancipation proclamations vacillated between giving the freed men and women complete autonomy and confining them to the houses to which they formerly belonged. Sometimes officials supported the ex-slaves' demand for complete autonomy and clamped down on former slave owners who tried to break the antislavery regulations, while at other times, the government tried to restrain former slaves from leaving. The dispute over the status of freed men and women, and the uncertainties surrounding their new relationship with their former owners, remained unclear until 1916 when the government passed the final law against domestic slavery in Nigeria. By this law, the colonial government abolished the legal status of slavery throughout the country and, at the same time, reenacted the Native House Rule Ordinance of 1912.[62] That law had declared that the government would no longer recognize the authority of heads of houses over their slaves, nor could the police be allowed to assist in recapturing those who left. The road to emancipation in Nigeria might have been paved with good intentions, but it was only achieved with much pain.

"WHEN THE SLAVES LEFT, THEIR OWNERS WEPT"

A chief of Aboh recalled the painful side of the end of slavery on the Lower Niger by observing, "When the slaves left, their owners wept."[63] Robbed of their slaves and therefore their investments, many owners became as poor as the "ordinary" citizens. A few persons tried to stop those they still regarded as their slaves from leaving but were arrested and then brought before the native courts where they were prosecuted for violating the law against slave dealing. Such disputes were reviewed by officials and in all cases the decisions favored the former slaves rather than owners. Many Aniomans, appalled by the humiliation of a military defeat and by the fact that they and those they still regarded as their slaves would be treated as equals under the new British laws, refused to press to be compensated for the loss of what had formerly been their property. In any case, no such provisions could be found in the antislavery regulations, for to compensate owners would have meant that the colonial government recognized owners' rights over other human beings in the first place.

Meanwhile, despite the obvious shortage of labor, the Christian missionaries continued to entice boys and girls from the family farms to the mission schools. Worse still, youths who graduated or dropped out of these schools hardly ever returned to the family farms, instead, wandering off to the new administrative, commercial, and mining centers in search of wage labor. Many who could not immediately find employment joined the ranks of the *lumpenproletariat* that began to emerge in colonial Nigeria, a throng whom Frantz Fanon has characterized as a "horde of starving men, uprooted from their tribe and from their clan."[64] Those who did find jobs returned to their hometowns half a century later, as H. Vaux observed, "in enjoyment of pension."[65] Indeed, with a stroke of the pen, colonial administrators dissolved two social classes (slaves and the ruling class of chiefs) and created two (workers and *lumpenproletariat*).

It is needless to emphasize that the departure of former slaves and educated youths compounded those labor and food crises which the British imperial conquest had set in motion. The chiefs and elders of Anioma faced considerable turmoil in terms of social status and economic welfare. Having capitalized on the sudden expansion of palm oil exports, together with the spread of the Islamic jihads in the mid-nineteenth century, to amass wealth through cheap labor, they had risen to higher levels on the social ladder; now, however, they must grow their own yams, fish for themselves, and paddle their own canoes. Indeed, it was not for nothing that owners wept when the slaves left.

One can see in British enterprise in Anioma the creation of a vicious circle of poverty, food scarcity, and loss of prestige. Food shortages and harsh taxation gave rise to labor migration; labor migration resulted in the dislocation of the social relations of production, which further depressed the people's capacity to produce food. Heads of households were beaten and sent to prison for tax evasion. Some parents had to pawn their sons and daughters to raise tax money.[66] In the 1930s, during the worldwide depression, Anioma men who could neither feed their families nor pay colonial taxes fled to northern and western Nigeria, following the railway lines. Some settled in the tin mining districts around Jos, some in the railway junction towns of Kaduna and Zaria, some in the trading entrepot of Kano, and others in the cocoa belts around Ondo, Ibadan, and Lagos. There, they hoped, perhaps, to build new homes, but another upheaval awaited in the form of the Nigerian civil crisis of 1966 to 1970. Life was very trying for the people of Anioma brought up in the harsh years of the colonial period.

INFLUENZA EPIDEMIC: COMPOUNDING THE LABOR AND FOOD CRISIS

It is important to remember that throughout the colonial period yams remained the major staple food of the people of Anioma and were central to their world. As long as this crop remained in adequate supply, the Igbo would not willingly switch to other foodstuffs, nor would they show any inclination to experiment with other food sources unless convinced that the new crops had certain advantages or were a useful addition to the existing range of foods. Indeed, we have ample evidence that the people of Anioma remained attached to yams until the early twentieth century, when British enterprise ushered in a major famine. The food crisis that British conquest and rule set in motion was accelerated, first, by the labor crisis already examined, and then, by an influenza epidemic which broke out in 1918. This terrible epidemic killed more Anioma men and women in six months than had all the thirty years of war with Britain.

The final collapse of the palm oil trade in 1915 was caused largely by the beginning of the First World War, the reallocation of shipping toward the war effort, and the exclusion of the Germans, who bought the bulk of West Africa's palm kernels, from the West African trade. With the failure of the palm oil industry yams became once more the main source of household incomes in Anioma, as they had been in the period before 1830. But times had changed greatly. The cultivation of yams was very exacting, requiring dense bush to be cleared and burned during the last weeks of the dry season. When the rains finally came, men proceeded to make large yam mounds in readiness for planting, and for the ensuing four or five months the plants had to be closely cared for. The young tendrils had to be protected from heat with sisal leaves and stacked with bamboo sticks and tree branches. The field had to be weeded at least three times during the growing period, and after harvest, the crop had to be transported and stacked quickly. Only households who still had access to large supplies of labor could satisfactorily cope with these difficult tasks.[67] With the exodus of slaves and youths, heads of households found themselves in a most pathetic situation.

The First World War further drained the energies of colonial subjects, as they were subjected to all forms of exactions as part of the "war effort." In a bid to collect revenue, the colonial administration raised both import and export duties. Commodities that previously were exempt from taxation, now were taxed.[68] These measures resulted in further severe hardships, marked by rising prices of all commodities, food shortages, unemployment in the urban centers, and political unrest in many parts of West Africa.[69] A colonial administrator confessed that "it is unfortunate that while the price of all imported commodities had risen enormously during the war, the price of palm oil and palm kernels had been kept at the pre-war level: and this —to some extent, at least—by direct state control."[70]

Meanwhile, as part of the "war effort," all Nigerian communities made voluntary and involuntary contributions of cash and foodstuffs to the colonial administration, while able-bodied young men were conscripted into the armed forces. Some were shipped away to the Cameroon, some to East Africa, and others to the Sahara and the Far East to fight the enemies of His Imperial Majesty, the King of England, and to preserve the British Empire. A large number of these conscripts never returned to their motherland. When these European-instigated conflicts ended in mid-1918 humanity was visited by a terrible legacy: the influenza virus.

The influenza pandemic of 1918–19 was one of history's worst short-term demographic disasters. It affected the entire world, killing an estimated 22 million people in about twelve months.[71] Since the dawn of human history no other disaster, natural or artificial, has claimed so many lives within such a short period of time. In Sub-Saharan Africa nearly 2 million lives were lost.[72]

Virologists are not in agreement on the origins of the 1918–19 influenza pandemic. Most believe, however, that some localized forms of the disease had broken out in certain United States cities between January and March 1918, and were then carried to Europe by American soldiers engaged in the First World War. In April 1918, large numbers of cases of influenza occurred among American and Allied troops in France, Britain, Portugal, Italy, Greece, Switzerland, Germany, Denmark, Norway, Holland and Sweden.[73] The disease underwent a rapid recombination and in August a second violent wave broke out almost simultaneously in Boston in the USA, and Brest in France, and then spread to all parts of the world, killing an average of 60,000 people each day.

Another school of virologists has suggested that the virus developed independently in Asia and Europe, and that the disease might have been brought to France by Chinese laborers.[74] This thesis is not widely supported, however. Whatever its origin, by July 1918 the disease had become fully established in Europe, from where it began to diffuse to the rest of the world. In August, a ship that had docked in a British port carried persons suffering from influenza to Freetown, Sierra Leone, from where the disease was taken to the Gold Coast and then to Nigeria by passengers who travelled by ocean ships.

Having reached the Nigerian seaports, the epidemic made its way into the interior following the trade routes, such as railway lines, motor roads, river and caravan routes, progressing "according to the speed of normal transport prevailing on each highway."[75] Within a few weeks, cases of influenza began to appear in western and northern towns and villages, starting with those on the Lagos-Kano railway.

From the north, influenza veered southward and, following the course of the Niger River, entered southeastern Nigeria. On October 14, the disease was brought to Onitsha from Lokoja, and in a week or two, entire towns and villages in the Onitsha province were thoroughly attacked.[76] Also from the Niger, the epidemic spread to Asaba and the other towns of Anioma, causing much panic and consternation. A report of the Roman Catholic Mission at Asaba stated that the

people of this town, disturbed by the rumor that influenza was causing havoc in Sierra Leone, Lagos, and parts of northern Nigeria,
gathered each morning at the post office, expecting to hear from relatives who had emigrated to these places as wage laborers. One morning, while a large crowd assembled, news arrived that influenza had
broken out in Asaba itself and the gathering broke up.[77] In a few
days, the town was thrown into mourning as virtually every family
had someone to bury. From here, influenza spread to Agbor, appearing
there on October 19 and Ubiaja a few days later.

Also from Onitsha the epidemic rapidly spread east and southward. It eluded the observation of medical workers because it was not
often spread by patients with advanced symptoms, but by those with
mild attacks who continued to perform their daily tasks and mingled
with the healthy populations in public places, schools, churches, marketplaces and in the streets. There was also the problem of inadequate
supply of medical officers; only fifty-three were in the entire country
(thirty-two in the south and twenty-one in the north), most of them
bearing such official titles as sanitary officers. Another problem was
created by people attempting to escape from the epidemic. In Port
Harcourt, for example, nearly one thousand laborers deserted their
jobs and returned to their home towns and villages, thereby introducing influenza into the outlying settlements.

Altogether, the epidemic killed half a million people in Nigeria, a
very large number considering that the population of the country at
that time was only eighteen million. More important than the total
killed was the demographics of morbidity and mortality. The old suffered less than the young and men suffered more than women. Very
few cases of deaths of persons over forty-five years of age were recorded.[78] Mortality was greater among women who were pregnant
than those who were not. Similarly, children suffered less than adults.
The overall impression was that mortality was highest in the age
bracket of 20–45 years, the group from which the country's labor pool
was primarily drawn. With food already in desperately short supply
and the yoke of British imperialism straining the people of Anioma to
their limits, the epidemic dealt the final blow to the people's resistance to external rule.

THE SPREAD OF CASSAVA
CULTIVATION IN ANIOMA

We have in Anioma a very convincing historical linkage between
the influenza pandemic of 1918–19 and the spread of cassava cultiva-

tion, that is, a linkage between an epidemic disease and a food crop.[79] Cassava was probably introduced into the Niger Delta region in the seventeenth century by Portuguese explorers and traders, possibly from Brazil, where the food had been cultivated for thousands of years. Cassava, together with paw-paw and maize, are considered the primary foods brought into Africa from the so-called New World. Some seventeenth-century European visitors to the Niger Delta made mention of cassava fields they found there, but no similar reports were made of the cultivation of the crop in the hinterlands. Thus, we may conclude that for three hundred years after its introduction into the Nigerian region, cassava remained confined to the Niger Delta. It was only in the early twentieth century (perhaps beginning in the late nineteenth century) that the Igbo people began to cultivate the crop, at a time when it became increasingly difficult for most households to subsist on yams. Strictly speaking, therefore, cassava production in Igboland is a twentieth-century affair, a view confirmed by both oral and written sources, although there are hints that cassava made an uneventful appearance in parts of Anioma in the 1870s. Michael Onwuejeogwu made mention in his *Traditional Political Systems of Ibusa* of the cassava age-grade, *ogbo akpu nkono* (1876–78), which was reserved for all those who were born when cassava was introduced into Igbuzo.[80] It is not unlikely that cassava made its first appearance in the last quarter of the nineteenth century, but we must recognize the difference between the time when a crop is introduced and when it is generally accepted as a regular food item.

Today, most Lower Niger Igbo men and women in their eighties can tell fairly accurately when cassava was introduced into their districts. I investigated this matter in the 1970s and 1980s in Igboland and virtually every elder I spoke with insisted that cassava was introduced within their memory. They pointed out that cassava came with *enu oyibo*, European colonial rule; some said, more specifically, after the influenza epidemic of 1918–19. Some elders recalled that soon after the arrival of the British, the country was visited by a terrible sickness called *ifelunza* (influenza). They insisted that it was an experience they had not forgotten, when *unwu* (hunger) and *ugani* (starvation) overran the nation. To commemorate the occasion, the influenza age-grade, *ogbo ifelunza*, was declared; in some Anioma towns, such Igbuzo, all men and women born between 1918 and 1921 belonged to it. Also such leading economic historians of Africa as David Northrup, are strongly convinced that "it was only in the twentieth century" that yams were "replaced by cassava as the staple food in much of the hinterland" of southeastern Nigeria.[81] The shift from yams to cassava was the direct result of the British imperial presence in Nigeria as marked by the punitive expeditions of that period, the labor crisis, the First World War, and the influenza pandemic of 1918–19, influenza being the last straw to break the camel's back.

A number of facts are particularly interesting about Anioma reminiscences concerning the influenza pandemic of 1918–19 and the spread of cassava cultivation. The first is the almost unanimous insistence by informants that, even if cassava was known before the outbreak of the epidemic, the crop was hardly ever cultivated. They wondered why a person would bother to grow cassava when he had enough yams in the barn. They also thought that it would have been absurd for a household to grow a crop for which there was no market or demand.

The fact that the Anioma people should consciously substitute cassava (an inferior food) for yams (a superior food), is a clear indication of the drastic decline in the factors necessary for the successful production of yams. There was neither drought nor land shortage; there were an epidemic and a labor shortage, however. The high rate of influenza deaths among the most vigorous sections of the Anioma population, severely depleted the main agricultural labor force. More importantly, the epidemic killed more men than women, men being the main cultivators of yams, so that yams, whose cultivation demanded a great deal of manual male labor, became severely affected by the mass withdrawal of male labor from the rural economy. When the epidemic was finally contained, the people of Anioma were forced to reconsider their ancient attachment to yams.

They were quick to realize that the cultivation of cassava required less labor and could, together with processing, be left to women and children, while the few available men concentrated on yam production and house roofing. Furthermore, since the collapse of the palm oil business, some amount of female labor had been freed, but ancient customs did not permit them to be integrated into yam cultivation. Cassava cultivation seemed naturally to fill the gap created by the decline in palm oil and kernel production. Having finally decided to experiment with cassava, the various Anioma communities must soon have realized that a cassava field needed little or no weeding; that when growing, the plant required no staking; and that when mature, it could be left in the soil for several years. They also would have realized that cassava thrived on old farmlands that were about to be left fallow, and that, unlike yams, cassava could be planted and harvested continuously throughout the year.[82] With these natural advantages, cassava proved a welcome supplement in a situation of acute food and labor shortages.

All in all, cassava cultivation was late to arrive in Anioma because more acceptable foods had hitherto rendered experimentation with new staples unnecessary. Anthony G. Hopkins has written that "where new plants and seeds were adopted, it was not because they caught the fancy of a primitive people, but because they were seen as useful additions to the existing range of foods, being worth more than the extra cost of producing them; or alternatively because they were regarded as good substitutes, yielding a higher return for the same input than the crops they displaced."[83] This is an accurate observation, for as some Anioma elders clearly stated, when cassava was introduced, "no one was prepared to eat it," but when the people became used to eating it, "they began to grow it."[84] To the Igbos of the twentieth century, cassava was accepted because of the failure of yams, and only when they were convinced that cassava would yield a higher return for the same input than yams, did they begin to grow it.

The cassava farmers of Anioma, who were mostly women, were aided in the development of this new crop by the arrival of the motor lorry and the completion of the eastern rail line in the 1920s. This "revolution in transportation" facilitated the movement of both traders and foodstuffs from the producing areas to major population centers. By the 1930s, cassava products from southern Nigeria were being sold in distant northern markets—in Jos and Kaduna, and in Zaria and Kano—and cassava cultivation had spread to most parts of Anioma. One of the most important centers of production was Obiarukwu. Even in those areas where yams were held in great veneration or consumed due to culture preference, cassava was still produced for sale. Thus, whereas cassava was virtually unknown in Anioma before 1900, by the 1930s it was being cultivated by virtually every rural woman. Men continued to refuse to grow cassava, however.

ANIOMA WOMEN AND CASSAVA PROCESSING

The two most common cassava foods produced in Anioma were *gari* (grated cassava) and *akpu* (mashed cassava). Until the arrival of grating machines, these foods were processed by women using traditional methods. While the last three or four decades have witnessed the introduction of cassava-processing machines, most edible cassava is still produced by small-scale rural female farmers, using traditional methods that are both tedious and time consuming.

Virtually every Anioma woman produces *gari* for family consumption or for sale. The equipment required for this activity is simple and easy to procure. It consists of a cutlass and a knife, a head pan, a clean cotton or baft bag, a large fire pan, and a fireplace. The mature cassava can be harvested at any time of the year since the tuberous roots do not grow deep into the soil. The woman makes periodic trips to her cassava field and returns home with a headload of tubers. Sometimes with the assistance of her children, she carefully peels the skin with a sharp knife. The tubers are then washed and grated.

The grating device is an incredibly crude tool, a sheet of galvanized iron, perforated in a hundred or more places with a nail and then clamped onto a narrow wooden board with the sharp nail openings turned outward. When in use, this tool rests on the user's laps and is supported with one hand as the user vigorously rubs each cassava tuber against the sharp nail openings. The grated cassava is collected in a container placed on the ground between the user's legs. The user works in this fashion for approximately two hours to produce about fifty pounds of grated cassava.

After grating, the cassava has to be dried. The drying process is also very crude. The grated cassava is transferred into a clean baft bag and the mouth securely tied with a string or rope. This bag is placed between three or more wooden frames and then tied firmly. It is then left in the sun for three or four days during which the watery content drains from the grated cassava. Some efficient and inexpensive pressing machines are now in use to speed up the draining process.

The end product, *gari,* is produced when the dry, grated cassava is baked in a large baking pan over an open fire. A certain quantity of this material is placed in the hot pan and stirred constantly. Sometimes a small amount of palm oil is added to color and flavor the *gari.* This is important because unseasoned cassava has a sour taste and an unattractive look, and might be mistaken for sawdust. Since the woman has to bake the cassava in small quantities it might take four hours to produce fifty pounds of *gari.* Once the mealy *gari* is dried, it is prepared and eaten in various forms like *fufu* (a pasty dough), and when mixed with water and sugar it can be eaten with cooked beans, fish, plantains or coconut. *Gari* is very much coveted by urban dwellers not only because it is cheaper than most foods, but also because it is easier to prepare and store than the older staples.

The production of *akpu* or mashed cassava is the logical follow-up of the production of pounded yam, which is a favorite dish of most southern Nigerians. *Akpu* is made from mashed cassava. To produce it, the tubers have to be soaked in water for up to four days to make them soft. To be eaten, *akpu* must be cooked and pounded. *Akpu* is usually treated as pounded yam and is eaten with rich vegetable soup. Except that it has a somewhat odd smell, one could easily mistake it for pounded yam.

Be that as it may, by the mid-1950s, *gari* and *akpu* had become two important food types and two of the most attractive sources of household income in Anioma. Yams, the most important staple food, whose production had been monopolized by men, suffered further setbacks partly because of growing population pressure on available land, and partly because the crop remained labor intensive. On the other hand, cassava's popularity increased not only because of the advantages it enjoyed over other staples, but also because it was, and still is, a base for animal feeds and the source of a number of industrial raw materials such as starch for the textile industry and glue for the wood industry.

Although cassava could have been produced efficiently on a large-scale using hired labor on plantations, no attempt was made in Anioma to do so. Experience must have convinced the people of this region that the plantation system was undesirable because of certain problems associated with land scarcity, soil conservation, and labor supply. Cassava cultivation has remained in the subsistence sector of the economy even though the crop is also a cash crop. Today, about ninety percent of the cassava produced in Anioma is by household labor. Cultivated areas per household hardly exceed two acres and production techniques are well suited to the use of simple tools like hand hoes and machetes.

The food crisis in Nigeria enabled the "cassava women" of Anioma to improve their economic and social status in society. Their new-found wealth freed them considerably from economic dependence on men. Even though men are still regarded as heads of most households, actual economic power in the rural, non-wage sectors is almost entirely in the hands of women. All women who engage vigorously in cassava production are guaranteed high and steady incomes because about seventy percent of the population of southern Nigeria regard cassava products as the major source of food. During the Nigerian oil boom period (1970–82) most food items were in large supply and cassava was still treated as "a poor man's food" in certain sections of the country. But after the decline of the oil boom, the more favored foods, like yams, rice, and wheat bread, were removed from the reach of the vast majority of the population. Today, cassava is no longer despised; it is almost the only food available at reasonable prices.

Most Anioma women now use the funds they accumulate from cassava production to care for their households. Without female labor, many households would starve. Women now pay local taxes and other forms of community levies on behalf of their families. They control the running of the local markets and finance the education of their children and other dependents. In some of the large communities, I found that most women grew cassava with hired labor. This was particularly the case in certain districts where large numbers of seasonal migrant laborers poured in from eastern Igboland and Urhoboland at the beginning of each farming season. Most of these migrant farmers were men who would not grow cassava in their own home regions.

THE DECLINE OF POLYGAMY

Because the spread of cassava cultivation brought changing roles to Anioma women, no examination of gender relations in this region is complete without considering the decline of polygamy at the end of the colonial period. Polygamy among the Igbo was both a social and economic institution. It was prevalent in the precolonial period, not because men wanted many sex partners, but because it was a major source of labor for peasant cultivation and commercial enterprise. As we have seen, the vast majority of local traders in West Africa were women who combined trading with farming and such other household chores as cooking, cleaning, and teaching young people the culture of the society. Large amounts of labor were required for the system of shifting cultivation prevalent in peasant agriculture, but wage labor was almost nonexistent and mechanized agriculture out of the question. Therefore one of the prime preoccupations of any household was to increase its size in order to augment its labor force, and polygamy was one of the surest means of doing so. Of course, like every other human-made institution, polygamy had its problems. Among those to be expected, though not always so, were the bickering of co-wives, witchcraft accusations, and occasional battering from a stressed husband. Nonetheless, the institution benefitted many households insofar as it enabled them to rapidly increase their size and wealth.[85] It also enabled them to forge a wide range of ties with many brothers- and sisters-in-law whose services could be solicited during the farming season or when the building of a large house was required. In the event of a personal tragedy, especially in a society that had no form of insurance, these brothers- and sisters-in law could be invaluable. As a chief of Asaba put it, a man with only one wife was considered a poor man and could not purchase the eze title.[86] Yet by the end of the colonial period, polygamy had lost its appeal. What happened?

Polygamy in Anioma was undermined by Christianity and British colonialism, through the conscious formulation and implementation of policies whose aim was to destroy it. The battle against polygamy was first championed by the Christian missionaries. As Jomo Kenyatta has pointed out, while the Africans saw polygamy as a fulfillment of a traditional custom, part of which aimed at preserving the clan, the Christian missionaries saw it as nothing but a device to amass sex partners.[87] Because Christianity upheld the principle of monogamy, every convert felt obliged to shun polygamy. Between 1900 and 1960, there was a noticeable switch from polygamy to monogamy as Christianity spread in Igboland. At first the relationship between the Christian missionaries and chiefs (who owned the most wives) was very bellicose. In due course, however, some chiefs converted, accepted the water of baptism, and cast away all their wives except one. Such requirements and the responses they elicited created confusion and undermined traditional customs (see chapter 4).

The British colonial administrators sided with the missionaries in this conflict, and working through the agency of the native courts, drove the indigenous marriage customs almost out of existence. Opportunities for divorce were consciously increased as few obstacles were placed in the way of petitioners. Akinjide Osuntokun has shown that the Iseyin people showed great resentment "against the British inspired judicial system which made divorce easier for African women."[88] Philip Igbafe has found that in one province of Southern Nigeria, seventy-five percent of the civil cases were concerned with divorce, that most of the petitions were granted, and that the petitions were nearly in all cases from wives against their husbands. Explaining the reason for the erosion of a system upon which the social relations of production were built, Igbafe noted that native laws which "did not pass the test of British morality were either considerably modified or rejected, while British concepts of justice led to the introduction of innovations."[89]

Christianity and the judicial system apart, the strain of the colonial economy, which forced men to seek wage labor in urban centers where public housing was designed for monogamous families, made polygamy almost unworkable.[90] In addition, the rearing of children became progressively more expensive, particularly when they were required to spend many years at school. Thus the polygamous life became more and more burdensome for the first generation of migrant Igbo laborers.

An example can be found in the life of Obi Okwuose who was born in Asaba in about 1875, the year that the Church Missionary Society built its first church and school there. As a boy, Okwuose witnessed the conflicts that raged between his people and the Christian missionaries, and was barely thirteen years old when half of Asaba was destroyed by the soldiers of the Royal Niger Company. Okwuose's parents were followers of the traditional religion and Okwuose never had a formal "western education." He was, however, one of the first Asabans to secure a place in the wage labor market that was slowly beginning to evolve on the Lower Niger.

Okwuose was first employed as a laundry man by the officials of the Royal Niger Company, and he devoted his entire energy to his job. His contacts with his European masters enabled him to speak English "tolerably well."[91] By 1925 he was fifty years old and had in his possession testimonials from military officers, residents, and judges. One of his employers was Judge V. N. Kener, the Catholic colleague of Sir James Marshall, who ordered the conquest of Asaba in 1888 and, in the same year, assisted Father Zappa and the Roman Catholics to establish themselves in the town. Like his parents, Okwuose remained faithful to the religion of his fathers.

When Asaba ceased to be the seat of government in 1904, Okwuose travelled to Benin City and Warri looking for work but in doing so, left behind in Asaba five of his seven wives. While away, Okwuose periodically sent money to the wives and children he left behind. However, considering the wage rate for laundry men and what money Okwuose could send home, the home remittance could hardly support five wives and several children. He also had to support the two wives and the other children who lived with him in Benin City and Warri. When eventually Okwuose returned to Asaba, he found out that four of his wives had deserted. Nevertheless, he invested his entire savings in the fulfillment of his dream; he took the *eze* title which, at this time had lost its ancient value, "except for the decorative." Although his eze title enabled Okwuose to occupy a place among other titled chiefs in the town council of Asaba, he could no longer fully reconcile himself with life in a purely traditional setting. He soon converted to Christianity and gave up polygamy. He also gave up the practice of offering sacrifices at the ancestral shrines. No one knows if his new-found religion gave him peace and joy, but the Roman Catholic Fathers at Asaba described his final adventure as "a remarkable conversion."

Okwuose was only one out of several thousand Anioma men whose traditional homes were broken up by the strain of the colonial economy. As the hardships of the colonial period continued to grind hard on the rural populations, so did men shy away from the prospect of having more than one wife. They certainly must have learned from instinct what Okwuose learned from experience, namely, that polygamy had no future in the new colonial situation. Similarly, with the spread of Western European values, Anioma women, like their counterparts in many parts of Africa, began to shun polygamous homes; hence, the number of petitions for divorce increased. Today, most Igbos look upon polygamy as a backward institution. In sum, as the indirect rule system undermined the indigenous political system of Anioma, so did Christianity and the crisis of the colonial economy disorganize the ancient economic order of the people. The three innovations of Christianity, indirect rule, and colonial economic policies were the most powerful agents of change in British colonial Africa.

NOTES

1. Richard N. Henderson, *The King in Every Man* (New Haven: Yale Univ. Press, 1972), 60.

2. NAI, CSO/26/4, File no. 3038X, J. Macrea Simpson, "Intelligence Report on the Agbor, Oligie and Emuhu Clans, Agbor District, Asaba Division," 1935.

3. Anthony G. Hopkins, *An Economic History of West Africa,* (New York: Columbia Univ. Press, 1973), 56–58.

4. MacGregor Laird and R. A. K. Oldfield, *Narrative of an Expedition into the Interior of Africa, by the River Niger,* (London: R. Bently, 1837), 164–67.

5. Daryll Forde and G. I. Jones, *The Ibo and Ibibio-speaking Peoples of South Eastern Nigeria* (London: Oxford Univ. Press, 1950).

6. Ukwu U. Ukwu, "The Development of Trade and Marketing in Iboland," *Journal of the Historical Society of Nigeria* 3, no. 4(1967): 648.

7. Ibid., 650.

8. Ibid.

9. See Hopkins, *An Economic History of West Africa,* 53–54.

10. B. W. Hodder, "Some Comments on the Origins of Traditional Markets in Africa South of the Sahara," *Transactions of the Institute of British Geographers* 36 (1965). See also B. W. Hodder and Ukwu U. Ukwu, *Markets in West Africa: Studies of Markets and Trade among the Yoruba and the Ibo* (Ibadan: Ibadan Univ. Press, 1969).

11. See Paul E. Lovejoy, *Caravans of Kola: the Hausa Kola Trade, 1700–1900* (Zaria: Ahmadu Bello Univ. Press, 1980); Hopkins, *An Economic History of West Africa,* and E. W. Bovill, *The Golden Trade of the Moors* (London: Oxford Univ. Press, 1968).

12. Duarte Pacheco Pereira, *Esmeralde de situ orbis.* Trans. and ed. George H. T. Kimble (London, Hakluyt Society, 1973), 123.

13. E. J. Alagoa, "Long-distance Trade and States in the Niger Delta," *Journal of African History* 11 (1970): 322.

14. David Northrup, *Trade Without Rulers: Pre-colonial Economic Development in South-eastern Nigeria* (Oxford: Clarendon Press, 1978), 22.

15. Note that cassava is not one of these food items. See Leo Wiener, *Africa and the Discovery of America*, vol. 1 (New York: Kraus Reprint, 1971), 231; W. O. Jones, *Manioc in Africa* (Stanford: Stanford Univ. Press, 1959); Northrup, *Trade.*

16. Kingsley Ogedengbe, "The Aboh Kingdom of the Lower Niger, c. 1650-1900," Ph.D. diss., Univ. of Wisconsin, 1971, 293.

17. Northrup, *Trade,* 177-80.

18. Richard and John Lander, *Journal of an Expedition to Explore the Course and Termination of the Niger* (New York: Harper & Brothers, 1858), 2: 237.

19. Laird and Oldfield, *Narrative.*

20. Northrup, *Trade,* 28.

21. Laird and Oldfield, *Narrative.*

22. CMS, G3/A3/1889/66, observations of Bishop Crowther, 1879.

23. Kenneth O. Dike, *Trade and Politics in the Niger Delta, 1830-1885* (Oxford: Clarendon Press, 1966), 97-127.

24. Mahdi Adamu, "The Delivery of Slaves from the Central Sudan to the Bight of Benin in the Eighteenth and Nineteenth Centuries," in *The Uncommon Market,* Henry A. Gemery and Jan S. Hogendorn, eds., (New York: Academic Press, 1979), 171-72.

25. Laird and Oldfield, *Narrative,* 100.

26. See, for instance, Joseph E. Inikori, "Historical Problems in the Assessment of the Impact of the Atlantic Slave Trade in African Populations," paper prepared for the international colloquium on the tricentenary of the Code Noir, Dakar, 1986, 25-41.

27. Susan M. Martin, *Palm Oil and Protest: An Economic History of the Ngwa Region, South-eastern Nigeria, 1880-1980* (Cambridge: Cambridge Univ. Press, 1988), 31-34.

28. PRO, CO 520/31/01663, enclosure in dispatch no. 258 of June 22, 1905, James Davidson to Walter Egerton.

29. Alan McPhee, *The Economic Revolution in British West Africa,* (London: G. Routledge, 1926), 56.

30. The tendency to develop Nigeria's natural wealth for the benefit of British industries is also well illustrated by the mining of tin on the Nigerian plateau, around Jos. See for instance, Bill Freund, *Capital and Labour in the Nigerian Tin Mines* (Essex: Longman, 1981).

31. See for instance, Frederick Lugard, *The Dual Mandate in Tropical Africa,* with a new Introduction by Margery Perham, 5th edition, (London: Cass, 1965).

32. Lord W. M. Hailey, "A New Philosophy of Colonial Rule," *United Empire,* 32, no. 7(1941): 146. For a debate on this matter see Cyril Ehrlich, "Building and Caretaking: Economic Policy in British Tropical Africa, 1889-1900," *Economic History Review,* 27 (1973): 649-67.

33. PRO CO 520/101/6586 of February 27, 1911, enclosed in confi-

dential dispatch to Colonial Office by the governor of Southern Nigeria, dated January 30, 1911. The ensuing account is from this source.

34. PRO, CO 520/99 extracts from the *Times,* December 30, 1910.

35. PRO, CO 520/103 of June 6, 1911, Walter Egerton to Colonial Office, May 23, 1911.

36. PRO, CO 520/99 extracts from *Times,* December 30, 1910. The Nigerian lignite was reported as "virtually identical with the German and Austrian lignite" in use at the time; the newspaper also reported that a German firm had made excellent briquettes from samples of the Nigerian lignite supplied by the Imperial Institute of London.

37. PRO, CO 520/18 of July 29, 1911, Imperial Institute to Colonial Office, July 28, 1911.

38. PRO, CO 520/103 of June 6, 1911, Walter Egerton to Lewis Harcourt, Colonial Office, May 23, 1911.

39. Ibid.

40. Ibid. The cost Egerton reported for Welsh coal was 34s. 6d. per ton.

41. PRO, CO 520/101/3774 of February 6, 1911, Walter Egerton to Colonial Office.

42. Enclosure in CO 520/110/10156 of March 29, 1911. The Niger Company Limited to Colonial Office, March 28, 1911.

43. Enclosure in CO520/110/10156 of correspondence connected with applications for mining licenses. The ensuing account and quotations from correspondence are from this source.

44. PRO, CO 520/110 of December 11, 1911, Charles Alfred Vant, consulting engineer, South Nigerian Exploration Syndicate, Ltd., to Colonial Office, December 9, 1911.

45. PRO, CO 520/98/15773 of May 26, 1910, Wyndham R. Dunstan, director, British Imperial Institute, to Colonial Office.

46. PRO, CO 520/104, Confidential dispatch, July 17, 1911, A. G. Boyle, Acting Governor, Southern Nigeria to Colonial Office, June 21, 1911.

47. PRO, CO 520/110 of December 11, 1911. South Nigerian Exploration Syndicate, Ltd. to Colonial Office, December 9, 1911.

48. PRO, CO 520/101, Confidential dispatch of March 7, 1911, disclosed in Walter Egerton's letter to Lewis Harcourt, secretary of state for the colonies.

49. Ibid.

50. PRO, CO 588/1 Proclamation No. 18 of 1902.

51. Draft comment on attorney general's report (p. 60) on Proclamation CO520/115/17924 of June 10, 1912.

52. Ibid.

53. Minerals Ordinance of 1912, amended in 1913 as Minerals Ordinance, 1913 (see CO 520/128 conf. 144642 of 19/12/13).

54. PRO, CO 520/115/17924 of June 10, 1912, (Signed) A.I.H., Colonial Office, January 2, 1912.

55. Confidential enclosure in Ibid. Lord Lugard to secretary of state for the colonies, December 11, 1913.

56. PRO, CO 583/23/27722 of July 29, 1914, "Mineral Survey Report," 1913. Prof. Wyndham R. Dunstan (director) to Colonial Office, July, 1914.

57. The Ogwashi-Ukwu uprising might have contributed to the sudden decision to discontinue mineral surveys in Anioma. See PRO, CO 520/91, Confidential enclosure of September 19, 1910, "Report on the Ogwashi-Ukwu Patrol."

58. PRO, CO 588/1, Proclamation No. 12 of 1903, "Master and Servant Proclamation."

59. PRO, CO 588/1, Proclamation No. 15 of 1903, "The Roads and Creeks Proclamation."

60. PRO, CO 520/13/83 of February 26, 1902, Ralph Moor to Colonial Office.

61. NAI, CSO/10, File no. 26769, G. B. William and E. A. Miller, "Intelligence Report on Aboh-Benin Clans," 1930–31.

62. NAE, CSE 1/85/2924, EP 5279, vol. 2, Cameron to Colonial Office, correspondence relating to International Slavery Convention, May 4, 1933.

63. Chief Ijoma Esumai Ugboma, interviewed in Aboh on December 23, 1982. For a full text of interview, see *Western Igbo,* ed. D. C. Ohadike and Rick N. Shain, *Jos Oral History and Literature Texts,* vol. 6 (Jos:Univ. of Jos, 1988), 146–150.

64. Frantz Fanon, *The Wretched of the Earth* (New York: Grove Press, 1977), 129.

65. NAI, CSO/26, File no. 30927, H. Vaux, "Intelligence Report on the Asaba Clan," 1936.

66. Don C. Ohadike, "The Decline of Slavery among the Igbo People." in *The End of Slavery In Africa,* eds. Suzanne Miers and Richard Roberts (Madison: Univ. of Wisconsin Press, 1988): 455.

67. See Paul Richards, *Coping with Hunger: Hazard and Experiment in an African Rice Farming System* (London:Allen & Unwin, 1986).

68. PRO, CO 583/48/02748 of August 31, 1916, Lugard's taxation proposals of 1916.

69. J. Ayodele Langley, *Pan-Africanism and Nationalism in West Africa, 1900–1945,* (Oxford:Oxford Univ. Press, 1973), 201–24.

70. Quoted in ibid., 210.

71. E. O. Jordan, *Epidemic Influenza: A Survey.* (Chicago: Univ. of Chicago Press, 1927).

72. For a detailed account of the diffusion of this epidemic in 1918–19 in Nigeria, see Don C. Ohadike, "Diffusion and Physiological Responses to the Influenza Pandemic of 1918–19 in Nigeria," *Social Science and Medicine* 32, no. 12(1991): 1393–1399

73. L. Hoyle, *The Influenza Viruses* (New York: Springer-Verlag, 1968), 255.

74. Ibid., 256.

75. PRO, CO 583/77 "Pandemic of Influenza: Experiences in the Northern Provinces of Nigeria," report by M. C. Blair, senior sanitary officer, northern provinces, September 19, 1919.

76. Ibid.

77. SMA, *From the Journals of Some Early Fathers of the Diocese of Benin.* Scribe: Father Krauth, Rome, October 25, 1918.

78. PRO, CO 583/77 "Pandemic of Influenza: Experiences in the

northern provinces of Nigeria." Report by M. C. Blair, senior sanitary officer, northern provinces, September 19, 1919.

79. For a detailed account of the linkages, see Don C. Ohadike, "The Influenza Pandemic of 1918–19 and the Spread of Cassava Cultivation on the Lower Niger: A Study in Historical Linkages," *Journal of African History,* 22 no. 3(1981): 279–91.

80. Michael A. Onwuejeogwu, *The Traditional Political System of Ibusa* (Ibadan: 1972), 51.

81. Northrup, *Trade,* 12.

82. Cassava is not a true annual; at any time of the year both new and old crops can be observed growing in the field. L. C. Uzozie, "Patterns of Crop Combination in the Three Eastern States of Nigeria," *The Journal of Tropical Geography,* 32 (1977): 66.

83. Hopkins, *An Economic History of West Africa,* 31.

84. Obi Onyemem, interviewed at Ogboli Igbuzo, July 30, 1974.

85. This was the response of almost all the Anioma males and females who were interviewed. However, most of them, both men and women, said they would not live in polygamous homes since such homes were usually the scene of endless quarrels between the women, on the one hand, and on the other, between them and their husbands.

86. Obi Nwobi interviewed of Asaba, on December 8, 1982.

87. Jomo Kenyatta, *Facing Mount Kenya* (New York: Vintage Books, 1965), 262.

88. Akinjide Osuntokun, *Nigeria in the First World War* (Atlantic Highlands: Humanities Press, 1979), 121.

89. Philip I. Igbafe, *Benin Under British Administration, The Impact of Colonial Rule on an African Kingdom, 1897–1938* (London: 1979), 224.

90. Some scholars have wrongly described this housing as "single family" units based of their Eurocentric notion that a family consisted of one man, one woman, and their children.

91. SMA, anonymous, "A Remarkable Conversion—An Asaba Chief," in *The African Missionary* (April, 1925), 13. The ensuing account is from this source.

CONCLUSION

≋

AS WE HAVE SEEN, the origins of the Anioma people can be traced to the tenth century A.D. or earlier, when rapid population growth and soil deterioration in the Igbo heartland compelled many groups to fan out in all directions. Those that crossed the Niger River and occupied what became, culturally speaking, the western part of the Igbo culture area secured excellent farming and hunting grounds. They were later joined by immigrants from other places and were variously known as *ndi Aniocha, ndi Ika, ndi Oshimili, ndi Olukumi* and *ndi Ukwuani,* names they retained until the end of the nineteenth century when the British colonized them and named them the Western Igbo people. However, in the 1970s, they consciously and unanimously chose to be collectively known as *ndi Anioma,* which in the Igbo language means "those who live in the good and prosperous land."

Wherever they settled, the early inhabitants of Anioma endeavored to reproduce the social, political, and economic practices of the communities from which they had been extracted. Although certain changes were introduced when non-Igbo groups began to arrive from the sixteenth century onward, the agricultural practices, belief systems, and political ideologies of Anioma remained essentially Igbo in character. One of these identifying characteristics was an apparent inability to evolve strong centralized traditional government that would unify a large group of clans.[1] Another was the tendency to cling to values derived from strong ties to ancestors. Simon Ottenberg has described others: "a strong attachment to the cult of achievement, the tendency to live in well-organized village structures centering around a system of age groupings and secret societies, and a marked discrepancy between the roles of men and women in social life."[2] Equally important was the profound respect for seniority of age, so that decisions in judicial matters were made by elders and important persons "acting as a group, rather than as single persons."[3]

While the people of Anioma evolved their own systems and customs, they nonetheless maintained strong cultural ties with the Igbo people on the eastern side of the Niger. These ties remained strong through the activities of Awka traders and craftspersons and, more especially, through the activities of travelling Nri spiritual specialists who were the main carriers of Igbo culture. It was easy for the travelling Nri to come to Anioma, not only because of its proximity, but also because most Anioma settlements were initially founded by men and women whose original homes were situated in the immediate Nri-Awka neighborhoods. The activities of the travelling Nri were proscribed by the British colonial government in 1911 and since then the entire Igboland has been left in a state of ritual siege.

In view of the scarcity of source materials, it has been difficult to reconstruct the early history of Anioma accurately. The existing oral traditions do not provide absolute dates. The result is that events that might have taken place in a given century are sometimes placed in another, depending on the attitude of the narrator and his or her audience. For instance, an elder might state that Odaigbo left Nri and settled in Ogwashi-Ukwu in the olden days, but it is left almost entirely to the audience to decide when the event took place. Michael Onwuejeogwu has devised a method of dating the various phases of Igbo cultural history,[4] but his method is very complex and difficult to apply to communities that had no divine kings or professional historians like the *griots* of the Western Sudan.

We do not know the exact date when the earliest immigrants entered Anioma, but by studying the homelands from where they came, it becomes clear that most had left the Nri-Awka area when land and population crises began to force migrations. By the ninth century A.D., Anioma, because of its proximity, fertile soils, and good hunting and trading grounds, was certainly one of the territories into which these groups moved. While it is uncertain whether the immigrants entered Anioma in the tenth century, clearly by the thirteenth they had formed thriving communities there.

ANIOMA-BENIN RELATIONSHIPS

With the rise of Benin, however, the historian finds a more reliable terrain, not only because oral and written records become more readily available, but also because they provide some dates with which to compare to oral accounts. Thus if one reads the account of the warrior

Agban and the subsequent changing of the name of the town of Igidi to Agbor in Jacob Egharevba's *A Short History of Benin,* it becomes possible to conclude certain things about Anioma. Since Egharevba dates Agban's conquest from 1577,[5] one could reasonably surmise that the area into which he was sent had been inhabited before that time, that its population was fairly dense, and that the society was already differentiated with chiefs or obis. If so, one would expect that the history of Eka (Ika) and other Igbo towns on the western side of the Niger River—that is, Anioma—could not have been founded in 1557 nor during the reign of Asije (Oba Esigie, c. 1504–50), when the Umuezechima people are believed to have left Benin City, but instead took place several centuries earlier. Despite the available evidence, however, some Igbo scholars have exhibited the tendency to date the origins of Anioma to the sixteenth century. The practice of consigning the origins of the Anioma people to the more recent centuries derives largely from the desire to equate Anioma history with Ezechima history, even though, as we have seen, when the Ezechima party began their migration during the reign of Oba Esigie, they settled near and among existing Anioma communities.

Benin history serves as a fairly reliable source of Anioma origins in other ways. The westward diffusion of the Anioma people had brought them not only within close proximity of Benin but also into Benin City itself, the metropolitan capital of an emerging kingdom in which many non-Edos lived; the Umuezechima might have been some of the non-Edo residents. When civil wars broke out it is only reasonable to expect that many residents would flee. It is also reasonable to presume that in withdrawing, each of the non-Edo groups would head toward its original homelands, which may well explain why the Umuezechima headed for the Igbo heartland and not toward Yorubaland or Urhoboland. One group of the retreating parties, led by Oraeze, crossed the Niger River and settled at Onitsha. Another group, led by Afe and Afekocha, also crossed the river and settled in Ogbaruland where they became known as *ndi gbahu agbahu,* that is, "those who came back" (implicitly, from Benin), an expression which was shortened to *Ogbahu* or *Ogbaru.* One other group, led by Esumai, travelled further down the river and settled in Aboh. Some of the groups that left Benin City or its vicinity never crossed the Niger but chose to remain in Anioma. Ezechima himself and many of his children and followers did not travel further than Onicha-Olona, Ezi, and Issele-Ukwu. Moreover, Kanagba, whose original hometown was Ogidi, and who emigrated from Benin in the company of the Ezechima party, founded Obamkpa. Thus by looking to Benin we can infer origins and movements.

As previously discussed, from the seventeenth century onward, these early Anioma communities became more and more infiltrated by non-Igbo-speaking groups, most fleeing violent or disruptive circumstances that created much turbulence in Anioma. Perhaps in no other part of southern Nigeria do we have more interesting, if conflicting, evidence of a long period of military clashes between two neighboring ethnic groups. The Igbo-Benin wars and the civil wars that the Edos fought in and around their capital city caused many Bini to emigrate from a sparsely populated area into the relatively more densely populated Igbo culture area. As they moved they took with them certain notions of Edo and Yoruba social and political organizations which they spread in Anioma. These disturbances and migrations went on for several centuries, compelling the Anioma people to accept a stream of social and political dislocations and subsequent readjustments. Certainly, we have a clear picture of how these non-Igbo-speaking peoples entered and settled in the western side of the Igbo culture area and introduced new social and political practices. We also know that they came in small groups at a time, that their arrival was spread over a period of two or three hundred years, and that, with the exception of the Olukunmi, they eventually lost their languages and rituals and adopted the Igbo. Thenceforth, they spoke the Igbo language, their major deities and emblems of worship had the same basic names and represented similar forces and concepts as those of the eastern Igbo people, and they performed certain rituals that were typically Igbo. However, before they were completely assimilated, they succeeded in causing some modifications in the Igbo language and culture. The result is that one encounters certain words and cultural elements that are both Igbo and Edo, or sometimes neither, as for example, in *ikeyi oba* (gentlemen) and *ikpoho oba* (ladies). Among the more widespread cultural elements assimilated were the *olokun* and *igbe* religious cults and the Benin-type institution of kingship and military titles.

This study corroborates the thesis that there were longstanding contacts between the Igbo and the Benin and that some of these contacts probably antedate the rise of the Yoruba influence and the Edo state of Benin.[6] The Yoruba influence refers to the twelfth or thirteenth century when Oranya was sent to Benin to establish a dynasty, while the rise of Benin refers to the period beginning in 1440 when Oba Ewuare ascended the throne of Benin and began a career of territorial expansion.[7] Before then, as we have seen, Benin was a small political unit, embracing no more than the capital (Benin City) and a few scattered villages within a radius of about fifteen miles.[8] In other words, even if we do not have sufficient evidence definitively to demonstrate early contacts between the Igbo and the Edo and Yoruba, we must open our minds to such a possibility and stop seeing their relationships only in terms of Igbo-Benin wars, *Aya Idu.*

Moreover, we observed that the power and extent of the Benin empire were not as effective and extensive as they are often portrayed; not even during the peak period of its fame did Benin establish any convincing and lasting control over its vassal states. Perhaps, their own interests led the rulers of Benin to maintain informal relationships with their vassal states, which made it possible for the ties of friendship to last beyond the periods of effective rule. Many Anioma communities, recognizing that relations of friendship were infinitely more enduring than relations of domination, responded accordingly. Such historical evidence as the Obi of Ubulu-Ukwu's sending of messengers to the Oba of Benin in 1876 to announce his coronation and to solicit the Oba's continued friendship confirm this assumption. Whether Benin's rule was effective or not, the fact remains that it was one of the most glorious kingdoms of the forest belts of Africa. It was the product of an African initiative; its rise cannot be attributed to any conquering oligarchies from "the east." Instead, it was the conquerors from "the west" who brought the kingdom to a sudden end in 1897. Till this day many groups in Igboland, Yorubaland, Ishanland, and Itsekiriland take pride in attributing their origins to Benin, and many more cherish their ancient associations with the Obas.

THE IMPORTANCE OF THE GEOPOLITICAL LOCATION OF ANIOMA

One of the major driving forces of Anioma social history was its geopolitical location. The region was situated along one of the busiest trade routes of Africa, the Niger River. This location brought the people of Anioma in contact with the numerous ethnic groups that travelled up and down the river in search of trade and fortune. As already demonstrated, long before the advent of the Portuguese, the people of this region had been gurus of long-distance commerce. Moreover, although Anioma was not a coastal community, its location on the lower stretches of the Niger River enabled it to participate in overseas commerce during the era of the Atlantic slave trade. In the nineteenth century, when the Europeans began to penetrate the African interior on steamboats, they had to establish contact with the Anioma communities who occupied this gateway to the interior. European traders and missionaries found it an indispensable region for trade and evangelization, and when the Europeans powers commenced their conquest of Africa, Anioma became a primary target of British imperial ambitions. Anthony G. Hopkins strongly believes that the conflicts that raged in this region in the 1870s and 1880s between the Africans and Europeans, on the one hand, and on the other, between European traders, contributed immensely to the scramble and partition of Africa.[9]

It is interesting to note, however, that Anioma history was not entirely predetermined by its geopolitical location. Although the people of this place profited from both internal and overseas commerce, they never cared to build large kingdoms themselves. Instead, they continued to live in small-scale, segmentary communities, ruled by their elders in association with titled chiefs, age-grades, secret societies, and women's associations. Thus, despite any possible attractions, they resisted those temptations that persuaded many West African ministates to experiment with large-state formation. Moreover, even though some Anioma polities, like Agbor, Ubulu-Ukwu, Issele-Ukwu, and Ogwashi-Ukwu, emerged as small-scale kingdoms which could have acted as the foundations upon which more ambitious political units might have been built, their ruling elite chose not to extend their power beyond the confines of their towns. This lack of large states in Anioma calls for a reexamination of the theories of state formation in precolonial Africa.

Closely related to the issue of state formation is the question of the Anioma attitude toward warfare. These people simply would not go to war unless provoked, although their strong resistance to Benin and British imperial conquests appears to contradict this claim. One might wonder how people who were so peacefully disposed could have been so prepared for war. Oral traditions confirm that the Anioma communities were generally amicable toward each other, exemplified by the ease with which immigrants from a wide range of places were admitted into existing communities. Additional evidence of this relatively pacific attitude is the complete absence of slave-raiding and head-hunting expeditions, even during the peak period of the Atlantic slave trade, when social violence and political insecurity characterized many African formations. By the last decades of the nineteenth century, however, some of this amicable disposition had begun to disappear and accounts of battles between the various Anioma communities became common. The new conflicts strongly point to the fact that the European presence, as manifested in the close of the slave trade and the arrival of European missionaries, traders, and gunboats, was already beginning to destabilize the region.

Although the Atlantic trade did not result in state formation, it nonetheless attracted to the Niger valley peoples of diverse origins and professions anxious to participate in that trade, which in time affected the region's social and political structures. Slaving, together with the provisioning and palm oil trades, stimulated the development of very complex relations of production and encouraged the emergence of social classes. As the society grew generally more affluent, so did it become more differentiated. At the top level of the social strata were the paramount and titled chiefs while at the very bottom were captives. This class differentiation became even sharper during the second half of the nineteenth century when the temporary economic prosperity brought about by the palm oil trade allowed for increased upward mobility. The large labor demands of the new palm oil trade created an internal demand for captives who continued to be ferried down the Niger River to feed a somewhat saturated slave market. The more resourceful men and women took advantage of the reduced prices to secure a large workforce. They became wealthy, purchased the highest titles, and amassed political and economic powers which virtually overshadowed those of the council of elders and the age-grades. They represented their respective towns in their dealings with Europeans. Indeed, some of the social transformations that took place in Anioma had their roots in the region's geopolitical situation.

THE MISSIONARY IMPACT

We have in Anioma a classic illustration of the fact that Christian missions were an agency of colonial penetration of Africa and that in many instances the Bible went before the flag. It was in Anioma, more than anywhere else in Nigeria, perhaps, that the two leading evangelical agents of colonial conquest—the Anglican Church and the Roman Catholic Church—almost overwhelmed peasant communities with their creeds. By attacking traditional religions, the missionaries ignored the vital role the Igbos' world and religion played in their culture. They recognized that Anioma traditional religions were mediative, tolerant, and friendly to other religions, but rather than reciprocate accordingly, they showed the greatest determination to destroy these same qualities. The religious conflicts that erupted raged for half a century, and despite the backing the Christian missionaries received from the British imperial government, Anioma religious belief systems were not completely stifled.

Moreover, while it is true that Christianity continued to make progress in Anioma as in other parts of southern Nigeria, there is no doubt that its impact on the overall society has been exaggerated and sometimes misunderstood. The compelling evidence is that the appeal of the traditional way of doing things was weakened but not destroyed. Sometimes historians invoke statistics to demonstrate that large indigenous populations converted to Christianity, but nothing can be more misleading, since numbers alone make no clear distinction between nominal and practicing Christians. Certainly, not every inhabitant of Anioma who bears the name Peter or Paul or John is a Christian. Accurate data is difficult to obtain, but from all indications, not more than two out of every ten Aniomans were practicing Christians by the end of the colonial period. Churches were hardly filled and a great number of churchgoers still took part in most of the traditional religious festivals and ceremonies of their towns and villages. Even after independence, a large number of Anioma people still had never been baptized and still rigidly followed the traditional religion. These pieces of evidence suggest that although the number of Christian converts steadily increased during the colonial period, Christianity had yet to displace traditional religion. This view was supported by H. Vaux when he wrote in 1935 that

> beyond the Asaba Union is the main body of the people. Illiterate and conservative . . . they have continued in their own way, following as closely as they have been able a life of their own based on ancient institutions and taboos. Large numbers of them have been converted to Christianity. This has affected them more than the laws and the governments superimposed. At least half the town own to a nominal Christianity, and more than one-eighth are practicing Christians. Many taboos have been weakened, but the main institutions have persisted to a remarkable degree.[10]

Further, as recently as 1982 the head of a leading Catholic family in Igbuzo, Patrick Uti, could declare that only one out of every five people in the town could be called a Christian. Uti said there were many churches in Igbuzo but these were hardly filled. Those who worshipped or kept idols were in the majority and included many of those who also went to church.[11]

If such could be said of Asaba and Igbuzo, which have been "evangelized" for so long, what can be said of other Anioma towns that never had a church or school until a hundred years after the historic meeting between Samuel Ajayi Crowther and Obi Ossai in 1841? The reality is that in some remote villages of Anioma, Christianity has yet to make an impact; the priests of the traditional religion are still nearly as powerful as they had been in the previous century, when Bishop Crowther lamented of Onitsha that "the inhabitants are entirely in the hand and control of the priests of the gods and medicine men, the king not excepted."[12]

In Anioma, certain religious practices were stopped, not necessarily because of the activities of the Christian missionaries, but because their legal prohibitions were backed by force. For instance, the Ordeal, Witchcraft and Juju Proclamation of 1903 promised death or imprisonment to those who indulged in certain religious practices.[13] Apparently the threat of death legislated by the colonial government was more persuasive in quashing traditional religious practices than any threat to the soul the missionaries could make.

Some of the implications of Christian missionary activities in Anioma require further examination. One of the professed objectives of the evangelical movements of this period was to spread western literacy, but as we saw in regard to the Roman Catholics, it was only after the First World War that their educational policy changed. Hitherto, greater emphasis was placed on conversion. Nevertheless, once a positive step had been taken to promote western education, it spread like a bush fire. As education advanced, so did certain changes naturally occur. The highly educated Aniomans entered the wage labor market with ease, sometimes achieving great success in life as if by a miracle. Further, the demands of life in a colonial educational environment militated against the practice of the traditional religions. A college student could not construct a shrine or offer animal sacrifices to his gods in the college compound, which were under the strict observation of the Christian missionaries, who ran most of the early educational institutions.

By the 1960s, some traditional religious practices had become anachronisms as populations became more and more heterogeneous, especially in the urban centers. Probably, only in the rural areas could people still maintain the customs of their ancestors and speak the languages of their fathers.

THE COLONIAL IMPACT

The disruptive nature of European colonialism in Africa has been a major theme of this book. The ruling classes of Anioma welcomed the Europeans with open arms but the visitors from Europe entered Anioma with preconceived notions of African barbarism. Understandably, the Africans felt betrayed when they found that the European presence was ripping apart every aspect of traditional life. First, Europeans established themselves in the Niger towns as traders and eliminated the African middlemen from their ancient roles. They went further to attack and plunder the principal Niger towns, causing fear and disquiet throughout the territory. Obi Egbuna, the paramount chief of Issele-Ukwu, is reported to have complained to Father Carlo Zappa that the battle which the British waged against Asaba disturbed him. "I know you are not a soldier and that you have brought the word of God but that not withstanding, the white man frightens me."[14] This was not just one man's fear, but that of everyone in the region.

Thus, while the missionaries were undermining traditional belief systems, the British imperial government was using the sentiments of "trusteeship" and the "white man's burden" to dispossess Africans of their wealth. They also used the slavery issue as a pretext to conquer and rule them. The so-called treaties of friendship and the proclamations of the period up to 1916 included the abolition of slavery, but the British, who wanted large amounts of labor to service the colonial economy, were not prepared to pay for it. Instead they tried to deprive slave owners of their subjects by violent means. The latter could not tolerate the emancipation of slaves without compensation, nor could they stand aloof and watch strangers destroy the accumulated values of the communities. The chiefs responded violently by launching a series of resistance and protest movements.

When the better-armed British forces defeated the leaders in the Aniocha, Kwale and Ika districts they stripped them of their political power, influence, and wealth. Many of the slave-owners' dependents took advantage of the political disturbances to desert, leaving the owners bereft of both a workforce and the basis for their prestige. Thenceforth, owners farmed for themselves and paddled their own canoes. Tensions grew, so that, strictly speaking, the Ekumeku, the Ika, and the Ukwuani wars were not a sudden eruption, but the culmination of a series of misunderstandings touched off by British cultural, commercial, and political ambitions in southern Nigeria.

The British incurrence brought other changes as well, some of them philosophical in nature. For example, while the people of Anioma were familiar with the military strategies of the Bini, they were totally unfamiliar with European gunboats, machine guns, and repeater rifles, and even less so with the military tactics of setting fire to farmlands and crops. Nor could they understand why the British would knock down the homes of peasants whose prompt flight into the bush might have indicated that they were not, at least for the moment, prepared to fight. Thus, while the Anioma communities sometimes underestimated the determination of the Europeans to conquer and rule, and while they tried to provide opportunities for dialogue, the British colonial agents preferred head-on confrontations, to demonstrate the effectiveness of their power. Frantz Fanon, with an exquisite understanding of the colonial mentality, later observed that "the settler-native relationship is a mass relationship. The settler pits brute force against the weight of numbers. He is an exhibitionist. His preoccupation with security makes him remind the native out loud that there he alone is master. The settler keeps alive in the native an anger which he deprives of outlet: the native is trapped in the tight links of the chains of colonialism."[15] In Anioma both the settler and the native would come to understand each other perfectly well and would realize that "between oppressors and oppressed everything can be solved by force," as Fanon convincingly argued.[16]

After their military conquest the British continued their brute force philosophy; they enforced the transition from the slave to the palm oil trade in Anioma and the supposed "civilization" of the people not with gentleness and love, but with great haste and hatred. Those who suggested that the ending of the overseas slave trade would bring social and economic development for Africa were disappointed.

The ensuing colonial period was marked by severe political strife and social insecurity. The imposition of indirect rule, based on the native courts and warrant chiefs, undermined the democratic principles of the people. The native administration reforms of the 1930s and 1940s did not signify a break with the past; they were simply an elaboration of the old undemocratic ways of handling local affairs. Elders and lineage heads, as well as the age-grades and secret societies, who had participated in clan governments, were elbowed into a state of insignificance. The secret societies and religious cults were under special scrutiny, to see if they would be the centers of new uprisings.

As an administrative convenience, the British introduced the indirect rule system, but this bizarre machinery ushered in a peculiar form of degradation and dependency. The most vital stewards of indirect rule were the warrant chiefs, who formed an indispensable link in the whole process of colonial conquest and consolidation. Like the colonial administrators themselves, warrant chiefs had no vision of economic development. As custodians of indirect rule, their role was to translate the wishes of colonial administrators into action and to ensure that the colonial estates were well looked after. The warrant chiefs, together with their small army of court clerks, policemen, interpreters, and messengers, often behaved like tin gods; their actions placed an undesirable wedge between the colonial government and the masses, thereby retarding the process of political development. As we have seen, the historic epic of indirect rule was a powerful instrument of colonial administration which enabled the British to centralize the very complex and fragmented political institutions of southern Nigerians. In Anioma, where these forms of complexity and fragmentation were most pronounced—where the Igbo, Edo, Yoruba, Igala, and Urhobo social and political systems had, to varying degrees, been brought together—indirect rule proved itself a useful administrative expediency, even if it was also faulty, disruptive, and burdensome.

In addition to nullifying the traditional political structures of Anioma, the working of indirect rule resulted in a permanent dissolution of the traditional fighting forces and a reduction of the importance of titles, some of which, as H. Vaux observed, became insignificant "except for the decorative."[17] It was through the warrant chiefs that effective political control was transferred from the precolonial ruling elite to a new ruling class composed mainly of district officers and British merchants. As power became concentrated in the hands of these men, so were the women's associations—the *otu omu, otu umu ada* and *otu inyeme di*—deprived of the opportunity to act in their ancient capacities as checks and balances in community life. Although the new colonial measures resulted temporarily in equalizing the classes, they nevertheless accelerated the marginalization of women, who were neither appointed warrant chiefs nor treated as trading partners of the European merchants, even when they produced most of the export cash crops. In addition, colonial officials and missionaries promptly allowed former male slaves to secure farmlands and western education to the almost total exclusion of free-born women, who were simply equated with former female slaves.

The history of the British enterprise in Anioma is a testimony that the British had no vision of developing their colonial territories beyond converting them into sources of cheap labor, cheap raw materials, and markets for manufactured goods. While pursuing their policy of self-preservation, colonial administrators took bold and prohibitive measures to discourage the development of any product that would compete with British industries or would not reinforce the necessary linkages between colonial raw materials supply and metropolitan industries. In Anioma, for example, the British colonial government refused to develop the lignite deposits because it feared that they would compete with the British coal industry.

It is almost impossible to quantify the casualties and other forms of disintegration that accompanied British colonization. On the one hand, during fifty years of British military expeditions in Anioma community leaders and their followers were shot or hanged after their surrender while others were sent to distant jails. The displacement of population, the looting of foods by British troops, and the disruption of agricultural cycles hurt the people of Anioma as a community, leading in the long run to the institutionalization of food scarcity and urban poverty.

On the other hand, the hardships and the demands of the colonial economy dislocated the ideologies and rituals that had previously regulated social relations quite successfully. Direct taxation and new forms of labor obligations provoked a strong tendency toward labor migration, which compounded the food crisis. The abolition of polygamy and the influenza epidemic of 1918–19 also depleted the available workforce and further undermined the struggling food supply system. To ward off hunger, the people of Anioma experimented with cassava, eventually devoting most of their energies to its production; thanks to the innovative spirit of women who were responsible for the colossal increase in cassava production, Anioma became the foremost cassava growing region of modern Nigeria.

Thus the food crisis in Nigeria did have one positive result; it enabled the "cassava women" of Anioma to improve their economic and social status in society. Because cassava is a staple food for over 70 percent of southern Nigerians and the plant is an important raw material for the wood, textile, and animal feeds industries, all women who engage in cassava growing or processing are guaranteed high and steady incomes. Their newfound wealth has freed them considerably from economic dependence on men and opened for them new avenues for upward social mobility. This is not an Anioma phenomenon alone. Similar trends have been observed in other parts of southern Nigeria. In the Afikpo village group, for example, Ottenberg observed that "it was not until the cash-cropping of cassava started in the 1940s and certain trading activities involving females arose that women became involved with status mobility to a considerable degree."[18]

But on a much larger scale in Anioma as elsewhere, colonialism sowed the seeds of its own destruction. By the 1930s, the old forms of resistance to European rule, which were based on peasant and rural communities, had given way to new forms of protest and resistance, thanks to the emergent Pan-African movement. The champions of these new strategies of political activism were western-educated Africans, mostly men who had been carefully hand-picked and then groomed by Europeans to support them in the exploitation of the masses. But over time these Africans showed a determination to substitute themselves for the Europeans as the ruling class. Under the leadership of

Dennis Osadebe, a militant Nigerian nationalist and a Pan-Africanist, many western-educated elite of Anioma participated actively in this modern struggle for freedom. They joined their fellow Africans in challenging the whole philosophy of colonialism. In the 1940s, they were already asking for the total dismantling of the imperial system. As their forebears had resisted the British conquest of Nigeria with an unsurpassed determination, so did these western-educated Anioma nationalists strongly oppose British imperialism. After 1945, the British government began to respond to international and local pressures to make concessions to the nationalists and to decolonize. In 1960, the government of Britain accorded full sovereign status to Nigeria. It was only then that the people of Anioma regained the freedom for which they had shed so much blood and so many tears.

All in all, this study has examined the precolonial and colonial histories of the people of Anioma. It confirmed, among other things, that the past of these people was not static but dynamic. Like most so-called small-scale African societies, the Anioma communities did not live in isolation and inactivity but interacted very vigorously with their neighbors. We saw how they advanced from one stage of development to another, and how each of the various historical periods of their history introduced new challenges. Nonetheless, the transformations that accompanied the British presence during the short period from about 1860 through 1960 far outweighed the innovations that had been evolving during the previous eight or nine centuries, confirming that European colonialism in Africa was a very powerful agent of change. What transformations still await the people of Anioma in an increasingly global community remains to be seen. What does seem certain, however, is that these people will, as they have throughout their history, adjust and survive.

NOTES

1. Simon Ottenberg, *Leadership and Authority in an African Society: Afikpo Village-Group* (Seattle and London: Univ. of Washington Press, 1971), 23.

2. Ibid., 3.

3. Ibid., 112.

4. Michael A. Onwuejeogwu, *An Igbo Civilization: Nri Kingdom and Hegemony* (London: Ethnographica, 1981).

5. Jacob Egharevba, *A Short History of Benin* (Ibadan: Ibadan Univ. Press, 1968), 32.

6. Daryll Forde and G. I. Jones, *The Ibo and Ibibio-speaking Peoples of*

Southeastern Nigeria: Ethnographic Survey of Africa (London: Oxford Univ. Press, 1950), 46.

7. Ade Obayemi, "The Yoruba and Edo-speaking Peoples," in *History of West Africa,* ed. J. F. Ade Ajayi and Michael Crowder, 207–8.

8. Alan F. C. Ryder, "The Benin Kingdom," in *Groundwork of Nigerian History,* ed. Obaro Ikime (London: Heinemann, 1980), 113.

9. Anthony G. Hopkins, *An Economic History of West Africa* (New York: Columbia Univ. Press, 1973), 152–56.

10. NAI, CSO 26, File no. 30927, H. Vaux, "Intelligence Report on the Asaba Clan," 1936, 2.

11. Patrick Uti, interviewed at Umuodafe Quarters, Igbuzo, December 7, 1982.

12. CMS, CA 3/04/76, from Crowthers's Journal, February 11, 1868.

13. PRO, C0 588/1, Proclamation No. 13 of 1903.

14. SMA, *Le Missions Catholiques,* No. 1279 (December 8, 1893), 586.

15. Frantz Fanon, *The Wretched of the Earth* (New York: Grove Press, 1977), 53–54.

16. Ibid., 72.

17. Vaux, "Intelligence Report on the Asaba Clan," 1936.

18. Ottenberg, *Leadership and Authority,* 314.

REFERENCES

≈

ORAL SOURCES

I have made use of numerous oral interviews I collected in Anioma and the adjoining Igbo districts, together with colleagues, like Elizabeth Isichei, and our students. Some of these interviews have been published under the title *Western Igbo* (volume six of the *Jos Oral History and Literature* series of the University of Jos in Nigeria), which I edited with Rick Shain.

ARCHIVAL MATERIALS

Local Government Archives, Benin City

Some intelligence reports were collected at the Ministry of Local Government Benin City. However, most of these reports are duplicated at the National Archives, Ibadan. Among those I consulted at the Benin City Archives are:

Beeley, J. H. "Intelligence Report on the Illah Village Group." File no. 15346A, March 1938.

"Ezechima Clan Administration: Instructions Concerning." File no. A.D. 632/A, November 13, 1944.

Jull, J. E. "Intelligence Report on the Akwukwu Village Group." File no. 1748C, April 1936.

———. "Intelligence Report on the Ogwashi-Ukwu Clan." File no. 1568C, April 1936.

Keer, R. N. "Intelligence Report on the Ibusa and Okpanam Clans." File no. 13402, April 1937.

Marshall, H. F. "Intelligence Report on the Ute-Okpu Clan of the Agbor District." File no. 13345, July 1936.

Miller, E. A. "Intelligence Report on Abo." File no. 26769, April 1931.

Vaux, H. "Intelligence Report on the Asaba Clan." File no. 188A, November 1934.

Whiting, N. E. "Intelligence Report on the Owa and Idumuase Clans" File No. 13301, April 1936.

Nigerian National Archives, Enugu

NAE, RIVPROF 2/1/42, C219. League of Nations Report and discussion on slavery, October 24, 1936.

NAE, CSE 1/85/2924, EP 5279, vol. 2, Cameron to Colonial Office, correspondence relating to International Slavery Convention, May 4, 1933.

Nigerian National Archives, Ibadan

NAI, ASA DIV, File no. 9/1, Danton, H. C. B. "Intelligence Report on the Ute Okpu and Ute-Ogbeje of Agbor District, Asaba Division," 1931–34

NAI, CSO/26, 31303, "Intelligence Report on the Oko Okwe Area of Asaba Division." 1935.

NAI, CSO/26, File no. 29300, "Intelligence Report on the Kwale-Ibo Clans, Warri Province."

NAI, Kwale District, File no. 62/1, Mackey, J. B., "Kwale district correspondents, 1928."

NAI, CSO/26 File no. 29300, Shelton, H. "Intelligence Report on the Kwale-Ibo Clan," 1933 (with an introduction by Mallison, to Resident)

NAI, CSO 26/4, File no. 3038X. Simpson, J. M. "Intelligence Report on the Agbor, Oligie and Emuhu clans, Agbor District," 1935.

NAI, Kwale Dist., File no. 10/8, "Taking of Eze and Ozo Titles in the Awka Division."

NAI, CSO/26, File no. 30927, Vaux, H. "Intelligence Report on the Asaba Clan," 1936.

NAI, CSO 26/3, File no. 26769, Vol. 1, Williams, G. B. "Intelligence Report on the Ibo-speaking clans of the Kwale Division, Warri Province," 1931.

NAI, CSO/26/4, File no. 30693, Woodhouse, F. M. "Intelligence Report on the Nsukwa Native Court Area, 1936" (with an introduction by Maddocks).

Public Record Office (PRO), London

The relevant Foreign Office and Colonial Office documents consulted include the following:

FO 2, volumes 167 and 178
FO 84, volumes 1487 and 2019.
FO 403, volumes 16-269.
CO 520, volumes, 2-131.
CO 583, volumes 10-141.
CO 588, volumes 1-6.

Proclamations:	Number	Year
Slave Dealing	5	1901
The Native House Rule	26	1901
The Master and Servant	12	1903
The Roads and Creeks	5	1903

(Note: For Proclamations 1894–1906, see CO 588/1)

≈≈≈

Anioma

232

Rhodes House Library, Oxford

Documents consulted include the following:
MSS. Afr. 701.17 S4/6. Brass Inquiry, 1895.
MSS. Afr. 100.441 S12/1930 (3) Colonial Office papers relating to labor
conditions in the colonies, protectorates and mandated territories.
MSS. Afr. S.544, Butcher H. L. M. "The Ika-Ibo People of the Benin Province,
Southern Nigeria."
MSS. Afr. S.1505 (8). Harris, (Jack). "Ibo Papers, 1938–39." Typescript.
MSS. Afr. S.413, Marshall, (H. H.). "Intelligence Report on the Ika, etc."

The Church Missionary Society (CMS) Archives, London

Documents consulted include those in the series:
G3/A3, CA3 and CA3/04.
The Church Missionary Intelligencer, and Niger and Yoruba Notes.

The Society of African Missions Archives, Rome

In addition to manuscripts, The Society of African Missions Archives
hold valuable periodicals, unpublished theses, books, and other relevant printed
materials. The following were consulted and used in this work:

14/.80302. Letters, mainly from heads of mission to the superior general.
14/80303. Letters and reports from the missionary holding the office of vis-
itor to the mission.
14/80404/15794. Strub, *"Le Vicariat Apostolique de la Nigerie Occidentale
depuis sa foundation jusqu'à nos jours"* (1928).
Annals of the Propagation of Faith
Journals of Some Early Fathers of the Diocese of Benin City. (Translated from
the French by Father J. J. Hilliard).
L'Echo des Missions Africaines de Lyon.
The African Missionary.
Annals of the Propagation of the Faith.
Les Missions Catholiques. (English version. Illustrated Catholic Mission).
EXIIT.
*Missionary Endeavour in the Diocese of Benin City from its Foundation to
the Present Day.* Compiled by J. J. Hilliard.

Theses, Dissertations and Research Projects

Afigbo, A. E. "Igbo Historians and Igbo History." Duplicated paper, University of Nigeria, Nsukka, 1972.

Agadah, B. C. "Migrations and Inter-group Relations at Illah." Research project, Department of History and Archaeology, University of Nigeria, Nsukka, June, 1974.

Anozie, F. N. "Archaeology of Igboland." Paper presented at a workshop on the Foundations of Igbo Civilization, University of Nigeria, Nsukka, May 20–22, 1980.

Chikwendu, V. E. "Recent Archaeological Discoveries in Igboland." Paper presented at a workshop on the Foundations of Igbo Civilization, University of Nigeria, Nsukka, May 20–22, 1980.

Ekwu, A. "The Establishment of the Catholic Mission in Western Nigeria by the Society of African Missions, 1868-1920." Ph.D. diss., University of Vienna, 1967.

Ijoma, J. O. "Igbo-Edo Borderland before 1897." Ph.D. thesis, University of Birmingham, 1978.

Inikori, J. E. "Historical Problems in the Assessment of the Impact of the Atlantic Slave Trade in African Populations." Paper presented for the International Colloquium on the Tricentenary of the Code Noir, Dakar, 1986.

Ogedengbe, K. "The Aboh Kingdom of the Lower Niger, c. 1650-1900." Ph.D. diss, University of Wisconsin, 1971.

Ohadike, D. C. "Western Igbo Communities Claiming Origin from Nri: A Cultural History." Research project, Department of History and Archaeology, University of Nigeria, Nsukka, June, 1975.

———. "Nri and the Foundations of Western Igbo Civilization." Paper presented at the Workshop on the Foundations of Igbo Civilization, Institute of African Studies, University of Nigeria, Nsukka, May 20–22, 1980.

Onianwa, C. N. "The Coming of Christianity to Asaba." Research project, History Department, University of Jos, 1980.

Walsh, M. J. "The Catholic Contribution to Education in West Africa, 1861-1926." Unpublished thesis, S.M.A. Archives, Rome.

Wren, R. M. "OZO in Achebe's Novels: The View from the Past." Duplicated paper, University of Houston, 1980.

BOOKS

Adeleye, R. A. *Power and Diplomacy in Northern Nigeria, 1804–1906; the Sokoto Caliphate*. New York: Humanities Press, 1971.

Afigbo, A. E. *The Warrant Chiefs: Indirect Rule in Southern Nigeria, 1891–1929*. New York: Humanities Press, 1972.

———. *Ropes of Sand*. Ibadan, Ibadan Univ. Press, 1981.

Ajayi, J. F. Ade and Michael Crowder, ed. *History of West Africa* 2 vols. London: Longman, 1976.

Allen, W, and T. R. H. Thomson. *A Narrative of the Expedition to the River Niger in 1841.* 2 vols. London: Richard Bently, 1848.

Anene, J. C. *Southern Nigeria in Transition, 1885-1906.* Cambridge: Cambridge Univ. Press, 1966.

Arinze, F. A. *Sacrifice in Ibo Religion.* Ibadan: Ibadan Univ. Press, 1970.

Ayandele, E. A. *The Missionary Impact on Modern Nigeria, 1842-1914.* New York: Humanities Press, 1968.

Azikiwe, N. *My Odyssey: An Autobiography.* London: C. Hurst, 1970.

Baikie, W. B. *Narrative of an Exploring Voyage up the River Kwo'ra and Bi'nue in 1854.* London: J Murray, 1856.

Bascom, W. and M. Herskovits, ed. *Continuity and Change in African Cultures.* Chicago: Chicago Univ. Press, 1959.

Basden, G. T. *Among the Ibos of Nigeria.* London, 1921.

————. *Niger Ibos.* London, Seeley, 1966.

Boahen, A. Adu. *African Perspectives on Colonialism.* Baltimore: Johns Hopkins Univ. Press, 1987.

Bovill, E. W. *The Golden Trade of the Moors.* London: Oxford Univ. Press, 1968.

Burton, R. F. *Wanderings in West Africa from Liverpool to Fernando Po: 2.* London: Tinsley, 1836.

Connah, G. *The Archaeology of Benin: Excavations and other Researches in and around Benin City, Nigeria.* Oxford: Clarendon Press, 1975.

Cook, A. R. *British Enterprise in Nigeria.* London: Frank Cass, 1964.

Crowder, M., ed. *West African Resistance: The Military Response to Colonial Occupation.* London: Hutchinson, 1971.

Crowther, S. A. *Journal of an Expedition up the Niger and Tshadda Rivers in 1854.* London: Frank Cass, 1970

———— and Taylor, J. C. *The Gospel on the Banks of the Niger.* London: Dawsons, 1868.

Curtin, P. D. *The Image of Africa: British Ideas and Action, 1780-1850.* Madison: Univ. of Wisconsin Press, 1964.

————. *The Atlantic Slave Trade: A Census.* Madison: Univ. of Wisconsin Press, 1969.

————, ed. *Africa Remembered: Narratives by West Africans from the Era of the Slave Trade.* Madison: Univ. of Wisconsin Press, 1967.

Davidson, B. *The African Genius.* Boston: Little, Brown, 1969.

Denon, V. *Travels in Upper and Lower Egypt: 2.* London: Longman and Rees, 1803.

Dike, K. O. *Origin of the Niger Mission, 1814-1891.* Ibadan: Ibadan Univ. Press, 1962.

————. *Trade and Politics in the Niger Delta, 1830-1885.* Oxford: Clarendon Press, 1966.

Egharevba, J. *A Short History of Benin.* Ibadan: Ibadan Univ. Press, 1968.

Ekechi, F. K. *Missionary Enterprise and Rivalry in Igboland, 1857-1914.* London: Frank Cass, 1972.

Equiano, O. *The Interesting Narrative of the Life of Olaudah Equiano* (abridged and ed. Paul Edwards). London: Hakluyt Society, 1967.

Fanon, F. *The Wretched of the Earth.* New York: Grove Press, 1977.

Flint, J. E. *Sir George Goldie and the Making of Nigeria.* London: Oxford Univ. Press, 1960.

Forde, D., and G. I. Jones. *The Ibo and Ibibio-Speaking Peoples of South Eastern Nigeria: Ethnographic Survey of Africa.* London: Oxford Univ. Press, 1950.

Freund, B. *Capital and Labour in the Nigerian Tin Mines.* Essex: Longman, 1981.

Gemery, H. A., and J. S. Hogendorn, eds. *The Uncommon Market: Essays in the Economic History of the Atlantic Slave Trade.* New York: Academic Press, 1979.

Gutkind, P., and I. Wallerstein, eds. *The Political Economy of Contemporary Africa.* Beverly Hills: Sage Publications, 1976.

Gwassa, G. C. K. and J. Iliffe, eds. *Records of the Maji Maji Rising.* Part 1, Nairobi: East African Publishing House, 1969.

Hafkin, N. J., and E. G. Bay, ed. *Women in Africa: Studies in Social and Economic Change,* Stanford: Stanford Univ. Press,1976.

Helleiner, G. O. *Peasant Agriculture, Government and Economic Growth in Nigeria.* Homewood, Illinois: R. D. Irwin, 1966.

Henderson, R. N. *The King in Every Man.* New Haven: Yale University Press, 1972.

Hodder, B. W. and Ukwu U. Ukwu. *Markets in West Africa: Studies of Markets and Trade among the Yoruba and Ibo.* Ibadan: Ibadan Univ. Press, 1969.

Hodgkin, T. *Nigerian Perspectives, An Historical Anthology.* London: Oxford Univ. Press, 1969.

Hopkins, A. G. *An Economic History of West Africa.* New York: Columbia Univ. Press, 1973.

Horton, J. A. B. *West African Countries and Peoples.* Edinburgh: Edinburgh Univ. Press, 1968.

Hoyle, L. *The Influenza Viruses.* New York: Springer-Verlag, 1968.

Ifemesia, C. C. *South-eastern Nigeria in the Nineteenth Century: An Introductory Analysis.* New York: Nok Publishers, 1978.

Igbafe, P. I. *Benin Under British Administration: The Impact of Colonial Rule on an African Kingdom, 1897-1938.* London: Longman, 1979.

Ikime, O. *Merchant Prince of the Niger Delta.* London: Heinemann, 1971.

_____. *The Fall of Nigeria.* London: Heinemann, 1977.

_____, ed. *Groundwork of Nigerian History.* London: Heinemann, 1980.

Isichei, E., ed. *Igbo Worlds: An Anthology of Oral Histories and Historical Descriptions.* Philadelphia: Institute for the Study of Human Issues, 1978.

————. *The Ibo People and the Europeans: The Genesis of a Relationship to 1960*. London: Faber and Faber, 1973.

————. *A History of the Igbo People*. London: Macmillan, 1976.

————, ed. *Studies in the History of Plateau State, Nigeria*. London: Macmillan, 1982.

Johnson, G. W. and M. Klein, eds. *Perspectives on the African Past*, Boston: Little, Brown, 1972.

Jones, W. O. *Manioc in Africa*. Stanford: Stanford Univ. Press, 1959.

Jordan, E. O. *Epidemic Influenza: A Survey*. Chicago: Chicago Univ. Press, 1927.

Kalu, O. ed. *Christianity in West Africa: The Nigerian Story*. Ibadan: Ibadan Univ. Press, 1978.

Kaniki, M. H. Y. ed. *Tanzania Under Colonial Rule*. London: Longman, 1979.

Kenyatta, J. *Facing Mount Kenya*. New York: Vintage, 1965.

Laird, M., and R. A. K. Oldfield. *Narrative of an Expedition into the Interior of Africa, by the River Niger in 1832, 1833, and 1834*. 2 vols. London: Richard Bently, 1837.

Lander, R. L. *The Niger Journals of Richard and John Lander*. Edited and abridged with an introduction by Robin Hallet. London: Routledge and K. Paul, 1965.

Lander, R., and J. Lander. *Journal of an Expedition to Explore the Course and Termination of the Niger*. 2 vols. New York: Harper, 1858.

Langley, J. A. *Pan-Africanism and Nationalism in West Africa, 1900–1945*. Oxford: Oxford Univ. Press, 1973.

Last, M. *The Sokoto Caliphate*. New York: Humanities Press, 1967.

Law, R. *The Oyo Empire c.1600–c.1830. A West African Imperialism in the Era of the Atlantic Slave Trade*. Oxford: Clarendon Press, 1977.

Leonard, A. G. *The Lower Niger and Its Tribes*. London: Frank Cass, 1968.

Leys, N. *Kenya*. London: Cass, 1973.

Lloyd, C. *The Search for the Niger*. London: Collins, 1937.

Lovejoy, P. E., ed. *The Ideology of Slavery in Africa*. Beverly Hills: Sage Publications, 1981.

————. *Transformations in Slavery: A History of Slavery in Africa*. New York: Cambridge Univ. Press, 1983.

————. *Caravans of Kola: the Hausa Kola Trade, 1700–1900*. Zaria, Nigeria, Ahamadu Bello Univ. Press, 1980.

Lugard, F. *The Dual Mandate in Tropical Africa*. With a new introduction by M. Perham. London: Frank Cass, 1965.

Lupton, K. *Mungo Park: The African Traveller*. Oxford: Oxford Univ. Press, 1979.

Mbah, N. E. *Nigerian Women Mobilized: Women's Political Activity in Southern Nigeria, 1900–1965*. Berkeley: Univ. of California Press, 1982.

McKenzie, P. R. *Inter-Religious Encounters in West Africa*. Leicester: Univ. of Leicester, 1976.

McPhee, A. *The Economic Revolution in British West Africa*. London: G. Routledge, 1926.

Martin, S. M. *Palm Oil and Protest: An Economic History of the Ngwa Region, South-eastern Nigeria, 1880–1980*. Cambridge: Cambridge Univ. Press, 1988.

Meek, C. K. *Law and Authority in a Nigerian Tribe*. London: Oxford Univ. Press, 1937.

Metuh, E. I. *God and Man in African Religion: A Case Study of the Igbo of Nigeria*. London: G. Chapman, 1981.

Miers, S. *Britain and the Ending of the Slave Trade*. New York: Africana Pub. Corp., 1875.

———, and I. Kopytoff. *Slavery in Africa*. Madison, Univ. of Wisconsin Press, 1977.

———, and R. Robert, eds. *The End of Slavery in Africa*. Madison, Univ. of Wisconsin Press, 1988.

Mockler-Ferryman, A. F. *Up the Niger: Narrative of Major Claude MacDonald's Mission to the Niger and Benue Rivers*. London: G. Philip, 1892.

Newbury, C. W. *British Policy Toward West Africa, Select Documents, 1875–1914*. 2 vols. Oxford: Clarendon Press, 1971.

Noah, M. E. *Old Calabar: The City States and the Europeans, 1800–1885*. Uyo, Nigeria: Scholars Press, 1980.

Northrup, D. *Trade Without Rulers: Pre-colonial Economic Development in South-eastern Nigeria*. Oxford: Clarendon Press, 1978.

Nwabara, S. N. *Iboland: A Century of Contact with Britain, 1860–1960*. London: Hodder and Stoughton, 1977.

Nzemeka, A. *One Hundred Years of the Roman Catholic Church at Illah*. Benin City: Bendel Newspaper Corp., 1980.

———. *British Imperialism and African Responses: The Niger Valley, 1851–1905*. Paderborn: F. Schoningh, 1982.

Nzimiro, Ikenna. *Studies in Ibo Political Systems*. London: Cass, 1972.

Ohadike, D. C. *The Ekumeku Movement: Western Igbo Resistance to the British Conquest of Nigeria, 1883–1914*. Athens, Ohio Univ. Press, 1991.

———, and R. Shain, eds. *Western Igbo: Jos Oral History and Literature Texts*. Vol. 6. Jos: Univ. of Jos, 1988.

Onwuejeogwu, M. A. *The Traditional Political System of Ibusa*. Ibadan, Odinani, 1972.

———. *An Igbo Civilization: Nri Kingdom and Hegemony*. London: Ethnographica, 1981

Orr, C. *The Making of Northern Nigeria*. With a new introduction by A. H. M. Kirk-Greene. London: Frank Cass, 1965.

Osuntokun, A. *Nigeria in the First World War*. Atlantic Highlands: Humanities Press, 1979.

Ottenberg, S. *Leadership and Authority in an African Society: Afikpo Village-Group*. Seattle: Univ. of Washington Press, 1971.

Pacheco Pereira, D. *Esmeralde do situ orbis.* Translated and edited by George H. T. Kimble. London: The Hakluyt Society, 1973.

Park, M. *Travels in the Interior of Africa.* New York: Arno Press, 1971.

Perham, M. *Native Administration in Nigeria.* London: Oxford Univ. Press, 1937.

Ranger, T. O. *Emerging Themes in African History.* Nairobi: East African Publishing House, 1968.

Richards, P. *Coping with Hunger: Hazard and Experiment in an African Rice Farming System.* London: Allen & Unwin, 1986.

Robinson, C. M. *Hausaland: Fifteen Hundred Miles Through Central Sudan.* London: S. Low, Marston and Co., 1896.

Rotberg, R. I., and A. A. Mazrui, eds. *Protest and Power in Black Africa.* New York: Oxford Univ. Press, 1970.

Ryder, A. F. C. *Benin and the Europeans: 1485-1897.* New York: Humanities Press, 1969.

Seligman, C. G. *Races of Africa.* London: Thornton Butterworth, 1930.

Shaw, T. *Igbo-Ukwu: An Account of Archaeological Discoveries in Eastern Nigeria.* 2 vols. Evanston: Northwestern Univ. Press, 1970.

Shelton, A. J. *The Igbo-Igala Borderland: Religion and Social Control in Indigenous African Colonialism.* Albany: State Univ. of New York Press, 1971.

Talbot, P. A. *The Peoples of Southern Nigeria: 2.* London: Frank Cass, 1969.

Tasie, G. O. M. *Christian Missionary Enterprise in the Niger Delta, 1864-1918.* Leiden: Brill, 1978.

Thomas, N. *Anthropological Report on the Ibo-Speaking People of Nigeria; Part IV: Law and Custom of the Ibo of Asaba District.* London: Harrison and Sons, 1914.

Trevor-Roper, H. R. *The Rise of Christian Europe.* London: Thames and Hudson, 1965.

Uchendu, V. C. *The Ibo of South Eastern Nigeria.* New York: Holt, Rinehart and Winston, 1965.

Uzoigwe, G. N. *Britain and the Conquest of Africa: The Age of Salisbury.* Ann Arbor: Univ. of Michigan Press, 1974.

Wiener, L. *Africa and the Discovery of America.* New York: Kraus Reprint, 1971.

Wolf, E. *Peasant Wars of the Twentieth Century.* New York: Harper & Row, 1969.

ARTICLES

Afigbo, A. E. "On the Threshold of Igbo History: A Review of Thurstan Shaw's Igbo-Ukwu." *The Conch* 3, no. 2(1971): 152-64.

———. "Patterns of Igbo Resistance to British Conquest." *Tarikh* 4, no. 3(1973): 14-23.

Akinjogbin, I. A. "The Expansion of Oyo and the Rise of Dahomey, 1600–1800." In *History of West Africa*, ed. J. F. Ade Ajayi and Michael Crowder, 373–412. London: Longman, 1976.

Alagoa, E. J. "Long-Distance Trade and States in the Niger Delta." *Journal of African History* 11 (1970): 319–29.

_____. "Ijo Origins and Migrations." *Nigeria Magazine* no. 9 (December 1966): 279–88.

Allen, J. V. " 'Aba Riots' or 'Igbo Women's War'? Ideology, Stratification, and the Invisibility of Women," in *Women in Africa: Studies in Social and Economic Change*, ed. Nancy J. Hafkin and Edna G. Bay, 59–86. Stanford: Stanford Univ. Press, 1976.

Asiwaju, A. I., and M. Crowder, eds. "Protest Against Colonial Rule in West Africa." *Tarikh* 5, no. 3(1977): 1–56.

Atanda, J. A. "The Iseyin-Okeiho Rising of 1916: An Example of Sociopolitical Conflict in Colonial Nigeria." *Journal of the Historical Society of Nigeria* 4, no. 4(1969): 497–514.

Ayandele, E. A. "The Missionary Factor in Northern Nigeria, 1870–1914." *Journal of the Historical Society of Nigeria* 3, no. 3(1966): 503–22.

Baikie, W. B. "Notes of a Journey from Bida in Nupe to Kano in Hausa Performed in 1862." *Journal of the Royal Geographical Society* 37 (1867): 92–107.

Bender, G. J. "The Limits of Counterinsurgency." *Comparative Politics* 4 (1972): 331–60.

Boston, J. S. "Notes on Contact Between the Igala and the Igbo." *Journal of the Historical Society of Nigeria* 2, no. 1(1960), 52–58.

Bradbury, R. E. "The Kingdom of Benin," in *West African Kingdoms in the Nineteenth Century*, ed. Daryll Forde and P. M. Kaberry, 1–35, Oxford: Oxford Univ. Press, 1969.

Coquery-Vidrovitch, C. "Research on an African Mode of Production," in *Perspectives on the African Past*, ed. G. W. Johnson and M. Klein, 33–51. Boston: Little, Brown, 1972.

Davidson, A. B. "African Resistance and Rebellion Against the Imposition of Colonial Rule," in *Emerging Themes of African History*, ed. T. O. Ranger, 177–88, Nairobi: East African Publishing House, 1968.

Ehrlich, C. "Building and Caretaking: Economic Policy in British Tropical Africa, 1889–1900," *Economic History Review*, 27 (1973): 649–67.

Ekechi, F. "Traders, Missionaries and the Bombardment of Onitsha, 1879–1880." *The Conch* 5, no. 1 and 2(1973): 61–81.

Ekejiuba, F. "Omu Okwei, the Merchant Queen of Ossomari: A Biographical Sketch." *Journal of the Historical Society of Nigeria*, 3, no. 4(1967): 633–46.

_____. "Omu Okwei: The Merchant Queen of Ossomari," *Nigeria Magazine* no. 90 (September, 1996): 213–20.

Eneanya, N. L. "The Eneanya Collection," in *Western Igbo*, ed. Don C. Ohadike and Rick Shain, Vol. 6, *Jos Oral History and Literature Texts*, 153–75, Jos: Univ. of Jos, 1988.

Hailey, Lord W. M. "A New Philosophy of Colonial Rule." *United Empire* 32, no. 7(1941): 146.

Hartle, D. D. "Bronze Objects From Ezira, Eastern Nigeria." *The West African Journal of Archaeology* 10 & 11(1980–81): 83–102.

————. "Archaeology in Eastern Nigeria," *Nigeria Magazine* no. 93 (June, 1967): 134–44.

————. "Archaeology in Eastern Nigeria," *The West African Archaeological Newsletter,* no. 5(Nov. 1966): 13–17.

————. "An Archaeological Survey of Eastern Nigeria." *The West African Archaeological Newsletter* no. 2(May 1965): 4–5.

Hilliard, J. J. "Father Zappa and his Mission." *EXIIT* 3, (May 1963).

Hogendorn, J. S., and P. E. Lovejoy. "The Reform of Slavery in Early Colonial Northern Nigeria," in *The End of Slavery in Africa,* ed. Suzanne Miers and Richard Roberts, 391–414, Madison, 1988.

Hodder, B. W. "Some Comments on the Origins of Traditional Markets in Africa South of the Sahara." *Transactions of the Institute of British Geographers* 36 (1965): 97–105.

Horton, R. "From Fishing Village to City State: A Social History of New Calabar." In *Man in Africa* ed. Mary Douglas and Phyllis M. Keberry, 37–58, London, 1968.

————. "Stateless Societies in the History of West Africa." In *History of West Africa,* ed., J. F. Ade Ajayi and Michael Crowder, 1: 72–113. Longon: Longman, 1976.

Horton, W. R. A. "The Ohu System of Slavery in a Northern Ibo Village-Group." *Africa* 24 (1954): 311–36.

Igbafe, P. A. "Western Ibo Society and Its Resistance to British Rule: The Ekumeku Movement, 1898–1911." *Journal of African History* 12, no. 3(1971): 441–59.

————. "Slavery and Emancipation in Benin, 1897–1945." *Journal of African History* 16, 3 (1975): 409–29.

Ikime, O. "The Anti-Tax Riots in Warri Province, 1927–1928." *Journal of the Historical Society of Nigeria* 3, no. 3(1966): 559–73.

————. "Native Administration in Kwale-Aboh, 1928–1950: A Case Study." *Journal of Historical Society of Nigeria* 3, no. 4(1967): 663–82.

Isichei, E. "Historical Change in an Ibo Polity, Asaba to 1885." *Journal of African History* 10, no. 3(1969): 421–38.

Jeffreys, M. D. "The Divine Umundri Kings." *Africa* 8 (1935): 346–54.

Kirk-Greene, A. H. M. "A Preliminary Note on New Sources for Nigerian Military History." *Journal of the Historical Society of Nigeria,* 3, no. 1(1964): 129–47.

Nwabuisi, A. "The Nwabuisi Collection," in *Western Igbo,* ed. Don Ohadike and Rick N. Shain, vol. 6 *Jos Oral History and Literature Texts,* 228–50, Jos: Univ. of Jos, 1988.

Obayemi, A. "The Yoruba and Edo-speaking Peoples," in *History of West Africa,* vol. 1 ed. J. F. Ade Ajayi and Michael Crowder, 196–265, Longon: Longman, 1976.

Obue, P. "The Peter Obue Collection," in *Western Igbo* ed. Don Ohadike and Rick N. Shain, vol. 6 *Jos Oral History and Literature Texts,* 207-27, Jos: Univ. of Jos, 1988.

Ohadike, D. C. "The Influenza Pandemic of 1918-19 and the Spread of Cassava Cultivation on the Lower Niger: A Study in Historical Linkages." *Journal of African History* 22, no. 3(1981): 379-91.

_____. "Father Zappa and the Ekumeku Movement: A Study in the Christian Missionary Contributions to the British Conquest of Nigeria." *Odu: A Journal of African Studies* no. 22(Jan/July 1982): 188-205.

_____. "The Rise of Benin Kingdom and the Settlement of Edo-speaking People in the Igbo Culture Area." *Ivie, Nigerian Journal of Arts and Culture* 1, no. 3(1986): 19-35.

_____. "The Decline of Slavery Among the Igbo People," in *The End of Slavery in Africa.* ed. Suzanne Miers and Richard Roberts, 437-61. Madison: Univ. of Wisconsin Press, 1988.

_____. "The Don Ohadike Collection," in *Western Igbo,* ed. Don Ohadike and Rick N. Shain, vol. 6. *Jos Oral History and Literature Texts,* 63-152. Jos: Univ of Jos Press, 1988.

_____. "Diffusion and Physiological Responses to the Influenza Pandemic of 1918-19 in Nigeria." *Social Science and Medicine,* 32, 12(1991): 1393-99.

_____. "Benin-Igbo Wars," in *Warfare and Diplomacy in Precolonial Nigeria: Essays in Honor of Robert Smith,* ed. Toyin Falola and Robin Law, 166-75, Madison, 1992.

Okonjo, K. "The Dual-Sex Political System in Operation: Igbo Women and Community Politics in Midwestern Nigeria," in *Women in Africa: Studies in Social and Economic Change,* ed. Nancy J. Hafkin and Edna G. Bay, Stanford: Stanford Univ. Press, 1976.

Onianwa, N. "The Onianwa Collection," in *Western Igbo,* ed. Don Ohadike and Rick N. Shain, vol. 6, *Jos Oral History and Literature Texts,* 186-206, Jos: Univ. of Jos Press, 1988.

Onwuejeogwu, M. A. "An Outline Account of the Dawn of Igbo Civilization in the Igbo Culture Area," *Odinani: The Journal of Odinani Museum, Nri* 1, 1(March 1972): 15-56.

Oriji, J. N. "A Re-assessment of the Organization and Benefit of the Slave and Palm Produce Trade Amongst the Ngwa-Igbo." *Canadian Journal of African Studies* 16, no. 3(1982): 523-48.

_____. "The Slave Trade, Warfare and the Aro Expansion in the Igbo Hinterland." *Geneve-Afrique,* 24, 2(1986): 102-18.

Ottenberg, S. "Ibo Receptivity to Change," in *Continuity and Change in African Cultures,* ed. William Bascom and Melville J. Herskovits, 130-43. Chicago: Univ. of Chicago Press, 1959.

_____. "The Present State of Ibo Studies." *Journal of the Historical Society of Nigeria,* 2, no. 2(December 1961), 211-30.

Ranger, T. O. "Connections Between Primary Resistance Movements and Modern Mass Nationalism in East and Central Africa." Parts 1 and

2. *Journal of African History* 9, nos. 3 and 4(1968): 437–53 and 631–41.

Ryder, A. F. C. "The Benin Missions." *EXIIT* 4 (May 1964).

———. "The Benin Kingdom," in *Groundwork of Nigerian History,* ed. Obaro Ikime, 110. London: Heinemann, 1980.

———. "Benin and the Europeans," in *History of West Africa,* ed. J. F. Ade Ajayi and Michael Crowder, 373–412. London: Longman, 1976.

Sanders, E. R., "The Hamitic Hypothesis: Its Origin and Functions in Time Perspective." *Journal of African History* 10, 4(1960): 521–32.

Temu, A. J. "Tanzanian Society and Colonial Invasion, 1875–1907." In *Tanzania Under Colonial Rule,* ed. M. H. Y. Kaniki, 86–127. London, 1979.

Terray, E. "Long-District Exchange and the State: The Case of the Abrong Kingdom of Gyaman." *Economy and Society* 3 (1974): 315–45.

Toner, M. "A Co-operative in Nigeria." *EXIIT* 3 (1963).

Uka, N. "A Note on the 'Abam' Warriors of Igboland." *Ikenga: Journal of African Studies* 1, no. 2(1972): 76–82

Ukpabi, S. C. "The Origins of the West African Frontier Force." *Journal of the Historical Society of Nigeria* 3, no. 3(1966): 485–501.

Ukwu, U. U. "The Development of Trade and Marketing in Iboland." *Journal of the Historical Society of Nigeria* 3, no. 4(1967): 647–62.

Uzozie, L. C. "Patterns of Crop Combination in the Three Eastern States of Nigeria," *The Journal of Tropical Geography,* 32(1977)

Wilks, I. "The Mossi and Akan States," in *History of West Africa,* ed. by J. F. Ade Ajayi and Michael Crowder, 413–55. London: Longman, 1976.

INDEX

~~~

About the Author

~~~

Don C. Ohadike is from the Anioma region of southern Nigeria. He was educated in Nigeria and in England, specializing in African social and economic history. He had lectured at the Universities of Port Harcourt and Jos in Nigeria, and had been a visiting scholar at Stanford and Northwestern universities before joining the Africana Studies and Research Center of Cornell University. His research interests include African cultures and civilizations, the history and politics of religions in Africa, resistance and liberation movements, and African economic and labor history. He is the author of *The Ekumeku Movement: Western Igbo Resistance to the British Conquest of Nigeria, 1883–1914*, published by the Ohio University Press.